MOTHER-HEADED FAMILIES
AND WHY THEY HAVE INCREASED

MOTHER-HEADED FAMILIES AND WHY THEY HAVE INCREASED

Ailsa Burns
Cath Scott
Macquarie University, Australia

LEA LAWRENCE ERLBAUM ASSOCIATES, PUBLISHERS
1994   Hillsdale, New Jersey   Hove, UK

Lawrence Erlbaum Associates, Inc., Publishers
365 Broadway
Hillsdale, New Jersey 07642

Library of Congress Cataloging-in-Publication Data

Burns, Ailsa.
    Mother-headed families and why they have increased / Ailsa Burns,
Cath Scott.
        p.   cm.
    Includes bibliographical references and indexes.
    ISBN 0-8058-1440-X (acid-free paper)
    1. Single-parent family.   2. Women heads of households.
I. Scott, Cath.   II. Title.
HQ759.915.B86   1994
306.85 '6—dc20   93-34798
                                                              CIP

Books published by Lawrence Erlbaum Associates are printed on acid-free
paper, and their bindings are chosen for strength and durability.

Printed in the United States of America
10   9   8   7   6   5   4   3   2   1

Contents

Acknowledgments

We wish to express our thanks to the Australian Research Council and Macquarie University for support in the research for this book. We gratefully acknowledge permission for the use of figures and tables given by the *Journal of Marriage and the Family*, the *Journal of Family History*, the *Urban Institute Press*, *The Free Press*, and the *University of California Press*. We are especially grateful to Nancy Thomas and the *Social Policy Report* for assisting a first version of this material into print and for suggesting useful editorial changes.

We also wish to thank Susan Cairns for research assistance, Jodie Watson and Dugald Burns for translation of German and Swedish material, Elaine Higginson for secretarial assistance, the late Robin McKenzie for his invaluable help with anthropological material, and Peter van Sommers for his careful reading of the text and insightful advice.

Ailsa Burns
Cath Scott

Introduction

The last two decades have seen a dramatic growth in the proportion of families that are headed by women. Current figures for different countries range up to almost one quarter of all families with dependent children. Most of these families are poor, so that mother-headed families now comprise a large under-privileged class across the Western world. This book explores the causes and implications of this development. Father-headed single-parent families are not discussed, as their situations are usually different.

Mother-headed families are not new. Wars, natural disasters, and the migration patterns of human history have left many societies depleted of adult men. What is new about the present situation is that the absent fathers are in most cases still alive, and are generally not very far away. It is by choice—their own, their partner's, or both—that they stay away. After leaving, they mostly keep their resources, and their labor income, for themselves.

Single mothers do not necessarily remain single. Many re-partner, so that the incidence of mother-headed families in a population at any one time is a considerable understatement of the proportion of all children that will be father-less at some stage of their lives. Current estimates are that up to one half of all children born today will spend part of their childhood in a family headed by a separated, unmarried, or divorced woman (Garfinkel & McLanahan, 1989). If a new partner joins the family, he is not of course the father, so the two may not be regarded as interchangeable by the children. Partly because of this, second partnerings have a higher breakdown rate than do initial ones, particularly in the (increasingly common) situation where the new partnership does not involve legal marriage. Periodic single parenting has thus emerged as a new family form.

The countries in which this is happening are not well geared to deal with the situation. Their patterns of employment, housing, and child care mostly assume the presence of two parents. Women's wages are generally lower than men's, with the assumption that fathers will be mainly responsible for supporting the family. Nonfamily child care is only sometimes available, and usually expensive, on the assumption that mothers will be doing most of it for free. Housing has to be mostly sought in a market geared to income, not family needs. Uncles, grandfathers, and friends may act as surrogate male-identity figures but, if they fail to do so, no one else will necessarily take their place.

The situation is not as severe as it might be, or has been, in some cases. It is not so long since women were barred by law from entering the better paid jobs, or from staying in any kind of career once they married. It is not so long since men in some countries, married or single, were paid a wage supposed to support a whole family, whereas women, regardless of their responsibilities, earned less than half for the same amount of work. It is not so long since women without husbands were refused rental accommodation, bank loans, mortgages, or any kind of credit. It is not so long since divorce required proof of adultery or degraded behavior, and the divorcee and even her children were considered shamed. These and other discriminations still occur, but in recent years the industrialized countries have repealed much of the statutory discrimination against women.

The nonstatutory kind remains formidable, however. There are many important consequences, in particular:

1. the proportion of women and children living in poverty has greatly increased,
2. social security costs have greatly increased, and
3. there is concern about possible developmental effects on the children involved.

Because this is an international trend, an international perspective is adopted in this book. It is not of course possible to document developments in every industrialized country, and it would be overkill to do so. The discussion centers on selected countries where certain trends are most visible. Among the Western nations, particular attention is given to the United States, Sweden, and the former Soviet Union, because of their very high prevalence of mother-headed families; and trends in some countries with a middling prevalence are also discussed. Japan is included, because of its combination of advanced industrialization with a non-Western tradition and a low incidence of mother-headed families. Other countries come into the picture where they report particularly high or low prevalence of certain kinds of female-headed families, for example those originating from out-of-wedlock births.

Specifically, the goals of the book are twofold. The first is to bring together information on the past and present prevalence of mother-headed families in different countries. This includes an exploration of the conditions under which such families have been many or few, and better or worse treated by their communities.

The second goal is to consider the various explanations (economic, demographic, cultural, sociopsychological) that have been offered for the recent increase, and to see whether these proposals fit the facts that we have gathered, and what they imply for the future—that is, whether the proportion of mother-headed families is likely to increase, stabilize, or decrease.

In the next section, we briefly describe the prevalence of mother-headed families in the industrialized countries. Chapter 1 considers the role of divorce and separation in their creation. Particular attention is paid to some countries in which divorce is or has been particularly high or low. This chapter describes the experience of the United States and the Soviet Union, and Sweden, Japan, and some other countries. It is noted that all except Japan experienced an upswing in divorce in the 1970s, providing a first wave of single-parent families, but that their divorce rates then stabilized during the 1980s. It is further noted that during the upswing of the 1970s the various countries mostly kept their position relative to the others, with the United States always substantially higher than the others. Chapter 1 offers a theoretical integration of these trends, and some predictions for the future.

Chapters 2–4 consider out-of-wedlock births as a source of mother-headed families, particularly since the stabilization of divorce rates in the 1980s. Historically, ex-nuptiality or illegitimacy is one statistic that has been very consistently recorded, so that it is possible to chart shifts over time as well as to make cross-national comparisons. Chapter 2 describes the current increase in selected Western nations in the light of their previous history and looks at some explanations that have been offered. Chapter 3 considers whether these explanations retain their validity when applied to non-Western nations where out-of-wedlock rates are substantially higher (or lower) than those recorded in the European or Europeanized countries. Chapter 4 offers an integration of the Western and non-Western material.

Chapter 5 discusses widowhood. Although widowhood is no longer a major source on mother-headed families in the West, it continues to be so in many other parts of the world, and the situation of the widow-headed family has much in common with that of the divorced/separated or unmarried mother. This chapter explores the experience and status of widows in different cultures, and suggests that their status depends on certain aspects of the status of women in the culture. The similarities and differences with the situation of other mother-headed families is then considered.

The second part of the volume (chapters 6–8) offers a critical discussion of various theories of the family and of parenting that might explain the various changes in the prevalence and status of mother-headed families that have been described. A good deal of writing about one-parent families has been quite narrow and oriented to practical ends, concerned, for example, with welfare dependency and the provisions that might increase or decrease it. General family theories are more expansive, but not usually particularly interested in single parents. The narrower approaches are mostly oriented to issues that are salient in the writer's home country, but not necessarily elsewhere. For this reason, we have favored the more expansive approaches and drawn our own implications for mother-headed families as required.

In doing so we have naturally concentrated on those approaches that seem to offer most ideas regarding the prevalence and status of mother-headed families. This means that our choice of approaches is not the usual one offered in family textbooks. The theories reviewed include sociobiological theories, demographically oriented theories, feminist theories, and what we are calling *decomplementary* theory. The decomplementary approach proposes that the increase in mother-headed families is the result of the fact that in Western societies men and women no longer have such complementary interdependent needs (i.e., they no longer need each other so much). We argue here that decomplementary ideas offer a particularly integrative and fruitful way of understanding the increase in mother-headed families and its relation to wider trends in family and social structure. We note that decomplementary theory, like most of the other theories reviewed, predicts that mother-headed families are here to stay, as long as social and material conditions provide a relatively high level of gender equality.

PREVALENCE

How many families today are mother-headed? What has been the rate of increase? The figures are not always easy to obtain. Different countries have collected information in different years, and have defined family types in different ways, making cross-national comparisons difficult. Some countries have published few figures of any kind. The reader needs to bear these caveats in mind in examining Figure 1, which depicts the incidence for eight industrialized countries for two time periods—early 1970s and mid- to later-1980s. Figures for all one-parent families are given, as not all countries separate out those headed by a lone mother from those with a lone father (generally some 10% of all one-parent families).

Figure 1 shows that Sweden reported the highest prevalence in the early 1970s (15%), although by the mid-1980s it had been outstripped by both the United States and the Soviet Union. Estimates are that the present high rate— 17%—of all families with dependent children will continue. Almost half of these families result from divorce, and a further 36% result from births to unmar-

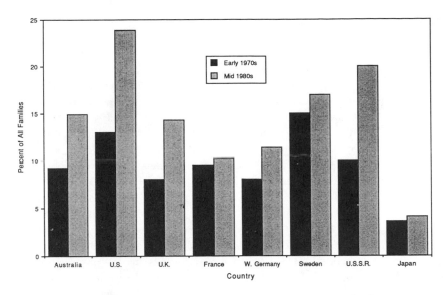

FIG. 1.   Single-parent families as percent of all families (from Australian Bureau
of Statistics, 1991; OECD 1987; Roll, 1989; Statistics Sweden, 1992).

ried women: Some 85% of them are headed by women (Statistics Sweden, personal communication, 1991). There are good historical reasons for this situation, which we look at in later chapters. Briefly, Sweden had low rates of
marriage in previous centuries, and a tradition of *de facto* marriages and
breakups. One writer attributed this to the fact that Christianity arrived late
and individualist liberalism arrived early (Rheinstein, 1972, p. 153). There
was a small boom in marriage after World War II, but since 1965 young people have increasingly chosen *de facto* relationships over marriage. There is a
high divorce rate, but breakups are even more common among cohabiting couples, including those with children.

    The highest current prevalence is found in a very different society—the Unit-
ed States. The number of U.S. children living with a single parent increased
from about 9% in 1960 to 24% in 1986 (Glick, 1988). Although in Sweden
women of almost every kind of background are equally likely to be lone parents, this is not the case in the United States. U.S. lone mothers are younger
than married mothers, are less-educated, and are likely to be African American. More than 50% of African-American families are mother-headed. U.S.
writers accordingly stress the importance of African-American culture, the des-
tructive effects of poverty on family life, and the shortage of young African-
American men due to high mortality and other causes.

    African-American teenagers are not the only lone mothers in the United
States of course. In absolute numbers there are as many Whites as African
Americans, and today's lone mothers are strikingly better educated than were

those of 1970. For example, the number of college-educated lone mothers tripled between 1974 and 1984. Projecting from present trends, it has been calculated (Norton & Glick, 1986) that of women who were in their late 20s in 1984, 37% could expect at some time to become single mothers; 8% because of an out-of-wedlock birth, 23% through divorce, 4% through widowhood, and 2% through long-term separation. From the child's point of view, this means that half of all U.S. children born in the 1990s will spend part of their childhood in a female-headed family (Garfinkel & McLanahan, 1989).

We have placed the former Soviet Union currently second (third in the mid-1970s), although the available figures are less detailed than for some other countries. Observers (Lapidus, 1981; Moskoff, 1983; Peers, 1985) put the figure for mother-headed families resulting from divorce, widowhood, or out-of-wedlock birth at between one in six and one in seven of all families. Among older cohorts, this was due to the special history of the Soviet Union, and the huge death rate among young men during World War II and its aftermath; but among younger people, marriage breakdown is the major cause. Soviet census figures show that some 94% of women of working age are either employed, mostly full time, or studying. Domestic life is also labor intensive, and the double workload carried by married women is considered by observers to be a major cause of marriage breakdown.

Of the other countries shown in Fig. 1, Australia and the United Kingdom had slightly lower rates in the mid-1980s, an estimated 15% in Australia in 1986 (and 16.3% in 1991; Australian Bureau of Statistics, 1991) and 14.3% in the United Kingdom in 1986 (and 16% in 1988; Kiernan & Wicks, 1990; Roll, 1989). In both countries, single mothers' average income is estimated to be about 40% of that of two-parent families. Single mothers are on average less well educated than married mothers, and less likely to be in the work force; and their work force participation declined during the 1980s. Comparisons with the United States have pointed up the high rate of single motherhood among Afro-Caribbeans in the United Kingdom (42.6%), but the great majority of single mothers (92.1%) are White. In Australia, aboriginal people have a similarly higher rate, but make only a small contribution in absolute numbers (Australian Bureau of Statistics, 1991).

France and West Germany reported a slightly smaller incidence, and a somewhat smaller but still significant rate of increase, accompanied in the case of France by a very low marriage rate and in West Germany by a very low birth rate (Ermisch, 1987; Roll, 1989). Other countries (not shown in Fig. 1) including Denmark, the Netherlands, Belgium, Switzerland, Luxembourg, Poland, Hungary, Norway, Canada, and New Zealand reported an incidence of one-parent families ranging between 10% and 15%, and rising. Roll (1989) estimated that at least 10% of families with children in the European Community are headed by a lone parent.

One interpretation is that this large latter group represents the typical modern pattern brought about by the social changes of our times. The above-average rates of Sweden, the United States, and the Soviet Union could then be seen to result from special national circumstances acting over and above the norm. Some other countries, with a lower but nevertheless increasing incidence (e.g., Ireland and Italy), can be similarly regarded as having cultural arrangements that have delayed the trend. We look at the viability of this explanation in later chapters. In doing so, we also consider the special case of Japan—non-European but highly industrialized—where the number of mother-headed families actually declined in the 1960s, and remains very low (Ermisch, 1987), a marked contrast to the Western industrialized countries.

CONSEQUENCES

The consequences of the increase in mother-headed families have been well documented (Garfinkel & McLanahan, 1989; McLanahan & Booth, 1991; Roll, 1989). Such families are generally poor, due to some combination of little or no paternal support, low social security payments, mothers' limited earning capacity, and the difficulties inherent in being both breadwinner and sole caregiver. They became poorer in most countries during the 1980s, due to social and economic changes, such as welfare cuts and increasing housing values, that especially penalized them. In Britain, for example, the proportion of lone parents reliant on supplementary benefits (available only to the very poorest) rose from 40% in the 1970s to 60% in 1991 (Kiernan & Wicks, 1990). In the United States between 1979 and 1988 the proportion of children living in poverty grew by 23%, to one in five, mostly because of lack of paternal support. Projections are that by the year 2000 this figure will have increased to one in four (Aldous & Dumon, 1990).

These families are mostly concentrated in the poorest inner-city areas of the big cities or in poorly serviced welfare suburbs on their fringes. In the Borough of Lambeth in London for example, one-parent families comprise one third of all families with children (Kiernan & Wicks, 1990). In Australia in 1986, there were five metropolitan areas where single-parent families comprised more than 35% of families with children (Australian Bureau of Statistics, 1991). By and large, the children of poor mother-headed families have reduced life chances (Garfinkel & McLanahan, 1989). The situation varies from place to place, as do the kinds of support services that have been developed. The issues involved are not the focus of this book, which concentrates on possible causes of the increase. However, it is impossible to overlook the consequences, so that the reader will also find some discussion of these in the text.

Ailsa Burns
Cath Scott

Chapter 1

Is Easy Divorce to Blame?

Are easier divorce laws responsible for the increase in mother-headed families? Their introduction into most Western nations between the late 1960s and the mid-1970s is often seen as the major cause of the increase. The new laws were not of course identical across countries, but in the majority of cases they represented a significant move toward consent or no-fault divorce. Is it true that the new laws have been responsible for the breakdown of the traditional family, as has often been alleged?

Figure 2 shows the divorce rates before and after the introduction of easier divorce laws in a selection of countries. Although absolute rates differ from one country to another, the pattern across time is quite similar—low rates until mid-century, a postwar jump, a plateau through the 1950s and 1960s, a rise in the later 1960s followed by a further rise in the 1970s, and a leveling out in the 1980s. The figures thus support the view that although divorce was on the rise before the laws were changed, the legal changes brought a further rise, followed by stabilization at a very high rate. This would obviously increase the number of mother-headed families unless all the divorcees were childless, or all remarried, or all had previously been single parents although not divorced. We know that none of these things is the case: Many divorcing parents do have children, many women (in particular) do not remarry, and most do not separate until a relatively short time before the divorce. Hence, the legal changes can certainly be said to have contributed to the increase in one-parent families, even if they did not cause it.

To say this only takes the argument one step back, of course. Why did so many countries change their laws at this time? And why did so many people take advantage of the changes? (And remember that Fig. 2 shows only a small

1

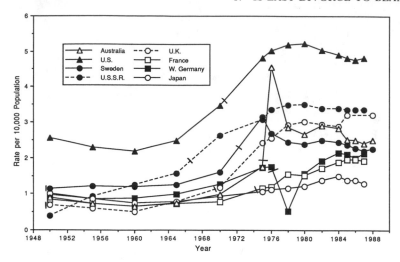

FIG. 2.   Divorce rates per 1,000 population, 1948–1988: selected countries (from U.N. Demographic Yearbook, various editions).

sample, many other nations did the same at this time.) Before we try to answer these questions, we need to point out that in some cases the changes came much earlier; and in other cases divorce law has been far freer in previous times than it is today. Japan in the 19th century allowed very ready divorce to husbands (although not to wives) and recorded a much higher divorce rate than any of the Western nations, and much higher than it has today. Following the Revolution of 1917, Soviet Union law swung between extremes of freedom and restrictiveness, and divorce statistics followed suit. Liberal legislation was first introduced into Sweden in 1920, although further changes were made in 1974.

Who sought change, and why? And who opposed it, and why? In most countries, both supporters and opponents were passionate about the issue, and saw consent divorce as bringing either great benefits or great disasters to their nation. And the two camps were often quite evenly matched. In Italy opposition to the 1970 law remained so strong that 4 years after it was brought in, a referendum was held as to whether it should be repealed. The result was a 59% to 41% vote in favor of retention, surprising a vigorous opposition that had confidently expected the silent majority to rise up in defense of the family. In other countries, the size of the vote for and against change has been roughly similar. The Australian no-fault Family Law Bill of 1975 was passed by 56% of Parliament, at the same time that public opinion pollsters were finding an almost identical degree of support among the public. In Ireland, the last European country without divorce, public opinion polls in the 1990s showed a majority in favor of it.

Despite large cultural differences between nations—which we look at later—

the writings of supporters and opponents indicate that the divorce issue drills into rooted, and opposing, views of human nature and society. To generalize, we can say that opposition has generally centered around two main elements. The first of these is a belief in the importance of the family as the basis of society. If the family weakens, then society may become decadent, and crumble. A recent statement of this belief was former U.S. Vice President Dan Quayle's comment following the 1992 Los Angeles riots that "the anarchy and lack of structure in our inner cities are testament to how quickly civilization falls apart when the family foundation cracks" (Yang, 1992, p. 1). The state therefore has a duty to support marriage. Ideally it should do this in many ways, but at the least it should make it hard for a parent to abandon a dependent family. This belief is often associated with the Christian doctrine of the sanctity and sacramental nature of marriage; but the two don't necessarily go together.

The second main element is a jaundiced view of the psychology of men, at least in respect to their commitment to marriage and family. This has involved the suspicion that many would rather readily abandon wife and children unless pinned in by moral and financial restraints, such as those embodied in the principal of marital guilt. Parliamentary debates contain many expressions of this view. For example, one speaker to the parliamentary debate on the Australian Family Law Bill of 1975 described abolition of the concept of *guilt* as an "open cheque to the Casanovas and tomcats in our society" that would invite men to walk out of their marriages "at the drop of a hat."

These views are expressed by both men and women, but tend to differ with the gender of the speaker. When expressed by men, they usually have a class ring about them—that of respectable men of authority being aware of the need to keep less responsible men under control. However, when expressed by women, the reliability of all men is commonly cast into doubt. For example, Barbara Ehrenreich (1983) cited a leading female anti-divorce reform campaigner's comment that "The men are going to leave their wives if they don't have to pay, because men are *this way*. Especially you know, when they get into middle age" (p. 165).

These two elements—society's reliance on the family and the unreliability of men—appear a little contradictory, but they are commonly found together in arguments mounted by opponents of ready divorce. The bridging concept generally offered is that of the redemptive power exerted by a good woman, when suitably buttressed by legal and economic sanctions. This way of thinking cuts across some of the obvious distinctions between conservatives and liberals. For example, it was adopted by U.S. sociologist and feminist Alice Rossi in her 1985 Presidential Address to the American Sociological Association, where she presented a chilling Darwinian picture of how

Unattached males roam the interstices between socially cohesive groups, kill, and are themselves killed and maimed, but the machine cultures of the West have

shown no inventiveness in developing new social institutions capable of providing individual loyalty and social integration to replace the bonds of family. Our
only answers have been armies and prisons. (Rossi, 1985, p. 168)

From the other side of politics and gender, the concept of marriage as a
valuable alternative to prison for unattached men has also been developed by
the right-wing writer George Gilder. Gilder (1974) viewed the single man as

disposed to criminality, drugs and violence. He is irresponsible about his debts,
alcoholic, accident-prone, and venereally diseased. Unless he can marry, he is
often destined to a Hobbsean life- solitary, poor, nasty, brutish and short. . .
(p. 10)

Gilder's views in particular seem extreme, but his writings have been popular, perhaps because they crystallize and dramatize a view of (male) human
nature that has been shared by many.

The pro-divorce reform groups have generally taken a more positive view
of both male and female nature. They have argued for ready divorce on the
grounds that both women and men would benefit by being able to end unsuccessful marriages painlessly and go on to happier lives. A clean break between
spouses would thus be to the benefit of both. Society would not crumble. On
the contrary, it would be strengthened by the fact that more of its citizens would
be happy. Regarding the protection of women and children, the divorce reformers of the 1970s were optimistic about the speed with which women would come
to have equal economic status with men. Equal opportunity, as they saw it,
would allow ex-partners to go their independent ways, with (usually) no need
for continuing paternal support for wives and children. With money wrangles
thus removed, better relations between children and their no-longer-resident
parent might even follow (Weitzman, 1985).

Today, we can see that neither supporters nor opponents had it quite right.
Ready divorce has proved very popular, and the idea that people should be
forced by the state to remain married against their will has come to seem ab-
surd. There is no support for return to a more restrictive law. At the same
time, many former supporters have reached the view that no-fault divorce has
been quite harmful for women and children. Large numbers of single-parent
families were created, but economic equality did not arrive, neither did adequate child care or other family supports. Ex-husbands continued unwilling
to pay child maintenance: Only some 30% pay even small amounts unless
forced to by the state (P. McDonald, 1986). The numbers of single-parent families created by the divorce boom strained social security budgets, and some
countries actually reduced the benefits they offered. At the 1989 International
Economic Consequences of Divorce Conference, speakers from various countries warned of the threat to national solidarity posed by a large underclass

of poor women, rearing the future generation in disadvantage while the rest of the nation including the fathers, lived well (Funder, 1989). Bernard (1985), a U.S. feminist, wrote that "no-fault divorce has failed young mothers, older housewives and women in transition, and has permitted a child-support situation that is a national disgrace" (p. 2). Bergmann (1986), also writing of the United States, described that nation as having fostered a "rogue elephant" image of the U.S. male as someone who is plundering the social system by using his own human capital to get the good life for himself while leaving his children poor and perhaps homeless. Paradoxically, the evidence is that the majority of divorces are now initiated by wives (P. McDonald, 1986). These outcomes indicate that the motives involved in the divorce boom are a good deal more complex than either side in the 1970's debate allowed.

Further complexity is illustrated by the national differences shown in Fig. 2. Although the trends are similar, the absolute levels are not. The U.S. rate is consistently the highest, followed by that of the former Soviet Union (Russia-only figures, which are not available, would undoubtedly be much higher, as the aggregated figures include rural and Moslem areas with little divorce). In the 1980s, divorces continued to increase in France and Germany, whereas the rate in higher divorce countries plateaued or even turned down. The lowest figures are for Japan, where a modest rise in the 1980s was followed by a downturn.

To understand what is going on then, we need to explore what the divorce histories of these countries have in common, and where they differ. Let us start with the nation with the highest incidence.

THE UNITED STATES

Some Background

Figure 2 describes only the period since 1950, but the U.S. divorce rate has always been higher than that of other industrialized countries. Throughout the 19th century, Americans annually obtained more divorces than were given in all of Europe (W. O'Neill, 1967). This divorce leadership has generally been explained by reference to the nation's liberal-individualist philosophy, which in the case of divorce has been able to override religious proscriptions. The geographic and social mobility of Americans have also been seen as predisposing them to end marriages that do not fit with a changed lifestyle (W. O'Neill, 1967).

Even so, until the middle of the 20th century the U.S. divorce rate was not massive, and nowhere near high enough to keep up with the increase in married life resulting from longer life expectancy. In 1860, 31.5 per 1,000 existing marriages were ended each year by the death of a partner, and a further 2 per 1,000 by divorce, making a total of 33 per 1,000. By 1954–1956, annual dissolutions by divorce had risen to 9.3 per 1,000, but those due to death had decreased to 17.5, giving a total of 27 per 1,000, that is to say 15% less than 90 years earlier (W. O'Neill, 1967). In addition, divorce was a state jurisdiction, and some states maintained very conservative laws. Not until 1966 was it possible to obtain a divorce in New York on any ground other than adultery.

It was the newer states like Nevada, Indiana, and Idaho that first offered easy divorces. This was a rational policy given the nature of the population that moved into these states. The young men who transmigrated west quite often left wives behind in the east. The new states and their courts took the view that they had the right to free themselves from these ties and to remarry. They accordingly introduced vague and hard-to-refute divorce grounds such as "invincible repugnance" or gave expansive definitions to apparently restrictive grounds like "mental cruelty." Access was further widened by requiring only a short stay to establish residence and therefore the right to divorce.

Once established, easy divorce proved a saleable commodity. Visitors could make use of the residence arrangement to establish instant domicile, and a divorce industry quickly arose that provided accommodation, dissolution and remarriage facilities, and accompanying entertainment. Nevada in particular was a poor state, underpopulated and lacking natural resources. The divorce industry became one of its few good earners, attracting consumers from the more prosperous and more conservative eastern states. Pro-family and religious groups continued to oppose it, and in 1913 were able to get the law changed so as to extend residence requirements to 1 year. But only 2 years later the previous residence requirement was reinstated, following angry lobbying by local people whose livelihoods depended on the industry. W. O'Neill (1967) considered that at this point the commercial advantages of the divorce industry were more important motives for legal liberalization than philosophical convictions.

Migratory divorce by nonresidents soon became famous, and its existence put pressure on neighboring states to loosen up their own procedures. As the number of states where divorce was readily available increased, it became more and more difficult for the remainder to maintain restrictive legislation. On the other hand, the antidivorce forces, usually led by the church, kept up the fight against "divorce-on-demand" legislation, particularly divorce on the demand of one party when the other wished to remain married. The nub of their argument remained much the same—the family was the basis of society and needed support; Christian marriage was a sacred institution; and men (and some women) could not be trusted with the decision whether or not to fulfill their obligations to their dependents. If divorce on demand were readily available, there were large numbers of irresponsible men (usually) who would take the opportunity to abandon their families, leaving many of these families destitute.

A common solution to these contending pressures was for the courts to institute a kind of *de facto* consent divorce, disguised as fault. Petitioners had to couch their cases in terms of marital fault, such as the adultery and cruelty of the partner; but the courts accepted weak and even obviously collusive evidence. The law at this stage had entered what some observers described as a state of "democratic compromise" between contending forces. The church, pro-family groups, and moral conservatives in general were pleased that they had been able to keep demand or consent divorce off the books. At a more strategic level, they believed that the maintenance costs associated with marital fault deterred men from leaving their wives. For example, a man who wanted a divorce either had to prove fault against his wife (which might be difficult), or persuade her to "give" him a divorce on the grounds of his fault. This allowed her to bargain for a reasonable settlement, which might give him second thoughts about abandoning his family; at the worst, it would provide the family with an income after his departure. The clients and their lawyers were more or less satisfied, as divorce continued quite easy to obtain. And governments were happy to avoid controversial legislation that might lose them office. The "democratic compromise" was seen by many as morally more desirable than client freedom of choice, because it kept ultimate power in the hands of the authorities (W. O'Neill, 1967; Rheinstein, 1972).

However, the compromise proved only temporary. As the number of petitioners for divorce increased, their tolerance for fictive legal practices decreased. The idea that marriage breakdown resulted from incompatibility rather than being the fault of one partner was by now well accepted, and respectable petitioners objected to hiring private detectives to incriminate their partners, or being themselves incriminated. Some conservatives who worried about the high divorce rate thought that more realistic laws complemented by conciliation procedures might actually reduce it. Many people worried about the destructiveness of the legal process and hoped to reduce this, if not the actual level of divorce. Thus, community groups with very different values began to converge in support of law reform.

Rheinstein pointed out that an important ideological input came from England, where in 1966 two prestigious bodies (the Archbishop of Canterbury's Group and the Law Commission) brought down reports concluding that the real issue for contemporary marriages was not one of marital fault but of whether the marriage was irretrievably broken down. The Church of England report was in fact very protective of marriage, and recommended a system of legal inquest into the viability of marriages that one or both partners wished to dissolve. However, it was the support given by the Church to the principle of irretrievable breakdown that received most publicity in the United States. Newspaper editorials asked: If the Archbishop of Canterbury thought that the concept of marital offense was out of date, and that current justifications for distinguishing between a guilty and an innocent spouse were "preposterous," then who could blame ordinary people for thinking the same?

By the late 1960s feminists had also joined the reform movement. They condemned fault law as hypocritical and unrealistic, and argued that legalized consent divorce, like legalized abortion, would give women more power over their lives. Discouraging experience since then has modified this perception, but at the time it appeared rational enough. Historically, Anglo-American divorce law has its roots in the Roman concept that the wife was her husband's possession, whom he could divorce as and when it suited him. Over the centuries, the law became less patriarchal, but U.S. feminists were able to point out that plenty of patriarchal echoes remained. For example, if a wife was found guilty of adultery she forfeited the right to maintenance, regardless of how poor she and her children had become, or how much she had contributed to the marriage. This was because, legally, she had defaulted on the marriage contract, which guaranteed exclusive sexual rights to the husband. She had therefore forfeited the rights of a matrimonially innocent woman, or more precisely one who in the (usually male) judge's opinion was matrimonially innocent. The very reasonable feminist interpretation of all this was that fault law perpetuated outdated notions of women as the possessions of men. They went further, to argue that no-fault law, by reconceptualizing women as independent rather than dependent persons, would be a step toward gender equality.

Ironically, one outcome was that feminists found themselves arguing for no-fault law in the company of a quite different interest group—a lobby of divorced men who objected to paying maintenance at all, and who proclaimed that "the divorce law and its practitioners were in league with divorced wives to suck the blood, not to mention, the money, of former husbands" (Weitzman, 1985, p. 17).

No-Fault Divorce

Pressure from all of these groups eventually led to the introduction of a no-fault divorce law in one state in 1970. Fittingly given its divorce history (47 divorces for each 100 marriages in 1960, compared to a national average of 26) this was California, which thus became the first state to eliminate fault grounds for divorce, and replace them by the single grounds of "irreconcilable differences." Divorce by mutual consent was now available, and so was divorce without the consent of one of the partners. The view of the law was that if one spouse thought the marriage was over, then it was. Furthermore, financial awards were disjoined from fault: Maintenance and property settlements were no longer to be considered a "reward for good behavior." Men and women were to be treated "equally" in these settlements, rather than in the terms of the "old sex-based assumptions" of the traditional law (Weitzman, 1985, pp. 17–20).

The other states soon followed California's lead, although around half chose to add a consent grounds to the already existing fault grounds, rather than to substitute consent for fault. In 1985, South Dakota, the last outstander, added a consent clause to its various fault grounds.

Glendon (1987) pointed out that the term *no-fault* was a misleading one invented by journalists, but that its adoption nevertheless had important consequences. At the time of the debate, no-fault automobile insurance had just been introduced, and the parallel was seized on. It did not mean that neither party was ever at fault, but rather that fault was not the relevant consideration. However, Glendon feels it encouraged attitudes of irresponsibility, by implying that no one was at fault when in fact one party often was; and that it thus victimized the weaker party. She and other critics saw further aspects of the legislation as victimizing women through their lack of realism. Where is the justice, for example, in telling a woman who has been a homemaker for 30 years and who has no other skills that the "old sex-based assumptions" regarding postdivorce maintenance no longer apply?

If the passage of the new laws did not in itself cause a surge in divorce, it certainly coincided with one. The U.S. divorce rate has risen 1,700% over the period (since 1867) for which statistics are available; but the sharpest rise occurred between 1970 and 1979. By 1973–1974, more U.S. marriages were being ended by divorce than by death. In addition, it is the youngest people who are by far the most likely to end their marriages. When the divorce rates for different age groups are looked at separately (Glick & Lin, 1986; Glick, 1988) we can see that there was some increase in all age groups, but it was those under 30 years of age who were doing most of the divorcing (see Fig. 3). This does suggest that those who have reached adulthood since consent divorce has been available are more ready than their predecessors to make use of it, so that the present high rate is likely to continue.

Remarriage and Single Parenthood

Up until 1975, newly divorced men and women readily remarried, apparently supporting the law reformers' belief that ready divorce would actually strengthen marriage by allowing new and better marriages to replace the old. Then there was a sharp turn away from remarriage among divorced people of all ages (Glick & Lin, 1986). Figure 4 shows that after 1965 remarriage at any age declined, but that the youngest women rejected it more. In consequence, the number of single-parent families resulting from divorce increased by 450%, from about 800,000 in 1960 to 3.6 million in 1983, including 12.6 million children living in mother-headed families. Over half the children whose parents divorce now spend at least 6 years with only one parent (Bumpass & Sweet, 1987).

Glick (1988; Glick & Lin, 1986), a U.S. demographer, believes these figures result from important changes in values. He found that those women who have traditionally had the best chances of remarrying—young and childless divorcees—have apparently lost interest in doing so. Better educated and better

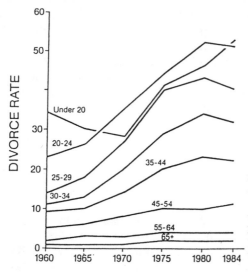

FIG. 3.   Divorce rates per 1,000 married women, by age: United States, 1960–1984 (from Glick & Lin, 1986, p. 739. Copyright © 1986 by the National Council on Family Relations, 3989 Central Ave., Suite 550, Minneapolis, MN 55421. Reprinted by permission).

able to support themselves than any previous generation, they evidently prefer cohabitation or single life to remarriage. It is now those in the weakest economic situation—poorly educated young women with dependent children— who are most likely to remarry, but even they do so in declining numbers. The best-educated women, who tend to marry late and consequently divorce later than others, are least likely to remarry, whether they have children or not. This, in Glick's view, is a matter of both choice and opportunity. On the one hand, such women may see little merit in a second marriage. But even

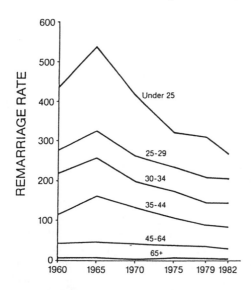

FIG. 4.   Remarriage rates per 1,000 divorced women, by age: United States, 1960–1982 (from Glick & Lin, 1986, p. 739. Copyright © 1986 by the National Council on Family Relations, 3989 Central Ave., Suite 550, Minneapolis, MN 55421. Reprinted by permission).

if they do, their relatively late age of marriage means that by the time they divorce there are few acceptable and available men, and those men who become available through divorce generally choose a new partner younger than their ex-wife. Whatever the cause, the result is that although today's mother-headed families are generally poor, they include a subgroup that is well-educated and often occupationally successful.

Not all of these divorcees are parents of course, and where they are, the children normally remain with one parent. Paralleling the rise in one-parent families therefore has been an even larger increase in adults living alone: from around 900,000 in 1960 to 4 million in 1983.

The Future

Trends in marriage and divorce are given to sudden and unexpected reversals, and the fact that U.S. divorce and remarriage rates were rather stable through the 1980s is no guarantee that they will continue so through the 1990s. Glick and Lin described a number of possible future developments that could maintain, raise, or lower the incidence of divorce and single-parent families in the future. Factors they see as likely to maintain or increase the incidence are more job opportunities and more education for women, the strengthening of equal rights philosophies, and the widespread social acceptance of divorce.

Of the factors that may lower divorce, perhaps the most important is the already apparent decline in marriage, and the increased acceptability of extranuptial births. Clearly, the person who is not married is not at risk of divorce, and incapable of remarriage. Another possibility is that the consequences of divorce may come to be seen as too costly: by women, by men, or by the state. The rise in divorce resulted in a severe drop in living standards for many women and children. Few mother-headed families received much or any child maintenance from the father, and by the mid-1980s around one half fell below the government's austere poverty line (Bergmann, 1986). By 1991, child poverty levels had risen still further (Kamerman, 1992; Strawn, 1992). It is possible, although on present evidence unlikely, that women in the future will turn away from divorce from fear of poverty, or that new social policies enforcing maintenance payments may dissuade some men from leaving their wives.

Another important but less predictable factor is the demographic one. The baby boomers—that large generation born in the years following World War II—will still be in age range for divorce and remarriage through the 1990s. Since 1970 the baby boomers have been the main contributors to the divorce increase. The sheer size of this cohort has itself been an important cause of divorce, as its entry into adulthood has meant that a large proportion of the total population has been in the age group in which most divorces occur. In addition, however, there may be something about the baby boomers that has made them specially divorce prone. By contrast, the postbaby-boom cohorts are generally depicted as a cautious lot. They are marrying at later ages, when they are more psychologically mature, and thus may be making better and more durable choices. However, there is not much evidence of this effect so far, as most breakups still occur in the first few years of marriage. The safest but unhelpful prediction is that generational effects could reduce or inflate divorce in the future, or that different trends could cancel each other out.

Summary

The U.S. divorce rate rose sharply in the 1860s and continued to rise until the beginning of the 1980s, since then it has stabilized around 5 per one 1,000 population per year. Remarriages increased up to 1965 but then declined. In consequence, the number of one-parent households resulting from divorce increased by 450% between 1960 and 1983, to 3.6 million. Although a proportion of mother-only families are headed by an unmarried woman, some two thirds of children in these families are living with a separated or divorced parent. For the majority of these, life in a mother-headed family will be a long-term arrangement. Thus, divorce has clearly made a major contribution to the increase in single parenthood. Consent divorce was opposed by many on the grounds that it would undermine the family, and damage women and children. It has certainly changed family structures, and children living in mother-headed families are five times as likely to be living below the poverty line as are children living with both parents (Bumpass & Sweet, 1987). Since 1967, their economic position relative to other families, never good, has further deteriorated (McLanahan & Booth, 1991). Nevertheless, ready divorce remains very popular, and the highest rates of divorce are now among the youngest couples. One expert observer (Glick, 1988) went so far as to suggest that today many young Americans may be reaching the conclusion that several years of marital experience is enough for them.

However, during the 1980s the divorce rate stabilized, while mother-headed families continued to increase. The discrepancy was mainly due to a rise in the formation of mother-headed families outside of marriage. Thus, as we see later, divorce is not the whole story.

THE SOVIET UNION

The Background

The (former) Soviet Union runs second to the United States in the prevalence of both mother-headed families (see Fig. 1) and divorce (see Fig. 2). The background of course is very different, so that we need to be careful about extrapolating "American" explanations to the Soviet Union or other countries. Some aspects of the Soviet experience are briefly described here, and we then make a comparison between the two countries.

In pre-Revolutionary Russia a wife was fully subordinate to her husband, who was considered responsible for her and her children "before the worldly and heavenly court" (Geiger, 1968, p. 218). Only the husband had the right to divorce, and only on the grounds of his wife's adultery. Following the 1917 Revolution, the early Bolsheviks instituted changes based on the view of Friedrich Engels that the bourgeois family is the prime site of women's oppression. As Engels described it, bourgeois marriage involves the trading of women for the purposes of men. "The modern family is founded on the open or concealed domestic slavery of the wife, and modern society is a mass composed of these individual families as its molecules" (Engels, 1884/1985, p. 102). Women were prevented from achieving independence by social arrangements that debarred them from education and job opportunities. It followed that the route to women's emancipation was through their full work force participation, improved family arrangements, and the minimization of domestic work.

After the Revolution, the new government therefore introduced equal pay for equal work, civil marriage, legal abortion, and a court-registration form of divorce. Engels' condemnation of bourgeois marriage did not extend to proletarian marriage, which was considered acceptable as, not involving property, it could not involve exploitation. In proletarian marriage there could be "no stimulus whatever to assert male domination." Therefore, marriage, and with it, divorce, were allowed to remain, but they were put as far as possible in the hands of the partners, rather than those of the law. When both partners agreed to divorce, a simple registration with a special agency (the ZAGS) was required. When only one spouse sought the divorce, it went to a People's Court, which could make orders regarding custody and child support, but had no right to refuse divorce or to explore issues of fault.

This first Soviet family law was considered an interim measure, and a new and further liberalized law was promulgated in 1926. Under the 1926 law, marriage was brought about by the agreement of the partners, and divorce was brought about by the decision of both or one. A marriage was deemed to have ended when one or both parties decided it had and told the other so, either orally or in writing. The communication did not in itself bring about a change in marital status: It merely provided evidence that the change had occurred. People who were reluctant to tell their partner the news in person could register their divorce with the ZAGS and the spouse would be notified by mail 3 days later, an arrangement known at the time as "postcard divorce." Having one's marriage and divorce registered could be useful with pension rights and other matters, but the existence of a marriage or divorce could be proved by other means, for example, evidence of a period of living apart (Moskoff, 1983; Rheinstein, 1972).

Postcard divorce invited abuse and many women and children found themselves abandoned. Geiger reported that it was not unusual to meet people in
the Soviet Union who had been married and divorced 15 times. A Moscow
registry that listed reasons why people divorce noted "many cases of instan-
taneous divorce as soon as 'he' learns that 'she' is expecting a baby." Housing was another issue. Revolution and civil war had produced a severe housing
shortage, and one way of gaining access to an apartment was through marriage. Following divorce, however, the original tenant did not automatically
remain in possession. One man told the following:

> The apartment situation often forced people into marriage—that is, girls mar-
> ried men with a suitable room and vice versa. They could then divorce and claim
> a part of the room they had married. It could often be heard said that someone
> had married a 20 square meter room. Then after two weeks or a month of mar-
> riage, the person concerned would divorce. The room would then remain in the
> possession of the least scrupulous, or the one with the strongest nerves. He or
> she would proceed to organize parties every night in his or her section of the room.
> These parties would usually be very noisy, smoky and drink-filled. As a final
> recourse, if his ex-wife had by that time not yet decided to move out, the man
> would bring in women. The ex-owner of the room would then attempt to find
> another man with a suitable room and the cycle would begin all over again. (cit-
> ed in Geiger, 1968, p. 209)

Despite abuses, the system served to legitimate the many separations and
desertions brought about by the turmoil and migrations of the times. But, after Lenin's death and Trotsky's exile, things changed. Stalin introduced a series of 5-year plans for a rapid build-up of heavy industry, and these required
a large industrial labor force. Women in particular were needed to be workers
both "by hand and by womb" (Peers, 1985, p. 116). The family was accordingly reconceptualized as the cornerstone of society. In 1936 a new Decree announced "the prohibition of abortion, the increase of allowances to women
after childbirth and to large families, the enlargement of the network of lying-
in clinics, nurseries, and kindergartens, greater severity of punishment for vio-
lation of duties of support," and some changes in the law of divorce (Rheinstein, 1972, p. 229). Divorcing parties now had to appear before a registrar,
and had to pay a substantial fine, which increased with the parity of the divorce:
Three times as much for a second divorce as for a first, and six times as much
for a third. As a result, the divorce rate dropped by more than one third between 1936 and 1938, and in the Russian republic by almost one half.

A much bigger change came in 1944, after the Nazi invasion had caused
millions of deaths. The 1944 Decree introduced special financial allowances
for pregnant and lone mothers, and established the honorary title of Heroic
Mother, the Motherhood Glory decoration, and the Motherhood Medal. The
distinction between legitimate and illegitimate children was re-established. The

claims of a legitimate child against its father were strengthened, but those of an illegitimate were wiped out. The state would, however, now pay a maintenance allowance for illegitimate children up to their 12th birthday.

Divorce was made much more difficult, by means of a two-stage legal procedure in which the courts were to be guided by "concern for the children and the mother and the strengthening of the institution of the family as one of the most important tasks of the Soviet state" (Rheinstein, 1972, p. 230). In the first stage, a People's Court had to determine the reasons for the divorce petition, call appropriate witnesses, and attempt a reconciliation. This occurred at a public hearing that the petitioner had to advertise in a local newspaper. If reconciliation failed, then the petitioner had the right to apply for a divorce in a higher court. The final decision could be argued all the way up to the republican supreme court. Cases could go on for many years.

The new procedures further reduced the divorce rate—from 1.1 per 1,000 population in 1940 to 0.6 in 1945 and 0.4 in 1950—and kept it down for the next 20 years. A main purpose of the 1944 law was population replenishment, on the premise that strong and stable families would raise a new generation of well-socialized citizens. In addition, by 1944 there were 50% more women of childbearing age than there were men. It was expected that many of these women would have affairs with married men, and bear their children. One outcome could be a new wave of divorce and re-partnerings, which the authorities feared could result in careless rearing and supervision of the new generation. By restricting divorce and taking responsibility for out-of-wedlock children, the state hoped to avert this outcome (Rheinstein, 1972).

The consequence was a vast growth in the number of de facto marriages and out-of-wedlock births. One observer estimated that there were 11 million illegitimate children in the Soviet Union in 1947, at which time 3,312,000 unmarried mothers were receiving state child support grants. The law made it especially easy for men to refuse support to these children, as only those born within a legal marriage had the father's name registered on the birth certificate (Geiger, 1968).

Despite the restrictions, people continued to seek divorce. For the courts the problem was one of deciding when divorce was "necessary" for the good of the spouses, the children, and the state. A working definition of "irretrievable breakdown" was gradually adopted, and when the law was finally liberalized, through 1965–1968, this became the criterion. The 1965–1968 reforms brought back the registration procedure for cases where both partners agreed to the divorce and there were no minor children. However, where there were minor children, or where one partner contested the divorce, the case had to go to court. A reconciliation procedure was also provided, and some 8%–12% of those coming before the court estimated as reconciled. There have been only minor changes to the law since 1968.

Causes of Divorce

Various studies show that the three most commonly listed official reasons for filing for divorce are alcoholism, adultery, and incompatibility of characters; that is to say, not too different from those in the Western nations. However, two other factors are usually described as particularly important—the housing shortage and the status of women (Moskoff, 1983). The housing shortage means that newly married couples are likely to share housing with their parents or others. The outcome is illustrated by one study (Chuiko, cited in Moskoff, 1983) which found that when the couple had lived with the wife's parents, it was typically the husband who filed for divorce, but when they lived with the husband's family, it was the wife who filed. In the new industrial towns, husbands and wives are often billeted in large and sometimes sex-segregated hotels, and divorce rates are also high.

The housing shortage also accounts for continued cohabitation after divorce, and for separations that are not registered as divorce, because the partners continue to live together for lack of other accommodation. Chuiko found that two thirds of all divorced couples in the city of Kiev were living in the same apartment after their marriages ended. Many of these families are effectively mother-headed although they are likely to be classed as two parent. Co-residence with the ex-partner naturally makes it more difficult to form a new family unit through remarriage.

Conflict over sex roles is also considered to make an important contribution to divorce. This is of course true in the Western countries also, but the Soviet picture is a little different. The Bolsheviks believed that women's liberation would be obtained through full participation in the work force, and the withering away of housework, which Lenin (1951) described as "barbarously unproductive, petty, nerve-wracking, stultifying and crushing drudgery" (p. 170). He proposed a system of collectivised domestic labor, public dining rooms, and universally available kindergartens and nurseries. Alexandra Kollontai (cited in Buckley, 1985) wrote:

> The individual household is dying. It is giving way in our society to collective housekeeping. Instead of the working woman cleaning her flat, the communist society can arrange for men and women whose job it is to go round in the morning cleaning rooms . . .
> [After childbirth], when the child is strong enough, the mother returns to her normal life and takes up again the work that she does for the benefit of the larger family—society. She does not have to worry about her child. Society is there to help her. Children will grow up in the kindergarten, the children's colony, the creche and the school under the care of experienced nurses. When the mother wants to be with her children, she only has to say the word; and when she has no time, she knows they are in good hands. Maternity is no longer a

cross. Only its joyful aspects remain; only the great happiness of being a mother. (pp. 34–35)

The first part of this program was quite readily enacted. Women were rapidly brought into the work force: By 1929, 27% of the work force was women; by 1930, 30%; by 1940, 38%; and by 1945, 55.3%. These figures reflect both the scope of the heavy industry program and the loss of men through revolution, famine, civil war, the German invasion, and internal imprisonment. Although these events impacted on the whole population, many more men than women actually died (e.g., in the Russian republic in 1959 there were only 58 men for every 100 women in the 35–59 age range). The high level of female employment has continued. The 1970 census found that 93.5% of women of working age were either working or studying, and even in the 1980s women still comprised over half the work force, and considerably more in some areas (Peers, 1985). Most women are in full-time jobs and most take little or no time out following the birth of children.

The domestic supports have been slower in arriving. Child-care services were never sufficient, and the communal dining rooms and domestic cleaning teams envisaged by Kollontai remained a fantasy. Few labor-saving or consumer goods were produced, and searching and queueing for food and domestic needs became a much-publicized feature of Soviet life. Taken together, this has meant a long second work day spent on housework by married women: an estimated 30–40 hours per week in the towns and cities, and up to 55 hours in some rural areas (Allott, 1985).

Although the Soviet Union from its beginning adopted an official policy of sexual equality, there is a continuing belief that domestic chores are women's work, and husbands' contribution remains limited. One study found that although women worked an average 80 hours week, men worked 50 (Peers, 1985). Another, in and around Moscow where attitudes are considered to be more modern, found that more than half the husbands sampled took no responsibility for children and two thirds did no cooking, everyday shopping, or household maintenance. A time budget study (Gruzdeva, cited in Peers, 1985) found that for women, marriage and parenthood meant abandonment of virtually all pursuits other than paid and domestic work, whereas for men it made little difference to overall leisure time. This held true for men of all education levels. Buckley (1985) noted that one impediment to change has been that complaints are often ignored on the grounds that equality has existed since the Revolution.

Given these inequities, it is easy to understand that many women may tire of marriage. However, studies of men's attitudes (Korolev, cited in Moskoff, 1983) show that many men also see marriage as restrictive and unsatisfying, and women as too bossy; and find the company of other men more rewarding. One consequence is that remarriage rates for both women and men are low, which maintains the high prevalence of mother-headed families.

Divorce and Fertility Decline

Although the state has tolerated fairly ready divorce since the mid-1960s, by
the 1970s it had become concerned about the associated decline in the birth
rate, which had fallen so low as to threaten labor force reproduction. Among
women married in 1970–1972 the desired number of children averaged only
1.7, and actual births paralleled this preference. The Census of 1979 showed
that 71% of all married women had two or less children.

Leonid Brezhnev put the demographic crisis on the agenda at the 25th Party
Congress in 1976, and at the 26th Congress in 1981 he outlined a package
of "important measures designed to increase the prestige of motherhood and
create an atmosphere of increased concern for families raising children . . .
and to raise the birth rate in most parts of the country" to two to three children per family. The measures included maternity and child-care leave, a baby
bonus on the birth of each child, priority for state housing to newlyweds and
families with young children, and a monthly child allowance for unmarried
mothers. The divorce law was not restricted again, as it was after 1936, but
a media campaign to encourage women to become more domestically oriented
and "feminine" was inaugurated. The media material provides an interesting contrast to counterpart publications in the west that were at the same time
telling their readers how to be more "masculine." One feature story for example explained the following to its readers:

> A woman only shows her worth, her essence, when she, alongside participating
> in production and socio-political activities, also fulfils her social role in the fami-
> ly, connected with the specific character of her sex. The character and structure
> of a woman's personality will be incomplete if she abstracts herself from her fam-
> ily functions, and especially from the function of maternity. (Peers, 1985, p. 138)

These various measures were associated with a stabilization of the divorce
rate, and a modest fertility increase occurred in the late 1980s. The 1989 Census showed however that this increase was mainly due to high birth rates and
very low divorce in the central Asian republics (Peers, 1985).

The Future

The liberalization of the divorce law in the mid-1960s was certainly responsible for a major increase in divorce, but only in the sense that it lifted a lid
previously firmly held down by state policy. Marriage continues to be subject
to multiple stressors and it is these stressors that are generally held responsible
for the high divorce rate.

The years since 1991 have brought such great changes that observers are reluctant to predict anything of the future, including divorce trends. Some likely influences have been noted, however.

First, the breakup of the Soviet Union has meant that the high divorce rates of Russia, Ukraine, and the Baltic states are no longer offset by the opposing pattern among the central Asian states. Recent divorce data are not available, but past trends suggest that when the figures for the Russian Republic are disaggregated, they will be very high by international standards.

Second, there is the emergence of a young adult generation whose men have not been decimated by war, invasion, and other catastrophes. A reduction in national service means that this larger group of young men are also more available. The sex ratio theory of gender roles (chapter 6) holds that an excess of women over men in a population, combined with strong male social power, results in a turning away from traditional family values and a high turnover in relationships. This certainly seems to have been the case through most of the 20th century, and if the theory holds, the attainment of a more equal sex ratio should see more stable marriages. However, the 1989 Census showed only a modest increase in the masculinity of the population (47.1% of the population in 1988 were men compared with 46.1% in 1971 and 45% in 1959). In explanation the Census notes that although deaths of able-bodied men from accidents and alcoholism decreased between 1984 and 1987, they remained unacceptably high. Thus, women may continue to predominate in the main marrying age brackets for some time to come. According to sex ratio theory, this means continuing instability of marriages.

Third, younger people are much better educated than their predecessors. Surveys show that younger men are more likely to believe in gender equality, and more willing to share domestic tasks. They also show that both sexes have higher expectations of marriage, and are more reluctant to tolerate disappointment. The first of these influences would be expected to promote marital stability, the second to reduce it. The evidence is that the latter effect is the stronger: Two thirds of divorces are of couples married 5 years or less (Peers, 1985).

Finally, there is the effect of recent political changes themselves, including the shift toward a market economy. Social life is already said to have changed considerably (Reddaway, 1993). The implications for marriage stability are as yet unknown.

COMPARISON OF THE UNITED STATES AND THE SOVIET UNION

Figure 5 illustrates the ups and downs in the two countries, and highlights the effect of both historical events and central policy control.

In the 1920s, for example, sympathy for divorce was growing in the United States but many state laws remained conservative, and the overall rate was

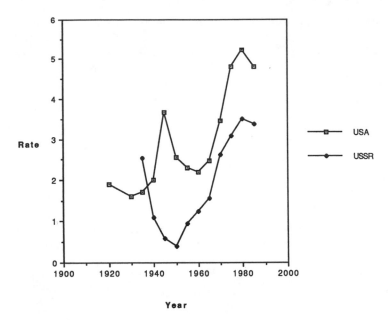

FIG. 5.   Divorce rates per 1,000 population: United States and Soviet Union
(from U.N. Demographic Yearbook, various editions).

quite modest. The Great Depression actually saw a decline in divorce. (In fact,
the stresses created by the Depression brought about an increase in family separations at this time, but the costs involved in divorce kept people out of the
courts until a later date.) The first big divorce wave came at the end of World
War II. There were no notable legal changes at this time, so that the rise can
be seen as the result of bottom-up pressure from those whose relationships had
not survived the war.

In the Soviet Union, by contrast, divorce was widespread during the 1920s,
due to both social policy and public demand. It declined sharply after 1936—by
government fiat—despite the far greater impact of World War II on the Soviet
population. The reason was the state's severe restrictions on divorce at this
time, imposed in an effort to stabilize the family. The figures come into parallel
in the later 1960s, when the law was liberalized in both countries. As in the
United States, the new legislation was partly a response to bottom-up pressure
from clients and court professionals, and the influence of opinion makers was
also important. For example, four of the Soviet Union's best known intellec-
tuals published an open letter arguing that mothers and children were being
penalized, and urging the Supreme Soviet to "repeal legally what life itself
rejects" (Geiger, 1968, p. 261). Observers consider that the Soviet authorities
were also influenced by a more pragmatic belief—that family life had become
more stable and that draconian controls were therefore no longer necessary
(Rheinstein, 1972).

The association with single-parent families also differs. It is generally considered that one reason why divorce in the United States has always been so high is because Americans who separate have been more likely to proceed to a legal dissolution than have separated people in other countries. In consequence, there has not been a large group of still married but permanently separated single mothers (Rheinstein, 1972). In the Soviet Union, the number of separations and mother-headed families has been consistently high, but the divorce tap has been turned on and off for policy reasons. In the later 1940s, when the U.S. figures rose, the Soviet Union's tap was screwed down precisely because of the large demand generated by wartime losses and movements. Since the mid-1960s there appears to be a much stronger association between legal and actual family status.

The United States and the Soviet Union thus present two pathways to a high incidence of mother-headed families. Changes in the divorce law have been important in both cases, but social and economic factors have been the motive force behind these. These are not of course the only pathways. In the next section we look at how some other countries have climbed their own paths up to slightly lower peaks. We then consider the common threads in these national stories, and describe some influences that seem to operate over and above cultural differences.

SWEDEN

We have seen how the United States and the Soviet Union have reached high divorce rates, and a high proportion of mother-headed families, by different pathways. Sweden presents a third pathway. As we saw earlier, Sweden has consistently reported one of the highest prevalences of mother-headed families among the Western European countries. Although the Swedish divorce rate is currently only middling, it was previously higher than any nation other than the United States and the Soviet Union, and it has dropped for a special reason—fewer marriages among younger adults, making for fewer people being at risk for divorce. Sweden has led the world in the move away from traditional marriage. Because of its reputation as a world leader in social welfare, social rationalism, and the rights of women, many people regard this as yet another way in which Sweden is showing other Western nations their own future. All of these features make Sweden an important reference point.

Background

The Scandinavian countries were among the last parts of Europe to convert to Christianity, among the first to accept the Reformation, and almost totally untouched by the Counter-Reformation. In consequence, their tradition is more strongly Protestant than most of Europe. In addition, the Swedish educated classes were greatly influenced by the liberal philosophers of 18th-century France and England. In the context of a small, homogeneous, and economically successful population, this resulted in a relationship between state and family that differs greatly from the Anglo-American and Soviet traditions.

Swedish law, like that of other European countries, initially embodied the Christian principle of the indissolubility of marriage. The clergy had the duty of overseeing sexual morals, using sanctions such as the stocks, the repenter's stool (a similar piece of furniture), and the public admonishment of sinners from the pulpit. When the country converted to Lutheranism, church and state remained generally hostile to divorce, but adultery and desertion became accepted as grounds that freed the innocent partner to remarry. The desertion grounds included "flight from the realm" where one party had left the country. In addition, a small number of (generally higher status) citizens were awarded a special royal dispensation to divorce and remarry (Rheinstein, 1972).

By the 18th century, military successes had made Sweden an important European power, with many links to France in particular. French and English rationalist and humanist ideas were adopted by the Swedish intelligentsia and by Lutheran theologians. Their commitment to social liberalism became still stronger after Napoleon's marshal Count Bernadotte was appointed to the Swedish throne in 1809. At this time, a committee of the four estates of the Swedish Diet proposed a reformed divorce law that would be based on the rationalist credo that "marriage, as a moral union is founded upon the mutual respect of the spouses, so that, once that mutual respect has vanished, the marriage has ceased to exist in their sentiments and in the conscience, even though there may still exist the appearance of the bond that had once been established."

The new law provided a gamut of fault grounds as well as "mutual aversion and hatred." The state reserved the right to inquire into the appropriateness of the divorce, and pastors retained their traditional obligation to name marital offenders from the pulpit and lecture them in front of the congregation. As the 19th century proceeded, however, the court moved steadily away from the fault concept and the guilty as well as the innocent were allowed to remarry. Because court proceedings were very slow, an alternative nicknamed the "Copenhagen divorce" became popular. This was the old flight from the realm grounds, now pressed into new service as a mutual consent divorce, and tolerated by the courts. One partner would leave the country, usually going to Copenhagen, and write from there announcing that he or she would not be coming back. The next day the other partner could start an action for divorce on the grounds of desertion, and this would usually be quickly granted. The traveller could then return home, and both were free to remarry (Rheinstein, 1972).

The Copenhagen divorce was no more hypocritical than equivalent devices in other countries that have aimed to protect marriage in principle by the use of strict laws, while in practice allowing a waiver to those who could afford it. But Swedish society put a high value on honesty and rationality, and the notion of a corrupt law favoring the wealthy was not as acceptable as it was in some other countries. Rationalist thinking also led to an early acceptance, by European standards, of the proposition that people are not persuaded to work harder at unsuccessful marriages by the knowledge that they cannot legally escape.

In addition, by the turn of the century the country was rapidly industrializing, creating a new bourgeoisie and a new proletariat, in both of which women were important. The mill workers, an important group, were mainly women, and women had early access to higher education. Women's rights became an issue, and it was argued these were damaged by strict laws that pushed many couples into *de facto* rather than legal marriages. The revolutionary ideas presented in Ibsen's and Strindberg's plays dramatized and strengthened an emergent belief that many of the rules that governed women's lives were not natural but oppressive. Ibsen's *A Doll's House* "fell like a bomb into contemporary life" wrote his biographer. "Perhaps no [work] in all literature had made such triumphal progress" (Meyer, 1962, p. 7).

In 1909, well before the Russian Revolution or the suffragette movement in England, the Swedish Parliament foreshadowed major reforms of the divorce law. The Copenhagen divorce was to go, the divorce procedure was to be completely secularized, the concept of irretrievable breakdown recognized, and the maintenance rights of women and children protected, even where a wife might be the guilty party. In 1915, the Law Commission, appointed to draft the new law, adopted the principle of consent that did not make its way into the law of most other Western countries for another 50 or 60 years.

> It is in general useless to try to maintain the formal tie between spouses whose inner relationship has deteriorated so thoroughly that no happy marital life can be expected any more. To require the parties to prove their discord to a court means to impose upon them hardship and discomfort. Very rarely would a judge find himself induced by such evidence to refuse the decree of separation. Dropping the requirement of such proof in cases of the parties' mutual consent simply means that their consensus is accepted as sufficient proof. (Swedish Law Commission, 1915, cited in Rheinstein, 1972, p. 139)

The new law allowed for divorce on the grounds of "deep and permanent discord" to be proven by joint petition for a judicial separation and followed after a year by grant of a divorce. A number of fault grounds were also retained, and desertion and separation were further grounds. In succeeding years, more than four out of five petitions were made through the mutual consent procedure, and another 12%–13% on the adultery ground, which did not require a waiting period.

Role of Social Security

An important feature of the Swedish law has been the accompanying provision of a package of social security, housing, education, employment, child care, and other aids. These arrangements were introduced as part of a full employment welfare state policy, but they had the extra effect of separating child support from marriage. Swedish sociologists point out that because the children of a single parent are guaranteed a home and income, there is no reason for a woman to stay in an unhappy marriage because she has nowhere else to go. The state expects fathers to continue to contribute to children's support, decrees what shall be paid, and collects it on the family's behalf, making up for shortfalls where necessary. These arrangements mean that for much of the 20th century the state has seen no need to use the divorce law to force men to stay married so that they can continue to provide for their dependents (Bernhardt, 1988).

As we have seen, the protection of women and children has been an important reason for keeping divorce laws restrictive in other countries. Of course, the law has never performed this task very well in any country, because divorced or married, a husband could always simply depart, leaving the family destitute. But where social security supports and women's economic opportunities are limited, the use of the law in this way may indeed provide women's and children's only protection. In consequence, even liberals who consider the concept of marital offense outdated have sometimes supported traditional divorce laws for this reason. Sweden, like the Soviet Union, broke the nexus between divorce and child support early in the century. Both countries have emphasized women's work force participation as essential to equal citizenship (by 1981 86% of Swedish women with preschool children were employed), but in Sweden this is complemented by many of the family supports that Kollontai envisaged but that the Soviet state failed to deliver. In addition, Sweden, unlike its neighbor, is small, homogeneous, remarkably united in social outlook and after World War II achieved exceptional prosperity.

Divorce and Marriage Incidence

The Swedish divorce rate rose from .03 per 1,000 population in the 1860s to 1.09 in 1947, at which time it was one of the highest in Europe. It continued to climb through the 1960s and came close to the U.S. rate in 1973. In 1974, the law was again altered. The waiting period was abolished for childless couples, and reduced to 6 months when children were involved. At the same time, the economic and other rights of women and children were strengthened. These changes were justified on the basis of two principles. The first was that divorce is a private matter in which the state has no concern, not even that of requiring parties to wait a while in case they should change their minds. The second

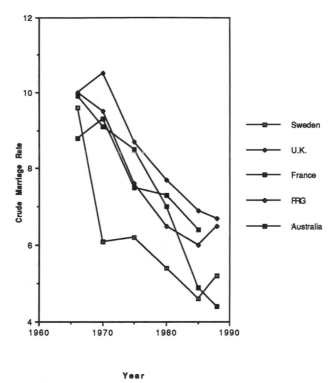

FIG. 6.   Marriage rates per 1,000 population, 1965–1988: selected countries (from U.N. Demographic Yearbook, various editions).

was that the continuing welfare of all citizens is very much the concern of the state, and that those who could suffer from the divorce—the children and the weaker partner—must have their rights safeguarded. Figure 2 shows that the divorce rate rose by two thirds in the first year of the new law (to 3.33 per 1,000) but then dropped back again, and has averaged around 2.5 per 1,000 throughout the 1980s (Hoem & Hoem, 1987, 1988; Popenoe, 1988).

These trends have to be seen in the context of marriage. Sweden, like most other Western nations, experienced a marriage boom in the 1950s and early 1960s and a subsequent marriage recession. But in Sweden the decline was particularly marked: In the 7-year period after 1966 marriages decreased by 40%, a drop that Swedish sociologist Trost (1985) believes has not occurred anywhere else or at any other time. (In the longer term, as Fig. 6 shows, the decline in France was just as great.)

In Sweden, the decline was steepest for the latest-born. Among women ages 20–24 the marriage rate per 1,000 was more than halved between 1966 and 1973, and by 1985 the figure was down to one fifth of the 1966 rate. For those a little older (25–29), the decline was almost as great. In consequence, the

TABLE 1
Marriage Rates for Women in Sweden and Comparison Countries
(per 1,000 Women)

	1966	1973	1980	1985
Women ages 20–24	194	91	53	40
Women ages 25–29	175	96	78	60
United States			127	
United Kingdom			168	
Australia			125	

Source: UN Demographic Yearbook (1982, 1986: Table 26).

average age of marriage has steadily risen, as has the number of people who seem unlikely ever to marry. Table 1 provides comparison data from several other countries, showing how dramatic the Swedish experience was.

These figures do not mean living alone. It is estimated that half of those born between 1956 and 1960 started living with partners as teenagers, that over two thirds of those in their early 20s are cohabiting, and that virtually all young people cohabit at some stage (Hoem & Hoem, 1987). In the early 1970s, these relationships were usually a prelude to marriage, but since then they have become more of an alternative. For example, one study found that only one fifth of childless women born in the 1950s had married their cohabiting partner within 8 years of starting to live with them, compared to 80% of those born in the 1930s (Qvist & Rennermalm, 1985). Furthermore, the birth of one or more children does not now greatly increase the likelihood of marriage. Somewhere over one quarter of all couples are currently estimated to be unmarried (Hoem & Hoem, 1987; Popenoe, 1987).

Part of the charm of cohabitation is that it involves less commitment and fewer obligations than marriage. So we would expect the breakup rate to be higher, and indeed it is. Hoem and Hoem (1988) found that among couples who had lived together and had a child, cohabitors were three times more likely to breakup than were the married. To Sweden's high divorce rate then must be added a much higher incidence of dissolution among that large proportion of marriages that are *de facto*. Taken together, it seems likely that they add up to the highest rate of family breakup in the industrialized world. An estimated 33% of women and 44% of men re-partner (either in marriage or, more typically, *de facto*) within 3 years, and some 50%–60% within 10 years (Hoem & Hoem, 1987; Popenoe, 1987).

These trends make for many single-parent families, many stepfamilies, and many single households. In 1980, for example, an estimated 16% of all families were headed by a single parent, a further 11% were in stepfamilies, and an estimated 18% of the total population were living in single-person households. In inner-city Stockholm in 1986, 63% of all households were reported to consist of a single person (Popenoe, 1987).

Causes of Breakdown

Why this flight from the traditional family? As in the Soviet Union, women's work force participation is high, but the conditions are far superior. Women with young children usually work part time, paid parental leave (which can be taken by fathers) is guaranteed, high-quality child care is provided, and health services are excellent. In consequence, Swedish women do not experience the work overload that pushes many Soviet women out of marriage.

Nor can the traditional risk factors of teenage marriage and pregnancy, shotgun marriages, and/or excessive unplanned births be blamed for the high divorce rate. Teenage marriage has practically disappeared, and Sweden currently has the lowest teenage pregnancy rate ever recorded in any country (Jones et al., 1985). Very few women give birth to more than three children, and even marriage and/or childbearing in the early 20s is relatively rare.

Another explanation often given for high divorce rates has been the relative inexperience of young people, which leads them to choose inappropriate partners, and to handle conflicts poorly. In the late 1970s, Trost (1977) predicted that the greater experience that young Swedes gained in consensual unions would result in more long-lasting marriages, because "the decrease in the marriage rate is the result of an increase in trial marriages, and therefore, those marriages being formed will be happier, and thus the divorce rate . . . will be lower" (p. 45). Trost subsequently pointed out that quite the opposite has occurred, and that although marriage continues to drop, the divorce rate remains high. Thus, relative maturity and relationship experience do not appear to inoculate against subsequent marriage breakdown.

Some answers are found in a study of legal and *de facto* marriages and breakups among 4,300 women born between 1936–1960.

As Table 2 shows, each birth cohort moved further away from the "traditional" pattern. Among the oldest (born 1936–1940), marriage was more likely than cohabitation to be the first family event, and those who cohabited first were most likely to choose marriage as the next event in their family careers. Births before marriage were relatively uncommon, and dissolution very uncommon. The next group (born 1941–1945) was more likely to cohabit as a first family event. Marriage was still the next most likely step, but a premarital birth had become more common. The next group (born 1946–1950) again was much more likely to cohabit as a first event, and premarital births and dissolution had become still more common. For those born from 1951 to 1955, marriage as a first event had become a rarity, and the next event after cohabitation was more likely to be a birth than a marriage. Finally, for the youngest groups, the most common pattern was cohabitation followed by a return to

TABLE 2
Family Careers of Five Cohorts

Cohort	First Event*			Next Event After Cohabitation*		
Born	Number	Marriage	Cohab.	Marriage	First Birth	Dissolution
1936–1940	490	234	187	143	33	9
1941–1945	990	360	505	334	116	45
1946–1950	1,014	155	698	358	210	112
1951–1955	1,030	66	832	269	280	179
1956–1960	699	16	493	67	124	136

*Those for whom no information was available are not included.

Source: Hoem and Hoem (1988. Reprinted by permission of the authors and the Union Internationale pour l'Étude Scientifique de la Population, Liege, Belgium).

single living. Those from middle and higher status families, and those who were themselves better educated, or in better jobs, were the most likely to follow the new pattern.

Across the group as a whole, the *de facto* marriages had four and one half times the dissolution rate of marriages, and the youngest women (born in the 1950s) had the highest breakup rate, even where partnerships had already lasted 3 years. The trends were similar for women with and without children, although the breakup rate was greater among the childless. The breakup rate of second partnerships (married or *de facto*) were again most common among the later-born and those from better-off homes (Hoem & Hoem, 1988).

Hoem and Hoem's figures thus show that looser and briefer partnerships have steadily gained in popularity over marriage. The incremental nature of the changes—each 5-year birth cohort less traditional than the last—suggests a steady shift in values, such that each new birth cohort has entered adulthood with less traditional attitudes toward the family. There seems no reason why the movement should reverse direction in Sweden or other countries with similar trends, unless social conditions themselves change considerably. Some observers suggest that loose relationships are in fact the natural preference of both women and men when they are not constrained by economic necessities, social stigma, or religious belief. Under such conditions, it is argued, the "weak" institution of cohabitation has more appeal than the "strong" institution of marriage, which makes demands of its own that are likely to infringe the autonomy and personal freedom of the partners (Bernhardt, 1988; Hoem & Hoem, 1987, 1988).

Summary

Sweden offers a third model of a high-divorce nation. The most striking feature is the state's early abandonment of divorce law as a tool for forcing fathers to support their children; and the state's provision of social services that give mothers and children relatively independent status. The decline in divorce since the mid-1970s is an artifact of the declining popularity of marriage. As in the quite different societies of the United States and the Soviet Union, a high proportion of families with dependent children are mother-headed, but due to the social security system's extensive provisions for children and parents, the consequences do not seem to have been socially damaging. The Swedish birthrate compares quite favorably with that of other European nations (Hoem & Hoem, 1987). Single parents are not heavily disadvantaged, and there is no evidence that the children of *de facto* and dissolved unions are any worse off than others. Nevertheless, it is certainly a different way of living. One observer has commented that

> From one point of view, living alone can be seen as a privilege of affluent people and as an active expression of individualism. But when living alone becomes a mass phenomenon, questions must be raised about the changing character and quality of social relationships, especially when single person households are considered together with such factors as low fertility and high family dissolution. In all of world history people throughout their lives have lived in the close presence of family members. That is, people have usually seen other family members at least each morning and evening, eaten most meals with them and slept nearby. In turn this generated a common domestic life and shared intimacy that has always marked the human condition, for better and for worse. What happens when this age-old aspect of the human condition is changed? (Popenoe, 1987, p. 179)

JAPAN

Background

Japan has always presented something of a puzzle to students of divorce and its causes. Whereas in most countries industrialization and urbanization led to increased divorce, in Japan the same social changes resulted in less divorce.

Figure 7 shows a very high rate in the late 19th century—well above that obtained in many Western nations today—and a decline from the 1920s, the very time when Japan began industrializing. This paradox particularly intrigued sociologist William Goode, whose 1963 book *World Revolution and Family Patterns* used the example of Japan to develop a theory of culture and divorce.

Japan remained a feudal society until the late 19th century, when the Meiji Restoration saw the beginning of modernization. Official divorce records were kept from 1882, and showed the rate to surpass that of any other nation at the time. The year 1883 recorded a divorce rate of 3.39, a figure that was not reached by the United States until the 1970s.

Goode argued that this was a natural outcome of a family system that did not support marriage except among the upper classes. Western divorce laws

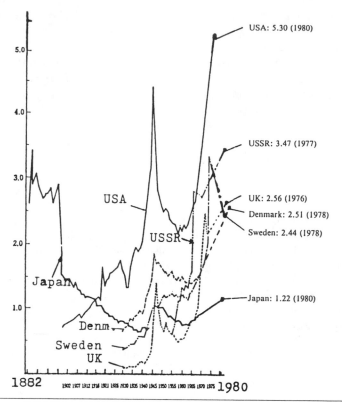

Sources: United Nations, *Demographic Yearbook*, vol. 30 (1979).
        Vital Statistics of the United States (1981).
        Vital Statistics of Japan, vol. 1 (1981).

FIG. 7.   Divorce rates per 1,000 population, 1882–1980: selected countries (from Kumagai, 1983. Copyright © 1983 by the National Council on Family Relations, 3989 Central Ave., Suite 550, Minneapolis, MN 55421. Reprinted by permission).

evolved within the Christian tradition of marriage as a sacrament ordained by God, not to be dissolved except in case of serious marital fault. In Japan, by contrast, the sacred institution was the lineage (the *ie*), whose continuity must be maintained through male heirs and the worship of the ancestors. Expelling an unsatisfactory wife was therefore an acceptable practice. However, as Goode saw it, the rich and powerful would not want to damage family connections forged through marriage, and would therefore restrict divorce and devise means to prevent it. In the Japanese system this was done by allowing husbands to take concubines if they were dissatisfied with their wives (or even if they were not), and by socializing girls into accepting (and subsequently enforcing on others) a subordinate and submissive status. The ordinary classes also gave women low status, but had less to gain from marital permanence, and did little to support it. In fact, official divorce rates for this period are higher than marriage rates, as marriages were often informally undertaken and unregistered (Kumagai, 1983; see Fig. 8).

There were regional and cultural variations, but in general a young wife passed at marriage into her husband's family, who regarded her as a labor source. If they were disappointed by her efforts, or disliked her, she was fired, like any other unsatisfactory employee. All family authority and property was vested in the head of the lineage, and descended at the death of a father to his eldest son. A husband's first loyalty was expected to be to his lineage, not to his wife, and the personal relationship between spouses was generally not very strong. A Western observer described the situation as one where "If you love your wife you spoil your mother's servant; it is almost as bad as flirting with your housemaid in England" (Hendry, 1981, p. 43).

In principle, both spouses could seek divorce, but as a wife was defined as inferior and duty bound to obey her husband, in practice divorce was a man's choice. After divorce the children stayed with the husband's family, and no maintenance was due to the wife, whose family was supposed to take her back, if it could. The written law provided seven grounds on which a man could

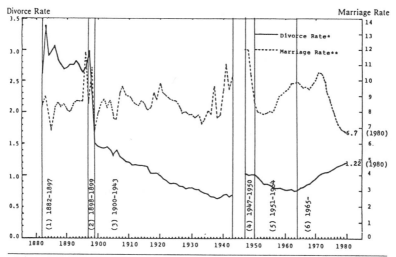

Sources: 1882–1899 Prime Minister's Office, Bureau of the Census, *Nihon Teikoku Tōkei Nenkan* (Tokyo, 1915).

1900–1979 Ministry of Health and Welfare, *Vital Statistics: 1979, vol. I* (Tokyo: Health and Welfare Statistics Department, 1980).

1980   Estimations of the Health and Welfare Statistics Association (Tokyo, 1981).

*Rate per 1,000 population.

**Rate per 1,000 population.

FIG. 8. Marriage and divorce rates in Japan, 1882–1979 (from Kumagai, 1983. Copyright © 1983 by the National Council on Family Relations, 3989 Central Ave., Suite 550, Minneapolis, MN 55421. Reprinted by permission).

divorce his wife—sterility, adultery, disobedience to parents-in-law, loquaci-
ty, larceny, jealousy, and bad disease. But the common practice of not regis-
tering a marriage for a time meant that a wife could be expelled even if blame-
less on all these counts. Official records show that the most common reasons
given for divorce at this time were poor choice of partner (sometimes a choice
made by parents or relatives), money problems, disagreements with in-laws,
and the ease of divorce and remarriage. The early period of the Meiji Restoration was a turbulent time, which may also have contributed to divorce (Hendry, 1981).

The Civil Code of 1898 introduced registration of marriage and divorce,
and required that people seeking divorce present written reasons for this. This
had the intended effect: Divorce declined, and in time it came to be seen as
shameful. The decline continued until 1943, with slight increases from time
to time associated with war and calamities like the Great Kanto Earthquake
of 1923.

Figure 7 illustrates the paradox that divorce declined in Japan at the very
time that it was on the increase in Western countries. Japan, like Western Europe and the United States was developing industry and national education
standards at this time, and a large proportion of the population was moving
into the cities. But although these factors seemed to promote divorce in the
other countries, the opposite occurred in Japan.

A possible reason was the development for the first time of a nuclear family, one that combined Japanese and imported ideas. In this new type of family
the husband–wife bond was stronger that under the *ie* system, but there was
a continuing emphasis on men's authority and freedom and female submissiveness and domestic virtue. Put briefly, this looks not too different from the
European tradition, but Japanese culture gave these marriages a different style
from the Christianity-influenced nuclear families of Europe; and many marriages continued to be arranged by kin (Kumagai, 1983).

Under the direction of General MacArthur, the new Japanese Civil Code
of 1947 officially abolished the *ie* system of parental control, redefined marriage as based on individual choice rather than parental permission, distribut-
ed inherited property equally among spouse and children, and modified the
grounds for divorce. The direction of change was in a sense the reverse of that
in the Christian countries, where the movement has been from fault-based to
consent divorce. Japanese divorce had always been a matter of mutual consent, with the wife however duty bound to consent to her husband's wishes.
The new law allowed a spouse (usually wife) who was not prepared to accept
the mutual agreement arrangement to go to court, and to demand that her
fault be established, or some form of compensation paid. In effect, she was
given the right to contest an unfair termination of employment. There was
a postwar rise in dissolutions, but as Fig. 7 shows, this was much more modest
than in the Western countries.

Contemporary Marriage and Divorce

The small nuclear family became steadily more dominant through the 1950s and early 1960s. Divorce continued to be seen as a disgrace, and could be a disaster for women who had nowhere else to go and no means of support (Stack, 1992). The rate declined steadily to a low in 1963, and has risen only modestly since then. The 1960s saw the appearance of Japan as an economic miracle, accompanied by a jump in education and job opportunities for women. Women entered the industrial work force, age at first marriage rose, and love marriages became the norm, increasing from 50.3% of marriages in 1966 to 62.8% by 1973. The proportion of divorces initiated by the wife, rare in previous times, steadily increased. By 1978, wives were the author of more than two thirds of all divorces, a figure similar to that in Western nations (Headlam, 1984; P. McDonald, 1986). Interestingly, research studies show the divorce incidence for arranged marriages and love marriages to be much the same (Kumagai, 1983).

The Japanese nuclear family continues to differ from the Euro-American nuclear family. Men spend a lot of time away from home, and being a mother is more central for women than being a wife. One study that compared U.S. and Japanese wives found that the Americans perceived that their husbands took more pride in them, cooperated more with them, showed them more respect and sensitivity, and accepted them more than did the Japanese (Durrett, Richards, Otaki, Penebaker, & Nyquist, 1986). At the same time, children have traditionally belonged to the father's lineage, and even as late as 1950 a minority of divorced mothers had custody of children. By 1978, an estimated 72% of divorced mothers with one child had custody, and 55% of those with three children had custody—still far lower than in most European countries. Children in the custody of their mothers are particularly likely to lose contact with their fathers, as the notion of joint responsibility for children following divorce has never had a part in Japanese law. Surveys show that divorced Japanese women are far less interested in remarriage than are men, and that their enthusiasm for it has declined over time (Kumagai, 1983).

Summary

Japan provides an example of a (previously) high divorce rate associated with low status of women: in effect, ready divorce of women by men without any need to prove fault. Whereas in Western nations divorce went up as women's rights increased, the opposite occurred in Japan because men (or rather, the man's lineage) no longer had such a free hand. The conditions usually associated with high divorce—industrialization and urbanization—are now well and truly in place, and divorce initiation has shifted from men to women; but the incidence is still low. Loss of the husband's income is often a key problem for women, and it is not uncommon for a wife to remain in a marriage because of her financial dependence. The incidence of mother-headed families is very low. These outcomes are attributed by observers to a strong continuing tradition of male supremacy that leaves little place for the independent woman. Kumagai (1983) concluded the following:

> The level of divorce in Japan will never become as high as that in America. Tradition in Japan is still so strong that the attitudes and behavior of the Japanese are consciously and unconsciously affected. The transformation of the family system from a stem to a nuclear type does not necessarily result in changes in family interaction patterns. Modernity and Japanese tradition may coexist without conflicting with each other. The modern liberal impulse to pursue divorce might be suppressed by the weight of tradition. (p. 105)

THE MID-RANGE COUNTRIES

So far we have looked at countries where for historical and cultural reasons divorce is or has been especially prevalent. In the United States, the influences of liberal-individualist philosophy and a mobile population have been seen as especially important; in Sweden, a social-liberal philosophy buttressed by welfare state provisions; in the Soviet Union, the official adoption of Engels' analysis of the family in the context of revolution and war; and in Japan a non-Christian patriarchy.

There are many other countries that have lesser rates than the United States, the Soviet Union, and Sweden, but show the same pattern of slow growth over the first half of the 20th century, a peak after World War II, a plateau or decline until the mid-1960s, and then a rise to new heights. Figure 2 included four of these—France, Federal Republic of Germany, United Kingdom, and Australia. A similar picture is found in other Western countries, including Austria, Belgium, Denmark, the Netherlands, Hungary, Luxembourg, Norway, Switzerland, Canada, and New Zealand. The four included in Fig. 2 can therefore be said to display the modal or midrange Western divorce pattern.

The midrange countries have some common features that have influenced this pattern. Each is or has been a Christian country with a philosophic allegiance to family stability, but also to individual freedom and happiness. Each has had a traditional form of family organization, with men holding superior authority and property rights, and women centered in domestic life. Each expanded its industry and technology after World War II and in the process expanded educational and job opportunities, especially for women. Each provides a variety of social services that make it possible, but not generally very comfortable, for mother-headed families to survive. Each has had a women's movement—some stronger, some weaker—that has pointed out that women's interests are not necessarily the same as those of the family, as defined by men.

There are also differences that have influenced divorce figures. Religion has been especially important. In the divorce debates between traditional Christian values and liberal individualism, the latter never achieved the ascendance in the midrange countries that it did in the United States and Sweden. More precisely, liberal individualism had short periods of ascendancy in France and Germany that were quickly followed by a return to marriage-protective legislation. In England, the great authority of the Church of England, and the network of powerful institutions that looked to it for moral leadership kept divorce low until after World War II. In Australia, the inheritance of English law and the presence of a large (mainly Irish) Roman Catholic minority had the same effect. Today, the Roman Catholic sectors of these countries have lower divorce rates than the general population, but a higher incidence of separation.

England

In England, the Church of England has dominated divorce law. Up until 1857 the Church held that marriage, as a sacrament, was indissoluble, and divorce was only available by means of a special Act of Parliament. In 1857 a reinterpretation of the Bible was made: It was now read as authorizing a man to divorce his wife who had committed a single act of adultery. In doubtful accord with the scriptures, but under the influence of the movement for the protection of women, a wife was also given entitlement to divorce, but only if her husband's adultery was accompanied by another offense such as severe cruelty, desertion, or rape. These modest reforms were instituted in the context of much anxiety lest the provision of easy divorce should damage the stability of marriage, the home, and the family. This fear was nicely summarized in the words of one judge who pronounced that "The possibility of freedom begets the desire to be free and the great evil of a marriage dissolved is that it loosens the bonds of many others" (Burns, 1980, p. 8).

Under the 1857 law, the "innocent" party was required to prove the other guilty, and the court made decisions regarding property, maintenance, and custody in light of guilt or innocence. One complication of the offense concept was that marital offenses committed by both partners canceled each other out, so that a couple who had proved adultery against each other could, at the end of the case, find themselves still married. This arrangement was satirized in A. P. Herbert's (1934) novel, *Holy Deadlock*, in which a long-separated husband agrees to "give" his wife a divorce by pretending to commit adultery, but the wife's honesty about her own feelings ruins the case. The husband's lawyer concludes

> "Queer thing," said Mr. Boom after his seventh oyster. "Just an ordinary English collusive divorce case—thousands like them every year. And all goes well

until people start telling the truth. Your part of it—the part that was all lies from
beginning to end—isn't questioned at all. . . .

You can go to Court and ask for a divorce yourself . . . the only thing is that
you'd all be charged with a conspiracy to deceive the Court and pervert the processes of justice . . . Your position is this, you see: either you have committed adultery,
in which case you can't ask for a divorce; or you have not, in which case you
can be sent to prison for pretending that you have. The Laws of England are
a continual joy.'' (pp. 304–305)

As *Holy Deadlock* makes clear, English court proceedings were expensive,
and mainly the prerogative of the wealthy. Most people settled for legal separations, which were adjudicated through the magistrates' courts. It was estimated that before 1937 divorce petitions made up only one tenth of all
matrimonial proceedings (McGregor, 1970); the other nine-tenths being legal
separations. In 1937 the grounds were widened, and the introduction of legal
aid in 1950 brought divorce within the reach of ordinary people.

The major change however came following the publication in 1966 of the
reports of the Archbishop of Canterbury's Group (1966) and the Law Commission (1966). Both of these recommended that the law be replaced by one
that emphasized the state of the marriage rather than the guilt or innocence
of the spouses. The Law Commission stated that the aim of the law should
be to dissolve ties with the ''maximum fairness and minimum bitterness, distress and humiliation'' and the Archbishop's Group, although not accepting
this role for church law, found that it was ''not an improper or unworthy conception for the law of a secular society to uphold.''

The Divorce Reform Act of 1969 followed these recommendations by making irretrievable breakdown the sole ground. However, breakdown had to be
proved either by fault, or by mutual consent or separation, and as fault-based
divorce is usually quicker, it has remained the most popular option. The court,
following the Archbishop's Group's recommendations, has in principle the duty
to inquire into the facts of each case to see whether the marriage has really
broken down. However, at the administrative level it has been decided that
undefended cases do not have to appear in court, and are merely reviewed
by a registrar and passed on to the judge for automatic issue of a decree. As
some 95%–98% of cases are undefended, this means that virtually all decisions are made by clients and their lawyers. Glendon (1987) commented on
the irony whereby a quietly introduced cost-cutting administrative procedure
had far more impact than the fiercely debated legal changes that preceded it.
However, as Fig. 2 shows, countries with other legal and administrative procedures showed the same divorce surge after 1970. Thus, the lawmakers' belief
that the court should have the right to establish whether a marriage had really
broken down was by this time way behind the thinking of the general public
and in practice not possible.

The divorce rate increased almost threefold between 1970 and 1988 (Fig. 2).

The proportion of single-parent families doubled and by 1991 was one of the highest in Europe. These developments were accompanied by a decline in marriage (Fig. 6).

France

Although British law has followed a fairly straight line toward greater ease of divorce, French divorce law has seen a number of turn abouts. Under the Edict of Nantes, French Protestants were allowed the right of divorce, whereas the Catholic majority were not. This provision was revoked two centuries later after the Protestants' rapid growth had alarmed Church and State and propelled the country into religious war. Another century on, and following the Revolution, the Revolutionary Law of 1792 proclaimed marriage a secular institution designed to promote the happiness of the partners, and terminable on a range of fault and consent grounds. Outside of Paris the law was not much used but in the capital up to one in three marriages were dissolved.

After the execution of Robespierre and the ascendance of Napoleon, conservative attitudes again became dominant, and the divorce law, now seen as recklessly radical, was a prime target of attack. It was revoked by Napoleon, who made divorce available only in case of serious marital offense, or by mutual consent, the latter by means of a procedure so complicated and expensive that it was rarely used (Rheinstein, 1972).

Things changed again after 1814, when Catholicism once more became France's official religion, and marriage once again proclaimed to be indissoluble. All that was now allowed was judicial separation, which allowed neither the guilty nor the innocent partner to remarry.

Divorce on the grounds of marital fault was reinstated in 1884, and as in other countries the various fault grounds were expanded *de facto* to cover many consent and incompatibility separations. In particular, the grounds of "maltreatment, excesses, and grave injury" were stretched to cover the same complaints as did mental cruelty in the United States.

The fact that divorce remained low has been attributed to the strong family base of French society—conservative, Catholic, and valuing respectability. A safety valve was provided by widespread tolerance of *de facto* marriages between partners who were still officially married to someone else (Rheinstein, 1972).

However, as in other countries, this arrangement gradually came to be seen as hypocritical and restrictive rather than realistic, and consent grounds were reintroduced in 1975. Divorce has risen moderately and steadily since that time, in the context of a marked decline in marriage. In the early 1970s, single-parent families were more common than in Britain, West Germany, or Australia, but the increase since then has been less (Fig. 1).

Germany

Germans also were able to obtain consent divorce in the late 18th century, in this case due to legislation introduced by Frederick the Great. Partners could mutually consent to a dissolution, or one could petition unilaterally so long as he or she could prove "through relevant facts the existence of so violent and deeply rooted an aversion that no hope remains for a reconciliation and the achievement of the ends of the marital state" (cited in Rheinstein, 1972, p. 25). As in France, this no-fault law was quickly repealed; and consent divorce did not reappear until 1976 in the Federal Republic of Germany (West Germany). The 1976 law instituted marital breakdown as the single ground for divorce, defined as 1 year of separation in the case of mutual consent, and a longer period where one partner contested the proposed terms.

The German legislators had the stated aim of improving on U.S. law by protecting the rights of dependent women and children while abolishing the concept of guilt. This was to be done by giving judges discretion to delay or deny divorce in cases where it was sought by one partner and contested by the other. The petitioner had to satisfy the court that adequate arrangements for custody and property division had been made, including superannuation and social security rights. Partners (read wives) who could show that they would be seriously financially damaged by the divorce could claim extra support for "marriage-conditioned" disadvantage. Although this was seen as a special case, in fact marriage-conditioned disadvantage was the norm in West Germany (as well as in most other countries). This meant that most cases fell in principle under the special case provision.

These proposals were extensively debated before the new law was introduced, and opposed by many on the grounds that husbands would face a crushing burden of repayments to ex-wives and children, even when they were the innocent party to the divorce. Several studies, however, have shown that this has not happened (Caesar-Wolf, Eidmann, & Willenbacher-Zahlmann, 1983; Willenbacher & Voegeli, 1985). Very few cases have been contested, even where the wife appeared to have a case for a better settlement; and those that were originally contested had mostly changed to mutual consent by the time the case came to court. One research group (Caesar-Wolf et al., 1983) concluded that the lawyers and judges proceeded much as before and that the intention of the law—to protect vulnerable ex-partners and children by financial equalization and compensation—has "fallen flat" (p. 26).

At the same time, the birthrate in West Germany fell to 1.29 births per woman in 1985—which was the lowest ever recorded for any country in the world. Almost one quarter of these births were out of wedlock, and it was estimated that one quarter or maybe more of the youngest women would remain childless. The "moderate" divorce rate has to be seen in the light of this reduction in the marrying population, and thus of those at risk of divorce (Hopflinger,

1985). There were fewer single-parent families than in France in the early 1970s, but more by the mid-1980s; however, the increase was not so great as in the United Kingdom and Australia. East Germany has for many years had more divorce than West Germany, so reunification may result in some increase for the former.

Australia

Australian law took up much of the English tradition, but was quicker to enlarge the number of marital faults that could be used as grounds for divorce. As in other countries a system of consent-disguised-as-fault evolved, with judges in the state of New South Wales being particularly willing to award divorces on the grounds of cruelty. (There is no other evidence that inhabitants of this state are crueler than other Australians.) As in France, there was reasonable tolerance of *de facto* marriages between partners one or both of whom were still married to someone else. For women, changing one's name by deed poll to that of the *de facto* husband was quite a popular option.

Comparison with the United States shows that the much higher U.S. divorce rate was not simply the result of more marriage breakdowns. It was also due to the fact that Australian couples who separated were much less likely to proceed to divorce. Thus, Census figures show that before the introduction of no-fault legislation in 1975 the number of Australians describing themselves as "married but permanently separated" was consistently higher than the number of divorced, whereas the reverse was the case in the United States. In 1947, for example, there were 2.4 times more separated than divorced Australians, at a time when there were 2.1 times more divorced than separated in the White U.S. population (Burns, 1980).

This situation led some anticonsent law campaigners in the 1970s to argue that there was something in the national character that made Australians prefer *de facto* separations over divorce. However, the divorce peak that followed the introduction of the 1975 law was exceptionally high—a rise of 260%—falsifying the national character argument, and ushering in a new fear that the Australian divorce rate would now outdistance that of England and rival that of the United States. This proved not to be the case, as once the backlog had moved through the courts, the divorce rate fell back to its previous rate of increase, and has since stayed close to the English rate.

From the beginning of the no-fault law's operation, a peculiarity of the Australian social security system meant that a special government pension available to single parents was actually reduced if a woman received more than a token amount of child maintenance from her ex-partner. Knowing that most men soon default on maintenance payments, the court accordingly mostly ordered that only "top-up" maintenance be paid. This has proved costly to social security funds and has some other disadvantages: and from 1989 a

Swedish-style system of garnishing of ex-partners' wages for child support payments was introduced.

One-parent families increased by 8% between 1966–1971, followed by a much larger increase between 1971–1976 (26%), an even larger increase between 1976–1981 (43%), and a further 10% between 1981–1986. Thus, the greatest growth was in the 5-year period following the shift to no-fault divorce legislation, but this was preceded by a substantial increase and followed by a further one. As in other countries, the divorce increase was accompanied by a decline in marriage.

CONCLUSION

Easy divorce was, for a long time, fiercely opposed in Western nations, and the law was used as a means of restricting it. This opposition collapsed in most countries at much the same time—in the late 1960s and early 1970s. Those opposed to no-fault divorce feared that such legislation would ''open the floodgates'' (to use the popular metaphor of the time) and some radicals hoped that it might. But the exact outcome—the divorce surge of the 1970s and the plateau of the 1980s—was not predicted or expected. The surge in divorce coincided with an increase in single-parent families.

There have been two basic arguments against consent divorce. The first is that dependent women and children will be abandoned and reduced to poverty, the second is that society needs a stable family as its base. The first fear has proved quite justified. Lack of adequate alternative supports have indeed disadvantaged single-parent families, even though single mothers in the 1990s have greater access to reasonable jobs and social security than ever before. Marriage-conditioned disadvantage has proved a hard condition to rectify. However, Sweden has gone a long way toward doing so, through a threefold policy of drawing women into the work force, providing a package of family support services, and insisting on continuing support from noncustodial parents. Comparison with other countries indicates that all of these policy directions are necessary. For example, simply increasing women's work force participation will not keep mother-headed families out of poverty. The full threefold policy of course requires a high level of state intervention.

The second ground of opposition is harder to evaluate. The nations we have looked at do not seem to have crumbled since consent divorce arrived. What has crumbled, with quite amazing speed, is the opposition to what were very recently considered deviant or even criminal alternatives to marriage (e.g., cohabitation, out-of-wedlock childbearing, and gay living). Opposition—on religious and other grounds—of course continues, but ordinary people seem to have accepted this huge social change very calmly. For the majority, despite national differences, marriage as a God-given institution has quietly subsided into marriage as a choice very similar to any other.

We have considered the reasons that have been given for changes to divorce law in different countries, and the arguments against these changes. What about the reasons of those who actually seek divorce for themselves. Why did so many people in so many different countries decide by the late 1960s that they needed to end their marriages? What are the reasons for the divorce surge of the 1970s, and the continuing high level? Some suggestions have already been made in our discussion of the divorce history of different countries. In the next section, we look in more detail at some sociopsychological explanations that have been offered for these trends.

SOME ANSWERS AND EXPLANATIONS

At this stage, we can conclude that the answer to whether easier divorce is responsible for more mother-headed families, is yes, to a degree. In most countries the legal changes were followed by a rise in the prevalence of one-parent families. Although single-parent numbers were on the increase before the introduction of no-fault laws, the big increase came after their introduction. On the other hand, the extent to which people make use of apparently similar laws varies quite a bit from one country to another, and sometimes within countries, indicating the importance of cultural and economic factors.

To the further question of whether easier laws are the cause of increased divorce, the answer is—no and yes. No, because divorce was on the rise in every country before the law was changed, and it was this groundswell that led to the changes, rather than vice versa. Larger social forces were at work, some of which have already been mentioned. Yes, for two reasons: No-fault legislation made divorce easier and faster; and the legal changes gave official approval to the concept of breakdown as a relationship problem rather than a crime committed by one partner against the other. Popular acceptance of this concept can be seen as feeding back into and strengthening the forces that brought about the change.

One interpretation then is that somewhere in the mid-1960s the Christian/patriarchal emphasis on the sanctity of the family was quite successfully challenged by the alternate view that unions are basically consensual, and that there is no great virtue in prolonging them once the consensus no longer exists. The nature and success of the challenge varied with the country, but most were forced to revise their divorce laws to reflect the new popularity of the consensual attitude. As more people divorced, the possibility of divorce became more accepted, leading at least for a time to a spiral effect.

The outcomes for men and women were, however, very different. Men suffered little financial disadvantage, and re-partnered quicker and more frequently than women. Women lost the family breadwinner but kept the family (P. McDonald, 1986; Weitzman, 1985). One result has been a growth in many countries in the proportion of women and children living in poverty (McLanahan, Sorensen, & Watson, 1989; Voegeli, 1993).

An important aspect is the fact that although it is wives who are most financially disadvantaged by divorce, it is they who are most likely to seek it. Most Western countries report that 60% or more of divorce petitions are now filed by women. Filing is not a very accurate measure of who originally sought the divorce, but surveys regularly show that divorced husbands and wives agree that the wife was the initiator in 55%–65% of separations and that a further 2%–20% were joint decisions (Burns, 1984; Headlam, 1984; Jordan, 1989). Thus, although the status of divorced single mother is not what the person might have chosen for herself in the first place, after trying the alternative she is more likely to choose it than is her husband.

It takes individual people to bring about a divorce. The explanations that are commonly offered for the divorce surge of the 1970s generally give important roles to the effects of increased urbanization, education, technology, and women's work force participation, along with the shift in values toward greater individualism, secularism, and feminism, among other things. However, the decision to divorce is a personal one, taken on personal grounds. If it is influenced by urbanization, most divorcing people are probably unaware and are unlikely to mention this as a cause of their marriage breakdown. How do these personal experiences mesh with the larger social trends that are so often blamed for increased divorce?

Marital Complaints

If you were to ask a friend the reasons for his or her divorce, you would almost certainly receive an explanation couched in personal terms—"We didn't communicate," or "He was always at the pub," or "She had another boyfriend." In his pioneering study of divorce, Goode (1956), a U.S. sociologist, found that the majority of explanations offered by his sample of divorced Detroit women could be placed into a relatively small number of categories, with husband's lack of economic support, domineeringness/cruelty, "helling around" with mates, drinking, and personality qualities being the most common complaints.

Later studies have reported quite similar findings, although there are some variations from one sample to another. When men respondents are included, sex differences in complaints emerge. In addition, women typically date the onset of the breakdown earlier than do men, perhaps because they usually carry most responsibility for domestic life and relationship work, and are thus quicker to note difficulties (see Fig. 9).

Table 3 presents the causes nominated by a sample of divorced or separated men and women. Most gave more than one cause, so that frequency of mention does not necessarily mean that this complaint is the most important. Thus, complaints of sexual incompatibilities and problems (top of the list for men

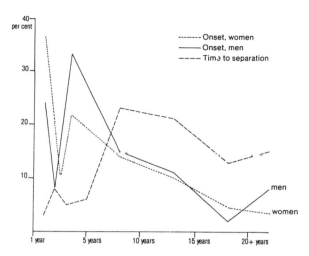

FIG. 9. Perceived onset of marriage breakdown, by length of marriage (from Burns, 1980).

TABLE 3
Perceived Causes of Marriage Breakdown

Causes[a]	% of All Respondents (n = 335)	% Men (n = 102)	% Women (n = 233)
Sexual incompatibility	45	56	40
Lack of communication[b]	40	41	40
Husband's lack of time at home	40	28	46
Financial	32	24	36
Husband's association with another woman[c]	31	17	37
Husband's drinking[d]	30	17	36
Husband's cruelty[e]	26	4	37
Wife's lack of interest[f]	26	25	26
Friction with relative	23	29	21
Disagreements over children	20	22	19
Wife's association with another man[c]	19	35	12
Husband's lack of interest[f]	13	15	12
Wife's ill health	13	13	13
Inadequate housing	9	4	13
Religious differences	5	5	5
Husband's gambling	5	3	7

[a]Percentages do not add up to 100: multiple complaints are included. Causes mentioned by less than 5% of the sample are not included.

[b]Includes lack of common interests.

[c]No homosexual relationships were mentioned.

[d]Includes husband's alcoholism.

[e]Includes wife's perception of husband as having sadistic or brutal personality.

[f]Includes statements of resentment about the lack of stimulation.

and an equal second for women) commonly accompanied other complaints, and the respondents often believed that the sexual problem was a result rather than a cause of their other problems.

In addition, the bald categories used to summarize replies do scant justice to the variety of situations described. "Husband's cruelty," for instance, includes attempted murder and violent assault, sequestering the family income, constant verbal abuse, insistence on conceptions unwanted by the wife, and absence during the illness and death of a child. Many complaints were expressed differently at different times by the same person. For example, a respondent might first refer to some specific incident in the marriage, but then describe the problem as "her whole attitude, really"; or a complaint of cruelty could be broadened to "his whole personality." As Goode noted, this means that the procedure of categorizing marital complaints is always somewhat arbitrary.

Despite these caveats, the set of complaints in Table 3 is quite similar to that given by Goode's Detroit sample 25 years earlier, and to other studies in the United States, Britain, and other countries (Hart, 1976; Kitson & Raschke, 1981; Thornes & Collard, 1979; Wolcott, 1984).

In the United Kingdom, for example, where "irretrievable breakdown" is defined as one of a set of fault and no-fault grounds, the majority of divorces granted to wives since 1972 have been on the grounds of the husband's "unreasonable" behavior, followed by his adultery; and the majority of those granted to husbands have been on the grounds of the wife's adultery, followed by a period of separation (*Social Trends*, 1991). In the former Soviet Union, although divorce is not based on fault grounds, petitioners are required to state the reason for the divorce, choosing from an officially provided list. As we noted earlier, the three most commonly listed reasons are alcoholism, adultery, and personal incompatibility (i.e., much the same as in Western studies), although alcohol abuse seems somewhat more important. One study found that almost half of the wives who filed for divorce (47%) did so because of their husbands' drinking (Perevedentsev, 1978, cited in Moskoff, 1983). The most common reason offered, however, is "incompatibility of character," equivalent to the "irretrievable breakdown" or "irreconcilable differences" provision of other countries, and like these, covering a variety of problems and complaints. Where petitioners have been allowed to give their own reasons as well as to choose one of the official categories, their complaints are very similar to those given by samples in Western countries—including lack of love, husband's failure to help with domestic chores, and interference from in-laws (Moskoff, 1983).

In modern Japan, too, the complaints offered are quite similar, although some differences have been found between the reasons given for the termination of love marriages and arranged marriages. Although petitioners from love marriages nominate incompatibility, adultery, and loss of love, those in arranged marriages cite disapproval of the wife by her husband's parents and grandparents as an additional factor.

Overall, therefore, there seems to be reasonable agreement over time and place in the kinds of things that people find objectionable in their spouses.

Which Marriages Break Down?

There are other factors that people are unlikely to mention as reasons for their marriage breakdown, but that nevertheless place them at risk of divorce. A number of these factors were first noted by Goode, and his findings have since been confirmed and added to by many other researchers (Lewis & Spanier, 1979; White, 1990). In English-speaking and other countries (Kumagai, 1983), these factors include not belonging to a church, being in a lower level job, being less educated, marrying young, not getting on well with one's parents, being married for a short period of time, and having daughters rather than sons (Morgan, Lye, & Condran, 1988). As we have noted, cohort is also an important factor, with couples who married in the 1970s and later being more at risk than those of preceding decades. Your divorced friend would no doubt be surprised if you suggested that being born in the 1950s had damaged his or her prospects of remaining married. But if we bear in mind that most breakdowns occur early in the marriage, and then look again at Fig. 2, clearly it has. Indeed, in some samples, year of birth may be a better predictor of divorce risk than spouse's cruelty, because many people continue to live with cruel and even life-threatening partners.

Divorce decisions can thus be seen to be influenced by both personal dissatisfactions and a variety of social influences of which the partners may not even be aware. How are we to understand the relationship between the two?

Nearly all researchers have tried to answer this question. One approach has been to look for associations between the causes that people offer for their marriage breakdown, and sociodemographic factors such as age, education, occupation, and religion. The connections that are found then suggest the ways in which certain conditions of life impact on marriages. In the sample presented in Table 3 for example it was found that those men and women who married under age 21 years were particularly likely to complain of friction with relatives and housing problems and (in the case of the wives) the husbands' drinking and cruelty. The inference is that starting marriage young and without assets renders couples particularly dependent on relatives and on hard-to-find cheap rental accommodation; and that husbands are likely to use alcohol to escape from these difficulties, thus compounding them. By contrast, disapproval of the wife's choice of partner by her parents was associated with her subsequent complaints of his cruelty, and of lack of communication. The inference here is that prospective in-laws are quick to notice personality defects and incompatibilities that only later become apparent to the bride. Further inferences can be drawn from the fact that this is not a gender-neutral effect. Men's parents were much less likely to disapprove of their prospective daughters-in-law, and even if they did, this did not predict to the reasons the son subsequently gave for the breakdown. Barry (1970) drew the conclusion that a wife's personality is not all that important to the success of the marriage, whereas that of the husband is. More specifically, an emotionally unstable or immature husband makes for an unhappy wife, but husbands are less affected by unstable wives; in Barry's view because husbands are less dependent on their partners for their quality of life.

The approach just cited operates at a common-sense level, offering interpretations for associations found through statistical analysis. A more ambitious approach has been the development of sets of principles or models to predict divorce-proneness. Goode (1956) proposed that marital stability was a function of five interacting factors: (a) satisfactions and strains within the marriage, (b) support for the marriage from the couple's reference groups, (c) the reference groups' attitudes to divorce, (d) alternatives open to the partners outside the marriage, and (e) precipitants of conflict or of the decision to end the marriage.

However, the classic model is that developed by Levinger (1965), and elaborated by Lewis and Spanier (1979), who were able to draw on the substantial body of research that followed Goode's work. This research is mainly American, but the literature from other countries indicates that much of it has wider relevance.

First, Lewis and Spanier pointed out the complexities that result from the fact that marriage breakdown and divorce are not synonymous. A couple may feel their marriage is over but continue to live together; or they may separate but not divorce. Both of these instances could be classed as marriage breakdown, but the couples involved, particularly the first group, are hard for the researcher to locate. Divorces by contrast are registered, and some characteristics of the parties recorded: Most research therefore concentrates on divorce, which is only one form of breakdown.

Lewis and Spanier proposed that we handle the definitional problem by using the terms *marital quality* and *marital stability*. *Stability* refers to whether the marriage is intact or not, with both legal and *de facto* marriages classed as intact, and both separation and divorce classed as nonintact. *Quality* is defined as the subjective evaluation of a married couple's relationship. Some low-quality marriages continue, and some high-quality ones break up, but quality is nevertheless the single greatest predictor of stability.

Marital Quality

Lewis and Spanier reviewed the literature in the area—some 300 empirical and theoretical works at the time they were writing—and listed 74 factors that had been found to be associated with marital quality. Lewis and Spanier grouped them into three broad categories, which are presented in the left hand side of Fig. 10.

Category 1: Premarital Variables

The first category comprises premarital variables (i.e., qualities that the partners bring to the marriage). This is made up of four groupings: premarital homogamy, premarital resources, exposure to adequate role models, and support from significant others.

Homogamy.   Homogamy—being similar to the partner—has consistently emerged as a very important predictor of relationship quality. Lewis and Spanier specifically referred to similarity in social class, ethnicity, religion, age, intelligence, and husband–wife status and personality traits, but later research has extended the list to include values, attitudes, interests, and aspirations (Kitson & Raschke, 1981; White, 1990). Prediction of course is probabilistic. It is not proposed that it is impossible to have a high-quality relationship with someone from a very different background—just that it is more difficult, because there are so many matters where the partner's ideas may be different from one's own, and where negotiation and even dissimulation may be required.

Premarital Resources.   This second grouping is also multifaceted. Lewis and Spanier specifically mentioned education, emotional health, physical health, self-esteem, interpersonal skills, higher social class, absence of neurotic habits, maturity, and greater acquaintance before marriage as important resources. This list covers so much that we hardly need to add to it, but later studies have described in more detail the kinds of social skills that are particularly valuable; for example the ability to discuss and negotiate sticky topics, and to abort conflicts by responding affectionately to cranky behavior (Duck, 1986/1992; Noller & Fitzpatrick, 1990).

Exposure to Adequate Role Models.   This grouping refers to early experience of a happy home in which parents gave affection and support to each other and to the children, and thus provided models from which to learn these manners.

Support From Significant Others.   This last grouping refers to the warmth and approval shown toward the prospective partner by friends and future-in-laws and, the partners' liking for them.

Category 2: Satisfaction With Lifestyle

Lewis and Spanier's second category, satisfaction with lifestyle, also comprises four groupings: socioeconomic adequacy, satisfaction with wife's employment, household composition, and community embeddedness.

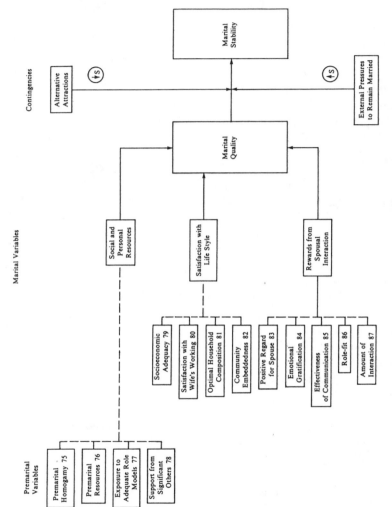

FIG. 10. A theory of marital quality and marital stability (from Lewis & Spanier, 1979. Reprinted by permission of The Free Press. Copyright © The Free Press).

Socioeconomic Adequacy. This grouping refers to the regular finding that marriages are more stable among the better off, although Lewis and Spanier emphasized the fact that it is *perceived* adequacy that is important—a quite reasonable income can be a source of strife among those who expect more, and conversely, low income is not necessarily a complaint among those with limited expectations.

Satisfaction With Wife's Employment. The next grouping refers to the conflicts that may arise when wives take employment against their husbands' wishes, or without his support; or alternatively, when they feel they have to go to work, but would prefer not to.

Household Composition. Household composition refers to the importance of not having more children than the parents want, and particularly not having children born sooner and closer together than desired; and to the frequently adverse effect of having other adults in the household.

Community Embeddedness. The last grouping describes the importance of a supportive network of friends, relatives, and neighbors. Church membership frequently provides such a network, and this is no doubt one reason why churchgoers often report happier and more stable marriages than others.

Category 3: Rewards From Spousal Interaction

The third category is made up of five groupings: positive regard for spouse, emotional gratification, effective communication, amount of interaction and role fit.

Positive Regard. Positive regard includes finding the partner physically, mentally, and sexually attractive, having one's values and actions validated by the partner, and seeing her or him as similar to oneself.

Emotional Gratification. Emotional gratification comprises mutual love, affection, equality, respect, sexual satisfaction, the encouragement of personal growth, and the construction of a "couple identity."

Effective Communication. Communication covers self-disclosures, other verbal and nonverbal communications, understanding, and empathy.

Amount of Interaction. Interaction refers to companionship and shared activities. The various components of these four groupings of course interact with the premarital variables: For example, people with similar characteristics (homogamous) will be likely to perceive each other as similar to the self and have fewer differences in background and values to negotiate; those with better communication skills will be able to communicate better with their partners, and will be better able to handle the negotiations that arise from differences; and greater love for the partners seems likely to lead to greater tolerance for their resource deficiencies.

Role Fit.   Role fit emphasizes that it is not so much the roles the partners fill that counts, but the fit between these and their expectations. However, Lewis and Spanier also pointed out that the research findings are not quite as value neutral as this might suggest, and that greater role sharing is generally associated with higher marital quality. This is an interesting area because gender roles have been extensively discussed and rethought in many countries since much of this research was done. One result has been that many people's expectations underwent sudden revisions when they decided that their old roles were not very rewarding. It is easy to understand that people brought up to believe in the value of traditional roles may be happiest when they and their partners are playing out those roles. But it is also understandable that when role beliefs are being rethought, fair shares should emerge as the arrangement most conducive to happiness (Scanzoni & Szinovacz, 1980).

Lewis and Spanier viewed all these factors as contributing to the overall level of marital quality. But quality is not the same as stability. Whether a low-quality relationship (or a high-quality one, for that matter) remains intact or not depends on two other factors—the Pressures to remain married, and the Alternative attractions (Fig. 10). The average quality of marriages has probably not declined since the 1960s; indeed it seems likely to have risen, given that young adults today are better educated, marry at a later age, have fewer children, particularly fewer unplanned children, and enjoy more equal status in marriage—all of which, as we saw earlier, have been found to make for higher quality. Therefore, the large rise in divorce (and mother-headed families) must be attributed to changes in the pressures and alternatives. What are these?

Marital Stability: Pressures and Alternatives

Lewis and Spanier referred to the pressures exerted by strict divorce laws, strong social disapproval, religious proscriptions, economic pressures, belief in the sanctity of marriage and the importance of staying together for the sake of the children, and fear of going it alone. Their alternatives include economic alternatives (employment or social security), another partner or other supportive people, housing, and alternative beliefs about what is best for adults and children (e.g., the belief that children are better off with one contented parent than two conflicted ones). Lewis and Spanier did not go into the relative importance of these pressures and alternatives for the surge in divorce. However, some stand out as strong candidates and are discussed here.

Divorce Law.   As we have seen, the increase in divorce predated the change to no-fault legislation in all countries, but the introduction saw a further increase. In part, this was due to a backlog or conversion of long-standing separations to divorces by couples not willing to divorce under marital offense law. But the law's redefinition of divorce as relationship breakdown in its turn strengthened utilitarian and nonsacramental attitudes to marriage, and thus increased the likelihood of divorce in low-quality marriages. The giant increase in divorce following legislative change provides ample evidence of this effect.

Another form of evidence is the movement to earlier divorce under no-fault law. This is partly a procedural effect. No-fault law generally speeds up divorce by requiring only a short period of living apart as evidence of breakdown. The early years of marriage are a high-risk period for breakdown, so that when legal obstacles are removed, they also become a high divorce time. However, something else has also happened. Divorce statistics in various countries show that under no-fault law the average period from marriage to final separation itself shortens (Australian Bureau of Statistics, 1984). Thus, it seems that consent law generates a climate in which people are quicker to abandon an unsatisfactory relationship as well as quicker in resorting to the law.

Social Disapproval. Public opinion polls and surveys show that there is now general acceptance in Western countries of the principle of no-fault divorce. In the 1990s, many people, looking back, wonder why the change was so slow in coming. A convincing answer comes from W. O'Neill's (1967) analysis of English and U.S. political debates on divorce

> The fundamental conviction that informed almost every attack on divorce was the belief that the family was the foundation of society (or the state, the race, or civilization, depending on the speaker) and that divorce destroyed the family as an institution and consequently threatened the existence of that larger entity of which it was the basic unit. (p. 58)

O'Neill's witty book details some of the directions in which this line of thinking took people during the early 20th-century debates on divorce in the United States and Europe. A common direction was toward urging couples to see their union as a lifetime commitment, and to work though their marital difficulties, on the grounds that each new divorce contributed to an "eroding of those values which buttress marriage and the family" (p. 58). O'Neill cited many British and U.S. legislators' rhetorical elaborations of the theme of it being their "stern duty" to permit the minority (the unhappily married) to suffer so as to preserve stability for the many. These attitudes of course survived the period that O'Neill described. One speaker to the Australian Family Law Bill debate, for example, demanded to know, "Who could honestly go about the task of helping one party, well knowing that hundreds and thousands would suffer as a result of that help?" (Hansard, 1975, p. 160).

Just how well these public statements have reflected the attitudes of the general population is impossible to say, but there is plenty of evidence from many countries that the divorced person, until quite recently, was treated by many as disreputable and even dangerous, and that both social standing and career prospects could suffer. Even the innocent party was not exempt from social disapproval because he or she could have been tainted by his or her unfortunate experience. As one writer put it:

> though not a shadow of blame should rest on her . . . it meant, none the less, that she had been through all sorts of unpleasant matrimonial experiences, which a properly married, or widowed, woman would know nothing about. Something of them might have remained clinging to her . . . the old saw about touching pitch. . . . (Richardson, 1925, pp. 241–242)

Why is it that this powerful hostility to divorce has dissipated so rapidly in recent decades? One explanation is that the hostility was powered by fear: fear of swarms of destitute women and infants requiring public support; of fatherless children growing up delinquent; of disorderly public behavior by adults unrestrained by family responsibilities; of hellfire and damnation; of uncontrolled sexuality; and of midlife husbands readily tempted to abandon a dependent wife and children for a new start with a younger partner.

The big change, according to this explanation, is that fear was reduced: by the pill, which took much of the threat out of sexual intercourse; by national prosperity, and particularly by the increase in jobs for women that lessened their dependency on men; by extended public education, formal and informal; and by the many well-publicized examples of public figures whose careers survived divorce and still less conventional doings undented. Of course not all the fears noted here disappeared; but rather they became sufficiently less pressing for sufficient numbers of people that more laissez-faire attitudes came to dominate. This was particularly the case among those born in Western countries after 1950, who grew up in times of national prosperity and security.

Religious Proscriptions.   As we have seen, the Christian Church has consistently opposed divorce on doctrinal grounds, but its influence has varied from one country to another. From the 1960s, the church in most countries softened its attitudes to divorce, and at the same time lost membership and authority. In 1990, even Ireland, the last country in Europe without divorce, elected a feminist woman president who announced that divorce legislation would be introduced.

An Important Alternative: Independence for Women.   The change in women's status in the last few decades has been truly spectacular in many countries. Women have flooded into the work force; their career opportunities and wage levels have risen; their standard of education and job training has increased; the pill and the decriminalization of abortion have given them control of their fertility; social security and child-care provisions have improved; and a variety of antidiscrimination, equal opportunity and affirmative action programs have been introduced.

Clearly, women in the 1990s are less dependent on the support of men than at any previous time, and divorce is therefore a far more viable alternative both for them and for husbands who are considering leaving them. This is not to say that women are not disadvantaged by divorce. They are, as many studies of the economic consequences of divorce have shown (P. McDonald, 1986; Weitzman, 1985). But the fact that it is women who initiate the majority of divorces tells us that they see the benefits as greater than the disadvantages. This suggests that a very important factor keeping divorce down in the past has been the unavailability of alternatives for women.

Women's work force participation is generally described as having been the crucial factor in improving their status in Western countries. But this of course depends on them owning their own labor and its proceeds. There is plenty of evidence that where women's labor is owned by the family, or the patriarch, or the state, no such benefit accrues. Changed attitudes to the ownership of labor are also therefore very important. Interesting evidence comes from surveys that have asked similar questions at intervals of a number of years. For example, in Australia the proportion of 18- to 34-year-old women who believed that "whatever career a woman may have her most important role in life is that of becoming a mother" declined between 1971 and 1982 from 78% to 46%. Those who believed that "wives who don't have to work (outside the home) should not do so" declined from 62% to 46%, and those who believed that "a wife should go where her husband wants her to go for his job" declined from 85% to 66% (Glezer, 1984b). In the Netherlands, the proportion who believed that "labor force participation of a married woman with school-age children is acceptable" rose from 17% in 1965 to 56% in 1970 and 69% in 1986 (van de Kaa, 1987). All of these changes indicate a significant shift away from the belief that the family owns the wife/mother's unpaid labor and that she has no right to withdraw any of it in order to seek paid employment elsewhere. The changes have gone much further in some countries than in others. Kumagai (1983), for example, pointed out that although Japanese women are now among the mostly highly educated in the world, cultural attitudes and arrangements keep their status modest compared to that of men.

Alternative Value Systems. "Marriage is a wonderful institution. But who wants to live in an institution?" quipped Groucho Marx. Observers in many Western countries consider that the big shift in popular attitudes to marriage has been from seeing it as an institution worthy of loyalty in its own right, to a piece of paper that means nothing if the relationship between wife and husband is not working (van de Kaa, 1987). This is an oversimplification of course, and even the most modern marriages have substantial institutional aspects, as anyone knows who has tried to divide up children, housing, belongings, and other assets. But the increased emphasis on the centrality of relationship is well evidenced. It follows that because relationships are by their nature more transient than institutions, this single shift in emphasis has been an important contributor to the divorce boom.

Other evolving value systems have also played a part. Feminist philosophy has played an interesting role for even not-very-feminist women, through providing them with a value system alternative to patriarchy: One that offers the divorcing woman far more dignity. The Christian-patriarchal assumption is that good people stay married, and that stable marriages make good people. From this point of view, it is hard to see marriage breakdown as other than a personal failure. Feminism, on the other hand, sees it as a more or less natural outcome of the unequal power of men and women in marriage, and divorce as often a form of self-liberation by the wife. Feminism, of course, cannot offer the same encouragement to men because it pinpoints them as the oppressors—witting or unwitting.

The other important area of competing value systems concerns what will be best for the children. The proportion of dissolutions that involve children has decreased considerably, but the actual number of children affected has been huge (more than 1 million every year in the United States alone), so that what is best for them has become a crucial question. The older Western value system sees the broken home as very damaging to children, and counsels considerable parental sacrifice to avert it. Newer attitudes emphasize the gain for children of being removed from a situation of conflict and unhappiness. Most people probably now believe both of these things to some degree because they are not really incompatible—divorce means the child may lose some advantages but gain others, and the balance, and the impact on the child, is hard to foresee. Nevertheless, the newer set of beliefs has steadily gained support in the professional and popular literature (Hetherington & Arasteh, 1988). Hence, the parent considering divorce may believe—and may be correct in believing—that the divorce will improve the children's lives.

CONCLUSION

Lewis and Spanier's framework provides an integration of personal and social dimensions, and a useful means for comparing divorce trends at different periods and places. For example, Japanese marriages under the old lineage system could be described as likely to be low on "rewards from spousal interaction" with few pressures to continue, and a range of alternatives available to husbands (if not to wives) and thus very divorce prone.

The model also implies that if one or two dimensions remain constant, and the others change, then predictions can be made. For example, if the marital quality and the pressures against dissolution in a population remain constant over a period of time, but the alternatives increase, then an increase in divorce is to be expected. If the pressures decline at the same time that the alternatives increase (as has happened since the late 1960s), we would expect a still larger increase. Thus, the Lewis and Spanier framework provides a neat explanation of the increase in divorce in modern Western societies, and the associated increase in mother-headed families. It is not, however, very precise in its prediction, as it does not specify the relative importance of the various pressures and alternatives, or the various components of quality. In fact, our proposal is that quality has increased since midcentury (due to greater prosperity, later marriage, fewer forced marriages, better birth control, and other factors), but that this improvement has been more than offset by the weakening of barriers to divorce, and the increase in alternatives to marriage.

A further difficulty for the understanding of mother-headed families is that these are formed by means other than divorce. Although divorce stabilized in many countries in the 1980s, or even turned down, there was no such downturn in female-headed families, which continued to rise in the 1980s (Fig. 1). Clearly, mother-headed families must be coming into existence by means other than divorce.

Figure 11 shows that this is indeed the case. It sets out for each country the proportion of all female-headed one-parent families that were headed by women of three different marital statuses—unmarried, divorced/separated, and widowed. In those countries that tally the divorced and separated separately, and where time series are available, it is clear that the divorced proportion grew considerably after the introduction of easier divorce laws in each country, whereas the size of the separated group shrank. By the mid-1980s, divorcees represented some 35% of all single mothers in Australia, and 42% in the United States.

The most striking feature, however, is the growth in the never-married group, which by the mid-1980s accounted for almost 60% of mother-headed families in Sweden and for more than 20% in the United States, the United Kingdom, and Australia. Figure 11 needs to be considered in conjunction with Fig. 6, which showed that marriage rates dropped by up to one half in the 20-year period between 1965 and 1985. Taken together, these figures suggest that many women in Western societies are increasingly choosing to bypass marriage altogether. Or is it more the choice of the men? In either case, does this mean a continuing increase in mother-headed families, even if the divorce rate remains stable, or wanes? In the next chapters we consider these questions.

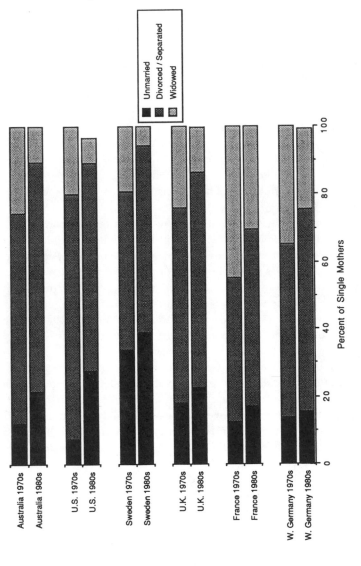

FIG. 11. Marital status of mother-headed families: selected countries (from Australian Bureau of Statistics, 1991; OECD, 1987; Roll, 1989; Statistics Sweden, 1992).

Chapter 2

The Contribution of
Out-of-Wedlock Births to the
Incidence of Mother-Headed Families

As we saw in the last chapter, the unmarried now comprise up to one half of all single mothers in Western countries. At the same time, the proportion of all mothers who are unmarried has greatly increased. This is illustrated in Fig. 12, which presents annual ex-nuptial (i.e., birth outside legal marriage) rates for selected countries since the late 1950s.[1]

As can be seen, out-of-wedlock births in the majority of countries rose in the late 1960s, and continued to rise through the 1970s and 1980s. As with divorce, although most countries showed an increase, those with originally high or low rates tended to stay high or low relative to other countries. Of the European countries, Sweden returned the highest figures and the Federal Republic of Germany the lowest. Japan reported virtually no out-of-wedlock births in any year, and figures for the Soviet Union were not available.

When out-of-wedlock births comprise up to almost half of all births, it is understandable that they should be making an important contribution to the rise in mother-headed families. So what has caused the worldwide increase in ex-nuptiality?

This proves to be a difficult question to answer. In one sense, there is plenty of information, because even when population statistics are poorly kept, exnuptiality is one thing that usually does get recorded. However, this tells us nothing about the relationship between the parents except that they are un-

---

[1]The terms *ex-nuptial* and *out-of-wedlock* are used here wherever possible. However, the United Nations Demographic Yearbook and some national statistics and publications continue to use the term *illegitimate*, which is used when citing them. For practical purposes the three terms can be classed as synonymous, although philosophically there is a world of difference between the pejorative concept of *illegitimacy* and the two neutral terms.

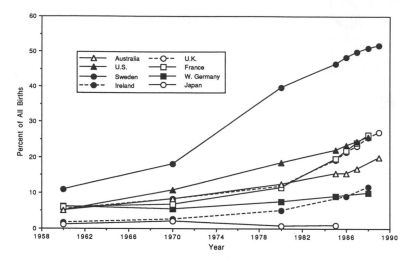

FIG. 12.   Ex-nuptial births as percentage of all births, 1960–1988: selected countries (from U.N. Demographic Yearbook, various editions).

married. Some out-of-wedlock births are to couples who regard marriage as unnecessary, or undesirable, but who have every intention of staying together, and who are "as good as" married. Other births are to cohabiting couples whose ties are weaker, and who are much more likely than a married couple to break up. Still others are to teenage girls with unreliable boyfriends, or no partners in sight. The different types vary in frequency from one country to another, and each country tends to offer different explanations in terms of local circumstances. Thus, in the United States most discussion has centered on teenagers, African Americans, and irresponsible or absent fathers. In the Scandinavian countries, by contrast, there is no significant Black population, teenage pregnancies are practically unheard of, and common law marriages are an acceptable alternative to legal marriage. In yet other countries, it is majority group members on low incomes, and the divorced, who are most likely to bear children out of marriage. There is obviously a world of difference between births within these various situations, but all are classed together as ex-nuptial. In this chapter we explore these differences and compare the explanations that have been offered. To do so we look first at Sweden and the United States, both of which have many out-of-wedlock births, and then Australia, a country with a middling level of ex-nuptiality. We point out that the nature of the populations bearing children outside marriage varies from one country to another, as do the explanations that have been offered. Nevertheless, as Fig. 12 shows, all show the same upward trend since 1970, and particularly since 1980, indicating some supranational influences.

SWEDEN

Sweden currently has one of the highest out-of-wedlock rates of all the European countries. This is not a novel trend. In the first quarter of this century around one sixth of Swedish children were born outside marriage. Ex-nuptial births then declined, but increased after 1960, reaching 45% of all births in 1984, and almost 52% by 1989. As we saw in the last chapter, this occurs in the context of the lowest marriage rate in the industrial world, one of the highest average ages for first marriages, probably the highest rates for nonmarital co habitation and family dissolution, and the lowest teenage pregnancy rate ever recorded anywhere in the world. These figures have created a popular image of Sweden as the world leader in the evolution of new family patterns: One that other Western nations will sooner or later follow.

As we noted, marriage in Sweden lost its popularity after 1966, and more than 25% of all couples are currently estimated to be unmarried. The figures show that the birth of a child does not greatly increase the likelihood of marriage. Partnering and childbearing outside marriage has become normal practice, whereas the number of births to women lacking a partner has in fact decreased. However, a high breakup rate among nonmarried couples is one reason for the high incidence of mother-headed families (Hoem & Hoem, 1988; Popenoe, 1987).

To some extent, the retreat from marriage can be seen as a throwback to an older tradition of childbearing within common law marriages. But the situation in the 1990s has many differences. The big change is that the nexus between marriage and reproduction has been effectively broken. Except for people with a religious commitment, living together and having children outside of marriage is socially acceptable. The average age for first moving in with a partner is around 20, but parenting and marriage come much later, and commonly in that order. Social security provisions protect the out-of-wedlock child from the possible disadvantages involved.

Swedish sociologists point out that effective sex education has a long tradition in Swedish schools, and contraception and abortion are readily available, so that unwanted pregnancies are relatively uncommon. This makes parenting largely a matter of choice, and it is typically postponed until the late 20s at least. Although there is very little conventional pressure to marry, there is a lot of pressure—and encouragement—for mothers to continue in the work force (usually part time). Becoming a full-time housewife is not considered meritorious, and those who do so incur taxation and other penalties. In addition, the housewife finds herself quite isolated, as most children and their parents are away for much of the day (Hoem & Hoem, 1987). One father reported that when he stayed home on parental leave with a new baby, his 4-year-old son lost his place in the local day-care center (which was for children of work-ing parents). The child soon became lonely as no other children were around, and hung over the day-care center fence until the staff (illegally) admitted him.

Popenoe (1987) was struck by the associated disappearance of the traditional rites of passage associated with marriage and family formation, and their replacement by personally chosen milestones. One couple he spoke to told him how they had met in 1967, moved in together in 1969, exchanged rings in 1973 around the time when their first child was born—as a public sign of attachment—and married in 1977. When asked what anniversary they celebrat-ed, they responded ''The day we met.'' In the study described in the previous chapter (Table 2), Hoem and Hoem (1988) compared the experience of two groups of women: those who moved in with a partner in 1965 and those who did so in 1977. Three years later, 83% of the 1965 group had married their partners, and more than 75% of these marriages contained children. Of the 1977 group, however, less than 25% were married 3 years later, and only 33% had children, most of them born out of wedlock.

Origins of This Pattern

Historians have pointed out that up to the 18th century, common law mar-riages in Sweden were recognized as legitimate provided that the parents' rela-tionship was established as a stable one. The church had difficulty in establishing the religious marriage ceremony as the sole source of legitimacy, and the pre-Christian custom of betrothal continued to be accepted. As a result, children who would have been classed as bastards in other parts of Europe were consid-ered legitimate in Sweden. Many examples are found in old parish records. For example, one entry describes a woman who although never married, was recorded as having two illegitimate and one legitimate child. The first child was born out-of-wedlock, but when the second was born the woman was ''un-der promise of marriage,'' which made the second birth a legitimate one. However, her fiance then spent some time in another parish, and while he was away, she ''let herself be bedded again, and thus had two bastards and one legitimate child, but was never married'' (Gaunt, 1980, p. 314).

Records from the early 17th century show that even allowing for the broad definition of legitimacy, illegitimacy rates were quite high by current Europe-an standards (although not as high as in other places like Denmark and Aus-tria where farm labor was in short supply and single women laborers with healthy children were popular with farmers). By the mid-17th century, however, famine and plague had reduced births to both married and unmarried wom-en. A little later, out-of-wedlock births were further suppressed by an outbreak of religious fervour, and the condemnation of fornication as inspired by the Devil. Anyone found guilty could find themselves in the stocks.

One hundred years later, things had changed again. Although marriage rates continued low, illegitimate births increased. Parish records show that the majority of these births were "true" illegitimates, in that the mothers were not betrothed, mostly left home for the birth, and did not subsequently marry. The records also show that conception patterns for legitimate and illegitimate births differed, the illegitimate being typically conceived at harvest festival time, the legitimate during the cold months. The reasons for the increase in illegitimacy are not fully understood. Among the explanations that have been offered are general background factors like better economic conditions and a less brutal treatment of unmarried mothers at this time; and more specific causes such as greater alcohol consumption (Laslett, Oosterveen, & Smith, 1980).

By mid-19th century, when cross-national figures became widely available, it was found that in illegitimacy, Stockholm (with a 46% rate over the period 1851–1855) was second only to Vienna (49%) among European capitals. Most commentators put the blame on moral degeneracy, but more mundane influences were also at work; for example changes in registration practices at this time meant that children of common law marriages were now classed as bastards.

The class system of the time also played a part. Men from the higher social classes were expected to postpone marriage until they had established themselves, but in the meantime it was acceptable for them to have affairs with working-class women. In some cases, a woman servant lived with her bachelor employer and was officially classed as his housekeeper or "house-mamselle," but was in fact his mistress, and often the mother of his children. When he married, she and her children would have to leave, although she might be paid off (Laslett et al., 1980). Plays and novels of the time describe some of the consequences. In Ibsen's *Ghosts*, Captain Alving marries off his ex-servant and mistress to a local villager when she becomes pregnant; and he marries a woman of his own class. Respectability is preserved through silence and lies, but disaster follows for the next generation. August Strindberg, himself the child of a mamselle marriage, took up another aspect in *The Father*. In this play, Captain Lassen (the father of the title) is tormented by the conviction that a man can never really know that a child is his own. He has no reason to suspect his fiercely respectable wife of committing adultery, but the fact that it would have been physically possible for her (or any other woman) to do so incites him to frenzy. When his wife asks him whether he wants to see his child, he cries out in bitterness, "My child? A man has no children! Only women have children!" This seems to have been how many unmarried mothers were perceived at the time.

At the start of the 20th century, barely half of Swedish women were marrying, and around one sixth of children were born out of wedlock. After that, marriage became more popular, and Sweden, like other countries, experienced a marriage boom (a modest one) after World War II, when more than 70%

of women had married by the age of 44 (a low figure compared to many other countries, but a high one for Sweden). After this, the nation returned to its previous status as a low-marriage country, and the proportion of children born ex-nuptially steadily rose.

Role of State Support

It is generally agreed that the support provided by the state is a very important factor behind today's family patterns. Unmarried mothers, like divorced mothers, are expected to continue in the work force or in further education, and receive an extensive array of social supports and special allowances that enable them to do so. As one result of this support, Swedish women continue to average two children, and by European standards, the birthrate is quite high. Hoem and Hoem (1987) pointed out that it is much higher than that of Denmark, a quite similar country, and attribute the difference to the fact that Swedish social services are particularly geared toward supporting parenthood (both partnered and unpartnered), for example through various forms of parental leave.

In an ingenious comparison with another neighboring country, Blanc (1987) analyzed the relationship patterns of women in Sweden and Norway. He found that although Norwegian women were more likely to marry a first partner, and, following a marriage breakdown, to move into a second cohabiting relationship that did not last, the Swedes were more likely to cohabit with both a first and a second partner, and to stick with the second one. Blanc explained this difference as reflecting differing values. In Norway, women still experience a good deal of pressure to marry and remain married. Female employment is low, social security is limited, abortion was only legalized in 1978, and divorced/separated women are financially disadvantaged. It is hard for them to find a suitable new partner, and their postdivorce relationships are therefore prone to dissolve. By contrast, Swedish women have economic and legal supports that allow them to cohabit early and to treat these first cohabitations as truly trial arrangements. Thus, they are able to screen out unsatisfactory partners at relatively little cost, even when children are involved.

For unmarried fathers the costs are both higher and lower than in some other countries. The state routinely collects maintenance, so that it is not easy for them to avoid contributing to their children's upkeep, as it has been in many other countries. On the other hand, if their second partner has children, the children's father will be paying maintenance for them, and the mother is likely to be earning an income.

It is often said (Hoem & Hoem, 1987; Popenoe, 1987) that the social services provided by the state in Sweden render men and women less dependent on a partner for material support than is the case in any other Western country. One outcome has been a popular movement away from the strong institution of marriage toward the weak institution of cohabitation, which removes, among other things, the need for divorce (Bernhardt, 1988). Many people have therefore concluded that given a really free choice, most men and women would choose the Swedish way, and that it represents the family of the future toward which other industrialized countries will steadily move. In this pattern, families typically will be formed and dissolved outside of marriage, breakups will be common, and marriage will remain as a rite of passage celebrated, often quite late, when the couple decides to make a public commitment.

A Caveat From Iceland

Before deciding that the popularity of ex-nuptial parenthood in Sweden is due mainly to a state policy of support for all births, we need to consider the situation in nearby Iceland. Iceland is still a largely agrarian country and has limited social security provisions compared to the other Scandinavian nations. However, it has recorded the highest out-of-wedlock birthrate of all the Scandinavian countries since at least the 1820s. In 1957, for example, 25% of all births were to unmarried mothers, while the next highest rates in Europe were 13.3% in Austria, 10.5% in Portugal, and 10.1% in Sweden. By 1975 the Icelandic rate had grown to 33% of all births, and by 1984 to almost 50%.

Why so? Although Christianity arrived late in Sweden, it arrived even later in Iceland, and the church was never able to control the practice of marriage. In consequence there was a continuance of the pre-Christian tradition of betrothal as the entry into co-residence (usually in the man's parents' household), and childbearing. Marriage came later, and marked the setting up of an independent household. Bjornsson, a sociologist, writing in 1971, distinguished three principal types of modern Icelandic marriage—the cohabitation family, the engagement family, and the marriage family.

Although each of the three types could be a permanent arrangement, they were more likely to succeed one another, with cohabitation being followed by formal engagement and eventual marriage. Cohabitation was the least approved status, but was never thought of as "living in sin," as it was in other European countries where the church was more powerful. In fact, a longstanding cohabitation family could often "pass" as married, as there are no obvious indicators of marital status: The formal title of Mrs. (Fru) is rarely used, and a woman does not take her spouse's name on marriage. The engagement family was inaugurated by the announcement of a formal betrothal. The couple then usually lived with one or the other set of parents, before setting up an independent household. Bjornsson distinguished here between couples born before World War II and those born after. Among the older group, the engagement period could be quite long, or even permanent, as they were expected to contribute to the extended family budget, and saving enough to set up an independent household could take a long time. Younger couples benefited from more prosperous times. Instead of expecting them to pay their way, parents were now prepared to largely support their adult children while they worked and saved for their own home. For this group, marriage usually followed the birth of the first child; although an average of 61% of first-borns were born premaritally, this was true of only 22% of second-borns. Even in older cohorts, however, most engaged couples eventually married and set up their own home. Following the wedding, the already-born children would be baptized, and all subsequent records then recorded the children as "legitimate," although their birth records continued to class them as born out of wedlock.

Rich (1978) pointed out that this system differs from both the traditional "European" marriage pattern involving late marriage, postponement of child-bearing, and the setting up of a new household on marriage; and the "Asian/ Middle Eastern" pattern involving early marriage, at least for women, and prolonged subordinate status within the extended family household. They see Iceland as providing the purest form of a third, "Scandinavian" form of marriage, in which ties between generations are strong and are not greatly changed by the formation of a new family of procreation.

From this point of view it can be argued that modern Sweden and Iceland are different developments from a traditional Scandinavian marriage form that emphasized betrothal rather than marriage, and thus produced many births that were ex-nuptial without necessarily being "illegitimate," in the Christian sense. The Swedish variant comes out of a liberal political tradition and 20th-century prosperity, and it has been able to support a relatively high level of family dissolution. In Iceland, the important factors have been a small, relatively isolated, and culturally homogeneous population, the late arrival of Christianity, and a domestic pattern where a period of three-generational co-residence was accepted as the norm. In consequence, in Sweden a high rate of ex-nuptiality is accompanied by a high incidence of single parenthood, but in Iceland by a relatively low one.

UNITED STATES

The Swedish figures suggest that a high incidence of mother-headed families resulting from a high out-of-wedlock birthrate is a sign of high choice. The United States has also seen a startling rise in out-of-wedlock births: From 5% of all births in 1960 to 18% in 1980, and to more than 25% in 1988. However, the causes are seen as very different. One important cause is the decline in overall fertility among U.S. families, such that out-of-wedlock births have come to make up more and more of the total. However, the actual number of out-of-wedlock births has also increased dramatically, tripling over the 20 years from 1960 to 1980. Rather than being the choice of privileged young people, these births are concentrated among African Americans and teenagers, with only some 20% being to women over the age of 24 years (see Table 4).

TABLE 4

Births to Unmarried Women as Percentage of All Births
(United States)

	1950	1955	1960	1970	1980	1985	1987
White	1.7	1.8	2.3	5.7	11.0	14.5	16.7
African American	16.8	19.4	21.6	37.6	55.2	60.1	62.2
Total	4.0	4.5	5.3	10.7	18.4	22.0	24.5

Source: U.S. Bureau of the Census: Statistical Abstracts of the United States, various editions.

Ethnic Group Differences

Ethnic group differences are very marked. African-American families have traditionally had more out-of-wedlock births and more marriage breakups than White families, but the present situation is something new. Whereas the proportion of White births that were ex-nuptial rose from 2.3% in 1960 to 16.7% in 1987, for non-Whites the jump was from 21.6% to 62.2%. In consequence, more than 50% of all African-American women who head families have never been married. This is in marked contrast to the White population, among whom most single mothers are divorcees, and only one in seven are unmarried (Hofferth & Hayes, 1987).

African-American single mothers are also younger than their White counterparts. In 1985, there were 87 unmarried pregnant African-American teenagers per 1,000 compared with 19 per 1,000 for unmarried White teenagers. In consequence, 41% of African-American women had given birth by the age of 20, compared with 19% of White women. Of the total population of African-American women with children, by the mid-1980s 56% were separated, divorced, widowed, or never married: Most of those under the age of 30 were unmarried (Hofferth & Hayes, 1987; U.S. Bureau of the Census, 1985).

Why? Marriage has traditionally been valued by African Americans, although it often came after the birth of one or more children. At times, the marriage rate has even been higher than for Whites; for example, among women aged 65 years or more in 1973, only 4% of African Americans had never married, compared with 7% of Whites. What then caused the massive move away from marriage?

The Welfare-Dependency Argument

As in other countries, a popular explanation has been the availability of welfare payments (in the United States typically described as welfare dependency rather than, as in Sweden, a citizenship right). By 1988, almost 1 in 8 of families with dependent children was on the welfare rolls, compared with 1 in 33 as recently as 1960 (Table 5; Hacker, 1988). The major U.S. welfare benefit

TABLE 5
U.S. Households Receiving Aid for Dependent Children (1986)

Race	1986	Status of Father	1973	1986
White	39.7%	Not married to mother	31.5%	52.6%
African-American	40.7%	Divorced/separated	46.5%	31.7%
Hispanic	14.5%	Unemployed/disabled	14.3%	9 %
Asian	2.3%	Deceased	5 %	1.7%
Other	2.7%	Other/unknown	2.7%	5.1%

Source: Hacker (1988).

for single mothers is Aid to Families with Dependent Children (AFDC). In 1973, less than one third of recipients were unmarried, most being divorced or separated. By 1986, however, more than one half were unmarried. The AFDC program was therefore accused of encouraging out-of-wedlock births by providing an income for unmarried mothers (MacDonald & Sawhill, 1978). As AFDC payments also went disproportionately to African-American and Hispanic women, they too were accused, the accusation here being that they were eager to seize on welfare as a way of life. (Only 21% of all U.S. women aged 15 to 44 are African American or Hispanic, but 55% of those receiving AFDC.)

Despite the popularity of the welfare-dependency argument, studies of the relationship between welfare payments and out-of-wedlock births have generally failed to support it (Aldous & Dumon, 1990). Figure 13 illustrates the typical findings of such studies.

Figure 13 shows that between 1955 and the mid-1960s the majority of mother-headed African-American families did not receive welfare payments. For a short period between the mid-1960s and the early 1970s both female-headed families and the rate of AFDC recipiency rose, suggesting some association between the two. From then on, mother-headed households continued to increase, but the proportion receiving AFDC fell (i.e., a negative association was recorded). Plainly, whatever was happening was not just a matter of more and more women seizing the opportunity to become welfare dependants.

Figure 13 shows that the value of welfare payments compared to average (African-American) male earnings also declined over the same period. The welfare-dependency argument is based on a theory of human nature that sees women as economically rational parasites. If welfare payments represent the best return available to them, they will have babies in order to become eligible; if male earnings go up, they will transfer their parasitism to husbands. Thus, an improvement in the value of men's wages compared to welfare payments should result in a decrease in the number of women who receive AFDC and an increase in marriage, which now becomes a relatively better

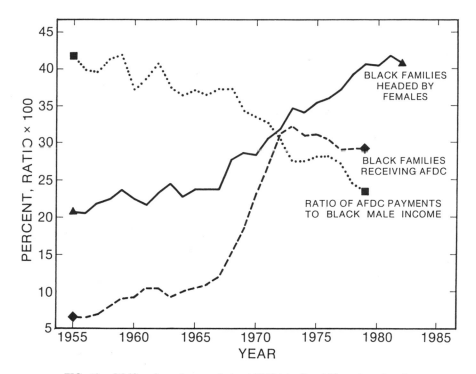

FIG. 13. Welfare dependency, relative AFDC benefits, African-American female family householders (from Darity & Myers, 1974, p. 769. Copyright © 1974 by the National Council on Family Relations, 3989 Central Ave., Suite 550, Minneapolis, MN 55421. Reprinted by permission).

economic investment. However, what actually happened was that many more African-American women became single supporting parents—both mothers and breadwinners—despite the fact that most could only obtain poorly paid work.

Further evidence against the welfare-dependency argument comes from the experience of former President Ronald Reagan's Omnibus Budget Reconciliation Act of 1981 (OBRA). OBRA placed more restrictive conditions for welfare program eligibility, and resulted in cancelled or reduced payments to low-income families, which involved 5–6 million children (National Council on Family Relations, 1990). However, as Figure 13 shows, no deterrence was effected, in fact ex-nuptial births continued to rise, as did the prevalence of mother-headed families in general. In a major review of the evidence, Garfinkel and McLanahan (1989) concluded that although single motherhood doubled between 1960 and 1975, increased government benefits could at most account for one-tenth to one-seventh of this growth.

Sex Ratios

If the welfare-dependency explanation does not work, what does? The increasingly accepted explanation (Majors & Gordon, 1991; Staples, 1985) is that although African-American women continue to value marriage, it is hard for them to find someone to marry. This is partly a problem of numbers. Virtually all (98%) African-American women marry African-American men, hence the field of eligibles is restricted to African-American men, and there has been a "virtual disappearance of men in the marriageable years" (Darity & Myers, 1984). By 1983, there were almost 1,500,000 fewer African-American men than women. More boys than girls were born, but by adulthood the numbers had been drastically reduced by homicides, accidents, suicides, drug overdoses, and war casualties (Edelman, 1987; Staples, 1982, 1985). McCord and Freeman (cited in Majors & Gordon, 1991) estimated in 1990 that the chances of African-American men living in Harlem surviving to age 65 were lower than those of all men in Bangladesh.

The main problem, however, according to Staples (1985) is employability. If the "minimum prerequisite [for a husband] is that he be gainfully and regularly employed, then . . . almost a majority of working-age black males" fail to qualify (p. 1007). In 1960, 75% of African-American men were working, but by 1982 the jobs they used to do had largely disappeared (Katz, 1989). Of the 8.8 million men ages 15–65, an estimated 46% were not in the labor force. Some 34% were unemployed, 11% were "missing" (not locatable by the Census Bureau), 2% were in prison, and 4.7% were in the armed forces with a high likelihood of unemployment following discharge. By 1990, among men ages 20–29, almost one in four was in prison, on probation, or on parole. A further number were in psychiatric and drug and alcohol institutions, and an estimated 9% were homosexual. Some observers have in consequence described the African-American man as an endangered species (Majors & Gordon, 1991). The minority who stay in school and achieve professional status are twice as likely as equivalent Whites to divorce, and less likely to remarry. In addition, African-American men who marry are twice as likely to marry outside their race than are African-American women (Staples, 1985).

Despite the shortage of men, younger African-American women are (compared to Whites) more sexually active, less likely to use birth control, and, in consequence, much more likely to conceive and to bear an ex-nuptial child while still in their teens. Staples and others emphasized that early childbearing is sought as well as accidental. He quoted a leading woman activist's comment:

> Having a child is probably the best thing that's ever going to happen to them in their whole lifetime and the only thing they can contribute—this is not true in most other countries in the world. But if you belong to a class or a group of

people who have no educational opportunities stretching out before them, no other goals, that's probably the single, best thing that's ever going to happen to you in your life. (Staples, 1985, p. 1009)

Other writers have emphasized the traditionally early start of sexual activity among African-American girls, their lack of sex education, and the force of peer pressure (Stark, 1986). Still others point to the influence of the previous generation of mothers. Although African-American women of this earlier generation mostly married, the combined effects of poverty, male unemployment, migration, and urbanization turned many into sole parents and breadwinners. Darity and Myers (1984) viewed them as thus acting as forceful role models to daughters who "grow up without the expectation of forming two-parent nuclear families" and to sons who "if they survive their youth, come to expect independence from any long-term familial obligations, except to their mother's family." They noted that all of these effects are accentuated by residence in segregated areas, where the pattern has become normative.

The African-American family has also been traditionally more prepared to accept the children of young unmarried daughters. Whereas White American families see an ex-nuptial teenage pregnancy as likely to ruin a girl's future, African-American cultures have typically seen childbearing as more important than marriage. In the 1970s, Stack (1973, 1974) described domestic life in The Flats, an African-American ghetto area of a midwestern city. The women she interviewed were the children of migrants from the southern states, and had been raised on public welfare, which continued to be their main source of support. She found that their families were not nuclear units at all, but made up of an extended cluster of kin, spread over a number of households with shifting membership. These households were typically formed around women, who had more regular access to jobs and social security payments than men. However, the households almost always had men around: jobless men living at home with their mothers or sisters, boyfriends, boarders, relatives or friends. Thus, children rarely lacked contact with men.

Marriage was not popular with Stack's respondents. Unemployed men (the majority situation) were regarded as poor husband material, likely to make trouble and to demand money and time that the kin group could ill afford. Even when a young woman was eager to marry and set up house, the man's family might be against it because they considered his first duty was to them. The women had a strong sense of independence from men, and in order to protect their own scarce resources had evolved ways of discouraging unwise marriages and of limiting the power of husbands and fathers. One young woman told Stack how her plans for marriage had been spiked by the matrons of the family:

Me and Otis could be married, but they all ruined that. Aunt Augusta told Magnolia [her mother] that he was no good. Magnolia was the fault of it, too. They don't want to see me married! Magnolia knows that it be money getting away from her. I couldn't spend the time with her and the kids and be giving her the money that I do now. I'd have my husband to look after. . . . (Stack, 1973, p. 124)

Since Stack's book appeared, multigenerational African-American households have increased threefold, mostly made up of a teenaged mother with one or two children sharing an apartment with siblings and a grandmother, herself often only in her 30s. The extended family network is less in evidence, and marriageable men even fewer, due to high mortality, ill health, and drug use among boys and young men. In addition, although the educational level of African-American women has risen, many African-American males continue to drop out of school early; and more and more of the jobs that were once open to unskilled men have disappeared. Observers see little likelihood of any change in the economy that would open up new opportunities for them (Wilson, 1987).

However, the women's economic situation has improved. A longitudinal study of African-American teenage unmarried mothers found that by the mid-1980s, when they were in their 30s, only 29% were still on welfare, and 71% had completed high school. By 1985, women held two thirds of all the professional positions held by African-Americans. Economic success did not increase the likelihood of marriage: The successful women were even less likely than other African-American women to be married. Among high-income earners, twice as many households were female-headed, and among college graduates three times as many. Current predictions, therefore, are for further movement away from the conjugal households toward women-headed households. It has been estimated that during the 1990s, three quarters or more of all African-American children will be living in such households (Taylor, Chatters, Tucker, & Lewis, 1991).

In a controversial revision of thinking about teenage pregnancies, Geronimus (1987) argued that the health of African-American women may deteriorate so rapidly from their mid-20s that teen childbearing is a rational decision. By this she means that it is not usually a conscious decision, but mediated through subcultural norms that have evolved from the realities of the situation. She found that African-American first-time mothers over age 23 had higher rates of neonatal mortality than teenage mothers, and attributed this to the women's early "weathering" due to poor diet, hypertension, lack of health care, and extensive tobacco and alcohol use.

Ethnic Group Similarities

Although out-of-wedlock births are commonly described as a minority group issue in the United States, Staples (1985) and others see that "these problems of the black family are only variations of the general problems of American families'' (p. 1010). White men were also in short supply as marriage partners in the 1970s and 1980s (see chapter 6, this volume); and low-skilled men lost jobs regardless of color. In just the 5 years between 1979 and 1984, 11.5 million U.S. workers lost their jobs due to plant closings or relocations, automation, or industry declines. The earnings of men younger than 30 dropped sharply after 1973, and the median income of families with children fell by 24% between 1973–1987, even though many more women entered the work force during this period (National Council on Family Relations, 1990; see Fig. 14).

Thus, African Americans and Whites share many of the same problems. Although African-American families are four times more likely to have below poverty level incomes, Whites still account for more than half the poverty population. In 1986, there were approximately the same number of poor White and African-American single mothers—some 1.43 million each. Although the increase in mother-headed African-American families may have been more noticeable (from 35% to 57% of all families with dependent children between 1970 and 1985), the rate for Whites almost doubled over the same period (from 9.6% to 17%; U.S. Bureau of the Census, 1985).

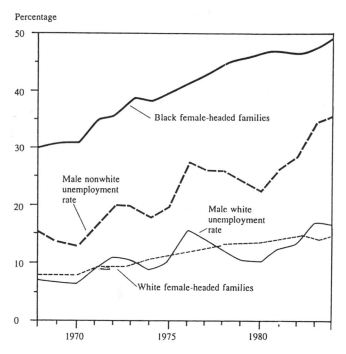

FIG. 14.   Trends in male unemployment and family headship by single women, by race, 1968–1984 (from Garfinkel & McLanahan, 1986, p. 74. Reprinted by permission of the Urban Institute Press, Washington, DC).

There are other similarities. Early pregnancy has become increasingly common among White girls. The birthrate for unmarried White teenagers increased by 50% between 1970 and 1981, whereas that for African-American teenagers actually dropped by 14%. One in 10 teenage girls in the United States is currently estimated to become pregnant every year, and almost half of these pregnancies result in a birth—over 30,000 of these to girls under the age of 15 (Stark, 1986; National Council for Family Relations, 1990). This is a startling change from the recent past. Before 1940, the U.S. out-of-wedlock rate was very low by world standards, and it only began to climb in the 1960s.

Although early pregnancy among African-Americans has been explained as a cultural tradition, the newer trend among White girls is usually attributed to increased polarization between the poor and the wealthy, and to the sexualization of the culture, including the use of younger and younger children in advertising and entertainment. Sex education is also poor by European standards. By 1983 the U.S. teenage birthrate was almost twice that of France, England, and Canada; three times that of Sweden; and seven times that of the Netherlands, all of which provide more sex education and more ready access to contraception (Stark, 1986).

However, many teenagers with good birth control knowledge still fail to use it. Several studies (Hanson, Myers, & Ginsburg, 1987; Yamaguchi & Kandel, 1987) found that knowledge has no effect on the likelihood of a U.S. teenager becoming pregnant, but that family values and aspirations do. Among girls of similar social background, pregnancy was greatest for those who were doing and behaving less well in school; and those whose parents monitored their children's activities less, and put less stress on responsibility and achievement. Having a steady boyfriend was also a strong predictor of teenage pregnancy.

McRobbie (McRobbie & Nava, 1984) described this constellation as one in which working-class adolescent girls without strong career, religious, or family values seek identity and self-esteem through success as defined by a peer group dominated by the boys. This means having a steady boyfriend, which requires sexual intercourse. However, it also involves being "a nice girl." Nice girls are in love with their boyfriends and they are also allowed to be "swept off their feet" or "carried away" by passion. But being too planful about contraception suggests premeditation, lack of romance, and immorality—to the girl herself as well as to others. One U.S. adolescent explained, "If I did [use a contraceptive] then I'd have sex more . . . then it would be too easy . . . I don't feel it's right. I haven't been raised that way" (Stark, 1986, p. 28).

Illicit drug use also contributes to teenage pregnancies, with adolescent users twice as likely as nonusers to conceive premaritally (Yamaguchi & Kandel, 1987).

An estimated half of all adolescent pregnancies are aborted, and some teenagers marry or continue in a *de facto* relationship. But some traditional solutions such as adoption and shotgun marriages are no longer popular. The result is a growing group of young, White, unmarried mothers, who are likely to drop out of school early, and to face many of the problems of African-American teenage mothers. However, the White girls are less likely to bear further ex-nuptial children, and their time spent in poverty is accordingly briefer (Hofferth & Hayes, 1987).

Combatting the "Epidemic"

The "teenage pregnancy epidemic" has received much public attention in the United States, and in the 1980s a range of inventive and successful sex education programs were developed, including image improvement for contraceptives. Programs to raise adolescents' self-esteem and their ability to succeed in the working world were also developed, on the premise that this provides a motivation for avoiding pregnancy. However, the general trend of federal policy under former Presidents Ronald Reagan and George Bush was to reduce funds for social programs rather than initiate new ones, an exception being the "workfare" program aimed specifically at moving clients off the welfare rolls and into the work force. Some of the legislation introduced was quite harsh. For example, under the Family Security Bill of 1988, single mothers who completed a work-training course were required to accept any "bona fide" job offer, and their welfare payments were terminated if they failed to do so.

Another obvious means of combatting the epidemic—through abortion services—has been bedevilled by the continuing strength of the anti-abortion lobby. Abortion as the choice of the woman was legitimated by the famous 1973 decision of the Supreme Court in *Roe v Wade*, and preterm clinics were set up around the country. However, in 1989 the anti-abortion forces were able to bring the abortion issue back to the Supreme Court, whose new ruling, although supporting *Roe v Wade* in general, gave more powers over abortion to the states, some of which have a strong record of opposing it (Aldous & Dumon, 1990). The much-contested appointment of Judge Clarence Thomas to the Supreme Court in 1991 was seen as likely to result in further legal restraints on abortion. However, President Bill Clinton in 1993, promised support for women's rights to abortion.

Comparison With Sweden

Both countries have experienced the post-1960s shift in attitudes that has legitimated sexual intercourse for unmarried teenagers and young people. However, although out-of-wedlock births have become a mainstream choice in Sweden, in the United States they are concentrated among those with least choice. In Sweden, the state through its sex education provisions, ensures that it is a choice, and there are very few teenage or even early-20s births; when the choice is made, the state through its social security provisions provides further support. Government policy in the United States has, by contrast, been grudging and even punitive, sex education is limited, and it is typically teenage minority group members who have babies outside of marriage.

Commentators on these differences make a number of points. Sweden is a small, prosperous, and cohesive state with a history of both liberal attitudes and anxiety over population decline: The outcome is a philosophy that sees everyone, including the newest-born baby, as a citizen with full rights to every service the state can provide (Hoem & Hoem, 1987). Hacker (1988), by contrast, argued that Americans generally are alarmed by the growth of a welfare underclass made up of school dropouts who, at an early age, bear children who are themselves likely to end up a "burden to society." None of the solutions tried so far have worked, and the public has lost patience. In this climate, draconian solutions are seen as acceptable, and justified by labeling the welfare recipients as irresponsible parasites who can perhaps be reformed by the discipline of work.

This comparison makes the unmarried mother population of the two countries appear poles apart. However, although U.S. out-of-wedlock births are concentrated among African-Americans and teenagers, the rate among mainstream women—older nonminority group members—has also increased markedly. Although births to women over 24 comprise less than one third of all out-of-wedlocks births, this is still some 300,000 per year, an increase of 416% since 1970. Therefore, the difference may not be quite so great as is usually represented, and can be seen as part of a transnational move away from the perceived need to preface childbearing by marriage.

A MID-RANGE COUNTRY: AUSTRALIA

Figure 12 showed that a number of countries have experienced a rather similar middling-size increase in out-of-wedlock births since the early 1970s. Australia is chosen to represent these. Australia has British law and institutions, a large Catholic minority, only a very small Black (aboriginal) population, and (since 1946) many immigrants (mostly European, Middle Eastern, and Asian) and their descendants. As one of the many countries that have experienced an increase in out-of-wedlock births in the absence of a large Black minority population or a long historical tradition of common law marriages, it thus presents a useful comparison to Scandinavia and the United States.

At the turn of the century, out-of-wedlock births were rather more common in Australia than in the United States, but by 1930 they had dropped to an equivalent level. They remained low in both countries until the early 1960s, when both rose steadily, in the case of Australia from 5.9% in 1961–1965 to 21.7% in 1989. As in the United States, the overall birthrate dropped during this period, so that out-of-wedlock births came to represent a steadily larger segment of a diminishing fertility. In the 10 years between 1976 and 1986, a drop of 14% in nuptial births was accompanied by a rise of 63% in ex-nuptial ones.

As in other countries, a common assumption has been that welfare payments are to blame, in this case the Sole Parent Pension (SPP). Introduced in 1974, the SPP is available (subject to a means test) to all single parents with dependent children. The SPP was introduced after the numbers of single mothers had begun to rise; but it is commonly depicted as having encouraged large numbers of unemployed teenagers to have illegitimate babies at the taxpayer's expense.

In point of fact, the rate of out-of-wedlock teenage pregnancies declined after the SPP was introduced, especially among younger teenagers. Most out-of-wedlock births are to women ages 18–31, which is also the peak age range for nuptial births. Ex-nuptial births as well as nuptial births to women in their 30s have also increased, particularly to those ages 35–39 years (Australian Bureau of Statistics, 1987, 1991).

Is this just a weaker version of the Swedish trend toward childbearing within common law marriages rather than legal ones? Not entirely. On the one hand, living together has increased steadily among people of all ages and social backgrounds. Contraception and abortion are readily available. Surveys show that a majority of the population regard teenage sex and cohabiting relationships as tolerable (Glezer, 1984a), and discrimination in employment, housing, and other areas on the grounds of marital status is illegal.

On the other hand, the people who choose legal or *de facto* marriages are not exactly the same. In the first place, separated and divorced people are particularly likely to live *de facto* rather than to remarry (Cotton, Antill, & Cunningham, 1983; Khoo, 1987), so that a subgroup of cohabitors are aged over 30 years, and many of these (a higher proportion than in the United States) have children living with them. They are likely to remain unmarried even after having children together. One study found that by 3 years after a divorce, 41% of divorced women who had had another child had conceived it out of wedlock (P. McDonald, 1986). When asked why they had not married, the majority said they saw little point in doing so. Census figures show that the men in these cohabiting couples had varied backgrounds: They were more likely to be unemployed than were married men of the same age, but those who were employed had above average income and job status (Australian Bureau of Statistics, 1985; Khoo, 1987).

Most cohabitors are young, however, and this is also true for those who have children. The childbearing age of both married and unmarried mothers rose steadily between 1976 and 1989, but the unmarried mothers remained consistently younger. By 1989, most married mothers were in their late 20s, whereas the unmarried were concentrated in the 18–25 age range, with the peak age being 20. Younger *de factos* include students, well-paid professionals, and business people, but overall they have below average income, job security, and job status, and are roughly twice as likely as the married to be unemployed (Australian Bureau of Statistics, 1985; P. McDonald, 1986). They are also usually native-born (despite Australia's large immigrant population), live in the cities, and lack religious affiliations (Khoo, 1987). One study (Cunningham & Antill, 1979) found that compared to married couples, the cohabitors were less committed to their partners, had less contact with their own and the partner's parents, had less traditional views on a range of social issues, shared domestic tasks more, and seemed generally more utilitarian in their attitudes to relationships. Another study (Glezer, 1993) found they were also likely to come from homes where they felt unhappy and not accepted, but where the parents tolerated the girls' premarital sexual activity (tolerance of boys' sexual behavior did not differ), to have become sexually active before age 18, and to have left home early. They also have above average likelihood of divorcing following marriage (Glezer, Edgar, & Prolisko, 1992).

The most common type of Australian unmarried parent then is young, working class and/or unemployed, and somewhat distanced from their own parents and their values. The breakup rate is very high, even when children are involved (Sarantakos, 1984). Glezer (1988) found that 45% of unmarried women who bore a child in 1984 did so while living with the father. Eighteen months later, 25% of them had married the father, but almost one in five had split up, compared with only 2% of those who were married when the baby was born. Thus, although nearly 50% of out-of-wedlock births are to women living with the father, the likelihood of these mothers subsequently becoming sole parents is very high: some 10 times higher than that of divorce among the married.

What about the 55% who were not living with the father when their child was born? Glezer's study found that 18 months later, 90% were still alone: Only 4% had married, whereas a further 6% were living *de facto*. This group included most of the teenagers, who were usually early school leavers from low-income families.

Given their youth, lack of support, and limited job qualifications, the most common outcome for both those alone at the time of the birth and those who subsequently split up, is the move onto welfare. When the SPP was first introduced in 1974, 15% of recipients were unmarried. By 1986, this percentage had risen only modestly, but the actual numbers rose by 642% (Raymond, 1987). Thus, the increase in out-of-wedlock births has, in the Australian context, been associated with a large increase in social security clientele. A number of studies have shown that many of these mothers don't expect any support from the father.

> When I was pregnant, I was interested in getting married, we both put in for this house I've got now, and we were going to get engaged and that. But he had

a temper, a bad temper, 'cos he drank a lot and we were living at Mum and Dad's and whenever he drank, and come home drunk, he'd always take it out on me, so that finished. . . . We tried again, but it didn't work, so we just went our own ways. (Montague & Stephens, 1985, p. 65)

I'd marry him if I knew he was going to treat me right, but he's got this idea in his head that if you're married or even just living together, his money's his— the only way I'm to support me and the kids is to go out to work or just stay like I am, on the pension, and live off that. (Montague & Stephens, 1985, p. 66)

We are friends but that is it. We are hardly on speaking terms. I do not want to live with (him). He has no sense of responsibility. He is absolutely useless with money. (Jordan, 1989, p. 32)

Originally, women on SPP were treated somewhat like widows, as dependent women in need of state support. Government policy is now to assist unmarried as well as other single mothers into the work force and their employment rate has increased after a low in the early 1980s. Nevertheless, they continue to be poorer, on average, than other single mothers.

Comparison With Other Countries

Ex-nuptiality in Australia increased over the same time period as in other countries, and to the same dramatic extent. However, it is neither as mainstream as it is in Sweden, or as concentrated among teenage minority group members as it is in the United States. Australian unmarried mothers are mostly either young, poorly educated and somewhat alienated (but not teenagers or minority group members), or previously married people disenchanted by marriage.

The evidence from other countries suggests that in populations with a middling degree of ex-nuptiality these are typically the people who are today most likely to cohabit rather than to marry (Balakrishnan, Rao, Lapierre-Adamcyk, & Krotki, 1987; Newcomb, 1986; Thomson & Colella, 1992; Trussell, Hankinson, & Tilton, 1992). For example, Newcomb carried out an interesting longitudinal study of a largely White U.S. sample, who were first contacted as high school students. It was found that those who subsequently moved into cohabiting relationships reported (at high school) greater drug use and more lawbreaking; earlier sexual activity; less religious commitment; poorer relationship with parents, other adults, and friends; greater dependency needs; and fewer inner resources. Those with these characteristics who married were more likely to subsequently divorce. Newcomb suggested that the very qualities that attract some people to cohabitation (nonconformity, suspicion of the value of marriage, and difficulty in resolving dependency and autonomy needs) are likely to disrupt their attachments. (This does not apply to the previously married, for whom cohabitation occurs within a different context; Demaris,

1984.) A dramatic finding from the United Kingdom is that babies born to unmarried couples are more likely to be underweight at birth, and are 39% more likely to die before their first birthday than children of married parents with fathers of the same social class (Her Majesty's Stationery Office, 1992). An obvious interpretation is that cohabitors, overall, have a lesser commitment to parenthood as well as to the partner.

CONCLUSION

Ex-nuptial births have increased in many Western countries over the last two decades, and particularly in the 1980s they made a significant contribution to the increase in mother-headed families. Removal or at least a weakening of social, religious, and economic restraints on unmarried sexuality is seen as the common factor. The most likely candidates appear to be those who do not particularly seek a pregnancy, but who lack the knowledge or the motivation to avoid it. However, the unmarried parent population includes very different kinds of people. In some cases, unmarried parents differ little from the married, except for their unwillingness to marry and their greater propensity to split up; or one or both parents have already been married and divorced, and see a second legal tie as pointless. For others, having a child is a boost to self-esteem, or to the father's self-esteem. Social differences between nations mean that the contribution of these different groups changes from one country to another—but in each case the total is increasing.

Our discussion has been mostly concerned with the period since 1960. But out-of-wedlock births have risen (and fallen) before, and many ideas have been offered for why this happens. In the next chapter we look at some explanations that have been offered for past rises and falls, and consider how these can further our understanding of the present.

Chapter 3

Why Out-of-Wedlock
Births Increase

We saw in chapter 2 that ex-nuptiality increased rapidly in the industrialized nations after 1970, particularly in certain subgroups. This was associated with a reduction in social, religious, and economic sanctions against sex outside of marriage. This brings up the question of why these formerly powerful sanctions collapsed so quickly, and why they were so strong before. As Fig. 12 shows, out-of-wedlock rates averaged only around 5% of all births in 1960, despite much poorer birth control than is available in the 1990s. Why the sudden change in so many countries? And why the variations within Europe, and the limited or nonexistent rise in some highly industrialized countries, notably Japan?

To explore these questions it is useful to take a longer term perspective. Most countries experienced periods of high ex-nuptiality before the 1970s, and other times when scarcely any such births were recorded. Is it possible to discern some logic in these changes? This is a question that has intrigued many scholars. In seeking an answer, comparisons over time and nations have been made, and the influence of religion, poverty, and many other factors explored. In this chapter we look at the major findings from these explorations. In chapter 4 we consider whether the same patterns occur in non-European societies and we reach some further conclusions.

SOCIETAL DISAPPROVAL OF ILLEGITIMACY

Malinowski (1930), an anthropologist, in a much cited passage, described what he called the "principle of legitimacy"

> The most important moral and legal rule concerning the physiological side of kinship is that no child should be brought into the world without a man—and one

79

man at that—assuming the role of sociological father, that is, guardian and protector, the male link between the child and the rest of the community. . . . The
form which the principle of legitimacy assumes varies according to the laxity or
stringency which obtains regarding prenuptial intercourse; according to the value
set upon virginity or the contempt for it; according to the ideas held by the na-
tives as to the mechanisms of procreation; above all, according to whether the
child is a burden or asset to its parents. . . . Broadly speaking, an unmarried
mother is under a ban, a fatherless child is a bastard. This is by no means only
a European or Christian prejudice; it is the attitude found amongst most bar-
barous and savage peoples as well. . . . I think that this generalization amounts
to a universal sociological law, and as such I have called it . . . The Principle
of Legitimacy. (p. 13)

Since Malinowski wrote these words, much evidence has been collected to
support his principle of legitimacy. All known societies seem to have made the
discrimination between legitimate and illegitimate births, and to favor the former (Hartley, 1975; Laslett et al., 1980; Rabb & Rotberg, 1971). One chilling
form of evidence comes from infant mortality rates, invariably higher among
the illegitimate. As we saw previously, recent British mortality statistics show
that this is still true today, even when the unmarried parents are living together,
and even when they are of the same social class as the married.

At the same time, the variations are huge. Some countries regularly record
very high out-of-wedlock birthrates, and some have none. In Europe, where
the longest standing records are available, there have been times when rates
were low in virtually all countries, and times when they have been high. Sometimes it is the cities that stand out, for example, 19th-century Stockholm and
the major French cities of the 18th century, where appalling rates of child abandonment and mortality were recorded. In other cases, illegitimacy has been
primarily an agrarian phenomenon. Almost one third of Austrian births in the
19th century occurred out of wedlock, and many more in some regions; and
these same regions still return very high rates. Some adjacent provinces within the same country have shown completely different patterns.

There are no simple or obvious explanations. At various times, characteristics like religion, race, or poverty have been suggested, but in each case there
are counterexamples that destroy the argument. For example, the Roman
Catholic religion is commonly associated with an ideal of virginity and fidelity, but the Catholic Central American countries rank second only to the Caribbean nations in out-of-wedlock births (Hartley, 1975). Similarly, poverty is
a frequent correlate, but the low-income Irish, both at home and abroad, and
even when they constitute the poorest enclave in English or other towns, produce
few illegitimate children (Laslett et al., 1980).

Furthermore, high rates of ex-nuptiality can occur when the status of wom-
en is very depressed, but also when it is relatively good.

There are, however, some trends that run through the findings, and that tell us something about the meaning of legitimacy and illegitimacy for individuals and for societies. These trends are intertwined, but for clarity sake they are presented here under separate headings.

CONFLICTING DEFINITIONS OF LEGITIMACY

We noted in the last chapter that the children of unmarried parents are officially classified as illegitimate whether they are born into consensual unions or whether the mother is on her own. There is obviously a world of difference between the two situations. Goode (1964) was able to discriminate not just these two but 14 types of illegitimate births. He went on to list them in descending order of social acceptability, from common law marriages and concubinage, to adulterous and casual unions, and finally to various kinds of incest. He found mother–son incest births the most universally deplored.

Most interest has centered around the distinction between consensual unions (continuing but not legalized partnerships, sometimes called common law or *de facto* marriages) and formal marriage. The distinction is not always clear-cut, but it is nevertheless an important distinction, because of the implications of the principle of legitimacy. A question commonly asked is whether the presence of consensual unions within a community denotes serious social disorganization or simply a preference for nonlegal or nonreligious unions, as seems to be the case in present-day Sweden.

In one sense, the very existence of common law marriages contradicts the principle of legitimacy. If legitimacy is defined as within-wedlock, as it has been in Christian societies, then the unmarried mother and her child are clearly disadvantaged, and it becomes a mystery why committed couples should choose such a situation.

The contradiction is partly explained by the fact that the Christian definition of legitimacy has very frequently been forced to co-exist with local definitions that accepted other kinds of commitments. These local definitions have not always shared the Christian requirements of premarital chastity, life-long marriage, and monogamy. The Scandinavian example of betrothal is one such local definition. As we have seen, before the period of Lutheran puritanism in Scandinavia, births to betrothed couples were generally classified as legitimate.

Local definitions such as betrothal usually serve a purpose and provide benefits, at least to some. Family historians have described how peasant families in many parts of Europe had a vested interest in a prospective daughter-in-law's fertility, on which the future of the family's estate could depend.

> They marry their women for a trial period. They do not conclude their marriage contracts in writing and do not receive the nuptial benediction until after having

lived with them for a long time, having closely observed their habits and verified their fertility. (d'Arrerac, cited in Burguiere, 1975, p. 45)

Where the local custom had this strong rational base, it could co-exist with Christian marriage for many centuries, or one or the other could gain ascendancy at different times.

Other examples of conflicting definitions come from colonized countries where the form of marriage defined as legitimate by the colonizing culture is difficult for local people to achieve, or unacceptable to them. The Central American and Caribbean states offer many such examples. An interesting aspect is that under these conditions, the legitimated form is generally considered to be better. Even in Jamaica, which has one of the highest illegitimacy rates in the world, surveys find that most people regard marriage as the most desirable state. However, for historical reasons, marriage in this part of the world requires the previous accumulation of considerable assets. A proportion of people finally acquire these by midlife, and marry then, perhaps as grandparents (see chapter 4, this volume).

It can be concluded that common law marriages have not, until the present, challenged the principle of legitimacy. In some cases they represent an alternative form of legitimacy; in others a step on the way to full legitimacy. Today's consensual unions may, however, represent something new. The whole basis of the principle of legitimacy is the belief that someone else—the church, the state, the community, the extended family—has the right to classify the relationship and the status of the children. This is precisely the principle that is now rejected by those who decide not to marry. Furthermore, in many countries the state is assisting in this by supporting their right of choice, and by guaranteeing the same legal, maintenance, and inheritance rights as exist in legal marriage. Language reflects these changes. Since the mid-20th century, sometimes earlier, official statistics in many Western nations have replaced the term *illegitimate* by *ex-nuptial*, *out-of-wedlock*, or some equivalent term, the intention being to affirm that although these children may have a separate demographic classification, they have the same social status and rights as anyone else. Under these circumstances it may be that the principle of legitimacy has lost its meaning; or even that marriage itself is losing its legitimacy.

PATRIARCHY AND PROPERTY

There is another way of looking at the principle of legitimacy. All babies are the legitimate offspring of their mothers. It is only in respect of paternity that differences arise. As men hold major social and economic power in all societies, this plainly puts the "unfathered" child at a disadvantage. However, even though all societies are patriarchal, variations in style and degree occur.

In general, the unfathered child is most stigmatized when descent is reckoned through the male line; when there is some family estate, however meagre, to be inherited; when women lack the means of economic independence; and when marriage connections are crucial to the maintenance and improvement of family prestige. When these conditions apply, an illegitimate birth brings dishonor to the entire family, so all members have an interest in preventing it. Unmarried daughters are likely to be chaperoned or claustrated, and a single compromising act, regardless of whether conception occurs, may be punishable even by death.

Interesting contrasts are found in complex societies where family inheritance and honor is important for some social classes but not others. For example, in 19th-century England and Scotland, prostitution was rife and out-of-wedlock births common, but women of the upper and middle classes were carefully chaperoned, were expected to conform to a strict code, and faced ruin if they contravened it. In consequence, illegitimate births, although commonplace among the lower classes, were very rare among the higher. The rationality of this double standard drew the following comment from Dr. Johnson to Boswell:

> Consider of what importance to society the chastity of women is. Upon that all the property in the world depends. We hang a thief for stealing a sheep, but the unchastity of a woman transfers sheep, and farm, and all from the right owner. (Boswell, cited in Smout, 1980, p. 214)

It follows that when the fate of women and children is less dependent on the social status conferred by their husbands and fathers, legitimacy will be less of an issue. This could be when both parents are poor and powerless, as in disadvantaged groups with high rates of illegitimate births. However, the importance of patriarchal inheritance is also diminished by a rise in the status of women, and their access to independent income. Under these conditions, births out of wedlock can be acceptable, but they will be most acceptable when the unmarried parents are most independent, or are least influenced by kin who might disapprove. In consequence, the people most likely to have out-of-wedlock children are those who are already of full adult status—like the previously married—and those younger couples who are somewhat alienated from their parents and their parents' values. As discussed in chapter 2, this is the case in the 1990s in countries with a mid-range incidence of ex-nuptiality.

RELIGION

Although Christianity preaches premarital virginity, monogamy, and fidelity, some Christian societies record high rates of illegitimacy, for example late 18th-century Catholic France. At other times religion has been the major force in

controlling out-of-wedlock sexual behavior, by one means or another including the threat of eternal hellfire. So religion per se is not a very helpful explanation of variations in illegitimacy rates.

However, family historians consider that certain changes wrought by the
Christian church in the middle ages made the European family forever different from other family types (Goody, 1983). A central factor was the church's
insistence that everyone, rich and poor, free and unfree, follow the same sexual morality, including monogamous marriage. Previously, polygyny and concubinage had existed side by side with monogamy, so that rich and powerful
men were able to accumulate women as well as other goods. Concubines were
commonly women who married without a dowry, as compared with fully legitimate wives, who came with a dowry. The concubines' children were acknowledged, and could inherit if the father wished. The church gradually
destroyed the previous status of the concubine. She became reclassified as the
"mistress" and her children as "bastards," without inheritance and other legal rights, even where the father was a nobleman or even a king.

In this way, the church actually increased illegitimacy. It is not hard to understand the disinherited children becoming embittered, giving bastardy its
bad name. Monogamy had another effect, however. It spread women more
evenly across society, and thus gave the majority of men an interest in marriage and its regulation. This in its turn brought further support for the church
(Goody, 1983).

A second major Christian innovation was the condemnation of marriages
between close kin, including those with a deceased spouse's brother or sister.
Within-kin marriages have the advantage of keeping family property and loyalties together, and were once very common in Europe as in many other parts
of the world. The church started by classifying first-cousin marriage as incest,
and by the 11th century had extended the prohibition to relatives seven times
removed. These seem strange rules, and they were often avoided or subvert-
ed. However, they had the important effect of weakening kinship bonds and
the power of lineages, and thus giving the church more influence over domestic and sexual morality. As a result of these and other influences, the European conjugal family (man, wife, and children) became somewhat disembedded
from its lineage group. It consequently developed special characteristics of independence, self-support, and late marriage in order to allow time to acquire
the resources necessary for initiating the enterprise (Goody, 1983; Macfarlane
1986).

Third, the church provided a divine rationale for the principle of male
supremacy and patrilineal descent. The European states were already robust-
ly patriarchal, but the Christian religion provided a wealth of symbols and
justifications for the belief that women were the vessels through which the family line passed down, rather than themselves the source of life and power.

Thus, the Christian Church pushed European societies toward particular forms of patriarchy, and out-of-wedlock births have to be seen in this general context, which varies in specifics from one region to another. In Scandinavia, for example, because Christianity was a late arrival, "legitimated" paternity has been less important than in western Europe (Goody, 1983; Herlihy, 1987). Within individual countries today, those people with a church affiliation continue to have fewer out-of-wedlock births than those without, but the proportion of the population with such an affiliation has dropped (Hartley, 1975).

SHORTER'S SEXUAL REVOLUTIONS

The historical pattern for Sweden described in the previous chapter is similar to that of a number of other European nations. Ex-nuptial rates were high in the early 17th century, then fell, rose again in the later 18th century, and remained very high until the mid-19th century, when illegitimate births comprised up to one third or even one half of all births in various regions. In the late 19th century, the rate dropped, then rose again in the late 20th century (Laslett et al., 1980).

A romantic explanation for this has been offered by U.S. historian Edward Shorter, who came up with the idea that there had been two sexual revolutions in western Europe, one in the early 19th century, the other starting in the 1950s (Shorter, 1975). The first was the more important, and it was brought about by young men and women moving out of the villages and into newly established manufacturing industries in the cities. As Shorter viewed it, sex and romance had received short shrift in village peasant life, due to the harshness of rural life, and the iron control of the elders.

> Sexuality in traditional society may be thought of as a great iceberg, frozen by the command of custom, by the need of the surrounding community for stability at the cost of individuality, and by the dismal grind of daily life. Its thawing in England and Western Europe occurred roughly between the middle of the eighteenth and the end of the nineteenth centuries, when a revolution in eroticism took place, specifically among the lower classes, in the direction of libertine sexual behavior. One by one, great chunks—such as premarital sexuality, extra- and intra-marital sexual styles, and the realm of the choice of partners—began falling away from the mass and melting into the swift streams of modern sexuality. (Shorter, 1975, p. 85)

In Shorter's view, it was the influence of city life—freedom from supervision, the right to keep one's own earnings, the day-to-day experience of a free market economy, the emphasis on individualism, and the crowd of similarly placed young people—that caused this thawing. Expressive sexuality ("true love" or "hit-and-run") came to replace manipulative sexuality (getting a hardworking, reliable, and fertile spouse for the long haul ahead). Expressive sex-

uality commonly involved romantic expressions and some interest in the partner as a person, but not necessarily much commitment. Soaring illegitimacy
rates were one outcome. For all the difficulties and distress involved, this was
an improvement on the peasant past, where sex as well as life was brutish and
short.

Oddly, Shorter made little distinction between the motivations of men and
women, implying a truly heroic romanticism on the part of the women, because the painful consequences of unmarried motherhood were all too visible.
Among these were poverty, prostitution, and child abandonment. For example, in Paris on the eve of the Revolution, one third of all infants were illegitimate foundlings whose mortality rates were so high that the practice of
abandonment has been described as a form of family limitation (J. Meyer,
1980).

In the 1950s, as Shorter saw it, a new wave in sexual expressiveness occurred in Western countries. In this case it was the suddenly acquired prosperity
of ordinary people that was responsible. Youth culture arose, and millions of
young people had access to smart clothes, leisure, entertainment, cars, and
music. Every young person was now his own Aladdin, gazing at a future of
ever-expanding riches—material, psychological, and sexual. The control of the
elders weakened further, youth demanded that unmarried sexual activity be
considered legitimate, and achieved this demand; and out-of-wedlock births
once again increased.

Shorter's expansive vision, the ingenious historical evidence with which he
documented his claims (in particular French and German parish and institutional records and contemporary accounts of village life), and his bouncy literary style, won him a large popular audience. His ideas have been less accepted
by those historians who since the 1960s have been analyzing European parish
and civil registers in order to explore the nature of family life in past times.
Their evidence suggests several other explanations.

RATIONAL PRENUPTIAL PREGNANCY

One of the unexpected findings of family historians has been the inverse corre-
lation in European history between age of marriage and extent of illegitimacy.
Europe here is an ill-defined term, emphasizing northwestern Europe, and allowing for multiple regional variations. Even so, a European pattern of family
formation has been described, in which couples have been largely expected
to support themselves and their children. In consequence, except in prosperous times, the European pattern involved delaying marriage until sufficient
assets were acquired or inherited; and many men and women remained single.

In the absence of reliable birth control, this might have been expected to
produce much illicit sexual behavior and many illegitimate births, but this was

not the case. Over the long period when much of Europe was in a no-growth situation, and marriages and legal births delayed, out-of-wedlock births were also few. Laslett, the doyen of British family historians (Laslett et al., 1980), viewed the nature of courtship practices as the crucial factor here. In one way or another, by various religious and social controls, local communities were able to divert their young people from "intense" courtship and consequent illegitimate births.

However, when real wages seemed to be improving, as was the case in England in the late 18th century, young working-class people saw earlier marriage as a possibility. They courted at a younger age and did so more intensely, married younger, and parented younger. In addition, more members of these birth cohorts entered the courtship arena, as pressure toward singlehood diminished. Parish priests noted that more brides were already pregnant than had been the case in previous times.

Inevitably, some partnerships broke down, and children conceived in expectation of marriage were born ex-nuptially to now partnerless mothers. Although these young women were categorized at the time as immoral, and treated as such, their behavior was in Laslett's view quite rational, as intense courtship increased the likelihood of marriage (their goal) as well as the likelihood of pregnancy. We can accordingly class this as rational prenuptial pregnancy, in which a risk is taken (intercourse) in pursuit of a desired goal (marriage). Laslett had no patience with Shorter's belief that an erotic revolution was under way among men and women.

Support for the notion of rational prenuptial pregnancies comes from Fairchilds' (1978) analysis of *Déclarations de Grossesses*, statements required by French law from women about to give birth to illegitimate children, detailing when, where, and under what circumstances they became pregnant. Declarations were generally taken in the seventh or eighth month of pregnancy, and were often detailed.

Fairchilds found that the majority of cases involved relationships between two workers or servants, where the major goal of the women was marriage. The records showed that marriage was of overwhelming importance to the women: It provided them with their only hope of economic security, gave them respectability, and saved them from the scorn accorded to spinsters. They believed (wrongly, as it turned out) that they were on the path to marriage, and were prepared to put up with some rough treatment from their men in order to attain it.

The number of women motivated by free-thinking attitudes or Shorter's "expressive sexuality" turned out to be rather few. Most lived sober and plain lives, kept in touch with kin, and sent money to their families. The exceptions were generally either inn servants and part-time prostitutes, or older servants who had become aware that their chances of marriage were slight and saw an affair as one of the few possible interludes in the drabness of their daily lives.

Although town and city servants bore many ex-nuptial children, Fairchilds and others found similar high rates in the countryside. Hence city life does not seem an adequate explanation: Indeed, a proportion of the city births resulted from rural conceptions. In a rural sample, Fairchilds found the same pattern of marriage plans gone awry and male partners who had moved elsewhere.

The *Déclarations* thus do not support Shorter's ideas about the rise of eroticism at this time. The courtship patterns described are particularly unromantic, usually involving a long engagement, promises of marriage and a ritual rape, followed either by marriage or abandonment. "In most of the cases we find brutality and an all-pervading masculine contempt for women. Instead of words of romance, there was verbal abuse. The best a woman could hope for in the way of tender words was the apparently standard line 'I have no other women but you' " (Fairchilds, 1978, p. 192).

Rational prenuptial pregnancy seems less important today, when marriage is no longer the only road to security, status, and respectability. But a variant of it seems to be responsible for many teenage pregnancies. In this case, it is not so much marriage that is sought, but a steady boyfriend, because for many girls this is the main way to achieve acceptance and status among their group. Achieving a steady boyfriend requires sexual intercourse without too much evidence of forethought in the way of contraceptive provision. This means risk of pregnancy, but the risk is considered necessary in order to achieve the goal.

STATUS-INEQUALITY ILLEGITIMACY

Rational prenuptial pregnancy generally involved men and women of similar status, mostly servants, laborers, and textile and retail workers. English records show that the more servants there were in a particular county, the higher was the illegitimacy rate.

A second common form of illegitimacy involves a higher status man and a usually younger poorer woman. Fairchilds found status-unequal illegitimacies to be the second most common type among her French sample. The typical picture was of a country or town girl who left home early—age 12 was not unusual—either because the father had died and left the family destitute, or because her wages were needed to supplement family income. She took whatever work she could find, was paid badly—about one third of that paid to men for equal work—and had little chance of resisting the master's advances, as he was likely to threaten "that if she didn't he wouldn't pay her wages" (p. 175). The women in these cases were usually younger than those with equal-status partners, and the men older. The pregnancies were sometimes caused by a single rape, but other times by liaisons that lasted years or even decades. Whatever the case, pregnancies were disastrous. A maidservant discovered by the mistress to be pregnant was dismissed without a reference, which meant

she would not get another job. Contemporary records show that a large proportion of prostitutes were former domestic servants.

The seduced servant girl is a universal phenomenon. However, the evidence
shows that the incidence increases when there is a rigid class structure, when
marriages are arranged, and when the women are isolated from their own families. Ironically, some epidemics have resulted from policies undertaken for
moral purposes, even very recently. The pre-World War II records of one Australian home for unmarried mothers, for example, show that many of those
admitted were young city or immigrant girls who had been sent as maids to
country families. It was assumed that the healthy country life would strength-
en their characters. But not knowing anyone, and often living on isolated
properties, they instead became pregnant by one of the men of the family, were
fired, and returned destitute to the city (Alexander, 1982).

The conditions conducive to these kinds of relationships are no longer very
prevalent in Western societies. However, they continue to be a feature in other
parts of the world.

TIIE "BASTARDY-PRONE SUBSOCIETY"

Laslett used the phrase "bastardy-prone subsociety" to describe minority
groups within a population who contribute disproportionately to local and national illegitimacy statistics, sometimes over many generations; and where these
births are not the result of common law marriages. Examples that have been
described were the "travellers" of Sweden, a gypsylike tribe, and in Scotland,
the Dumfriesshire shepherds who were at one time accused of having introduced
illegitimacy into the Highlands (Smout, 1980).

Such subsocieties seem to be present in many communities. Sometimes they
have comprised ethnic minorities, sometimes members of a particular occupational group, sometimes single families.

An interesting example comes from studies of the Alpine areas of Europe
(Khera, 1981; Viazzo, 1986). The formulator of population theory, Thomas
Malthus (1830/1970), pointed out long ago that "there is no land so little capable
of providing for an increasing population as mountainous pastures." This makes
Alpine populations an interesting test case of population control, and the records
show that over many centuries singlehood was very common in the Swiss and
Austrian mountain areas. At times, up to half the women failed to marry and
large numbers of men either emigrated permanently or worked outside the country for part of the year.

The Alpine areas also reported many out-of-wedlock births. The accepted
explanation has been that when marriage is not possible, people will have liaisons outside of marriage. It was assumed that the mountain regions offered
special opportunities for such liaisons during the summer, when unmarried

daughters took family flocks into the high country, and lived there unsuper-
vised by parents until the seasons changed.

However, close analysis of birth records show that the daughters of propertied peasant families very rarely had ex-nuptial children, and were usually prepared to accept a single life in order to keep the family estate together. The
women who became unmarried mothers were members of immigrant groups,
mainly miners, who had few assets except their ability to labor.

Describing such two-culture societies, B. O'Neill (1983) described the existence of an illegitimacy-prone subgroup as a socially functional arrangement,
whereby the landed families kept their estates and their status intact, whereas
the landless produced continuing generations of cheap labor devoid of inheritance rights. The situation of these minority group women can probably
be regarded as a special case of status-inequality, since the family's or the
group's reputation put them at particular risk of sexual assault and seduction.
The evidence is that this pattern can continue over many generations, and that
illegitimacy-prone subgroups continue to exist in many modern Western nations (Laslett et al., 1980).

POVERTY AND WOMEN'S WAGE LABOR

In the records cited previously, it is servants and laboring women who comprise the majority of unmarried mothers. This suggests that illegitimacy follows from poverty. This is a very common belief, but it is far from always true.
Some very poor countries have virtually no illegitimate births, and this is also
true of the poorest classes in some highly stratified communities (Hartley, 1975).

However, some features of life often associated with poverty are clearly more
likely to have an effect, for example (as in the instances cited earlier) culturally
accepted exploitation of poor women by higher status men, substantial male
mobility, and disadvantaged group status.

A different set of circumstances arises where women have been able to earn
reasonable wages in their own right. Before the 20th century, this has not been
a common situation for European women of the ordinary classes. They have
usually made an essential economic contribution, but their labor has been owned
by someone else, usually their husbands or father.

However, there are some instances of relative economic independence. These
generally occurred when young men and women servants worked and lived
together away from parental supervision, labor was in short supply, and the
women could earn good wages. A woman may have become pregnant in the
expectation of marriage (i.e., a rational premarital pregnancy), but her earning capacity meant that breakdown of the relationship was not a disaster, and
could even be her own choice.

Smout (1980) described the 19th-century Scottish Lowlands as providing such a situation. Young men and women worked away from home, finding constant employment by moving from one farm to another. They often lived in servant quarters away from the farm family so that surveillance by the farmer was limited. Girls could keep their jobs if they became pregnant rather than having to return as a shamed and economic burden to their families. The parents accordingly took a relaxed view: The clergy recorded frequent comments from parishioners along the lines that ''It's nae sae bad as steeling'' and ''Puir thing, it's a misfortune, but she'll get ower it'' (p. 207). This is a very different picture from that in Fairchilds' description of the destitute, deserted servant women who made their *Déclarations de Grossesses*; and closer to the unmarried motherhood of today.

Another example comes from the Austrian provinces in the late 19th century, when the introduction of the potato and other new crops meant that large tracts of previously fallow land were being brought under intense cultivation. These areas had previously followed the Alpine pattern of low population growth, but demand for labor now became acute. Farm workers were able to improve their conditions, and unmarried mothers fared better than usual. One observer commented:

> Even if the maidservant who has been seduced has her children with her, she will not stop working for the farmer, nor will she stop caring for the children. There is the instance of the girl who became pregnant seven times; she now has seven excellent sons who are in great demand as farm servants. She has brought them all up by herself and has also carried out her work as a servant. . . . she has never been in danger of not being able to work. (cited in Mitterauer & Sieder, 1983, p. 125)

The illegitimacy rate in the Austrian provinces reached 30% at this time, and 50% in some regions. These births were socially accepted despite the influence of the Roman Catholic church. Rural inheritance rights prescribed that only the heir had the right to marry, and only after the father died; but all children continued to live and work at home, and out-of-wedlock children were very welcome as extra labor for farm work. This pattern has continued among farmers and laborers and today close to half the births in some areas continue to be ex-nuptial (Mitterauer & Sieder, 1983; van de Kaa, 1987).

MODERN CHOICES

As ever, women today can bear an out-of-wedlock child within a variety of contexts, including every kind of unplanned pregnancy. However, two groups of today's unmarried or previously married women stand out as having made a positive decision to bear and raise a child or children outside of marriage.

The first, the great majority, are those who have children within a common law relationship. As we have seen, the composition of this group varies from country to country, but the breakdown risk is always higher than that of legal marriage. This group comprises a variety of household arrangements, including not living together, which can in some countries bring social security and taxation benefits, as well as having its own attractions. The evidence is that women in *de facto* arrangements are as likely as the men to have chosen this status, although they may have greater expectations of eventual marriage (Cotton et al., 1983).

The second and smaller group are those who want the least possible involvement of a man. These mother-only families may be formed by the birth of the mother's own baby or when she adopts an infant or child. The most publicized of these are lesbians who for ideological and personal reasons choose artificial insemination by donor (AID) to conceive a child. The phenomenon of single women resorting to AID appeared in the mid-1970s. Groups then evolved in the United States and the United Kingdom to facilitate the actions of women choosing this option, and to provide information and support.

Two recurrent themes appear in the publications of these groups. The first is human rights. One mother for example said of her decision:

> I knew I would be sorry if I never had children; sorry not only for giving up a part of life I really wanted, but for not making a decision I thought was right. I felt I was as worthy of having children as any other person. To not have children because I was a lesbian would have been giving up a goal that was dear to me (Hornstein, cited in Arditti, Klein, & Minden, 1984, p. 373)

The second theme is that of control of one's own body, reproductive capacity and life, freed of the interference of a man. AID is a choice that "is one that can remain in our control" and "takes back what is rightly ours" (Arditti et al., 1984, p. 373). Mainstream society is described as tyrannous in demanding that women bear babies only under certain conditions, one of which is the permanent presence of a "responsible" man. Traditional families are seen as intolerably restrictive and even informal relationships with men as imposing unwanted restraints. Because it challenges such controls, "donor insemination has been an enormously exciting step in breaking through the constraints placed on women by sexist prohibitions" (Hornstein, cited in Arditti et al., 1984, p. 373).

Contrary to the conventional view, literature on the lesbian mother does not view the lack of a male parent as a handicap. It stresses instead the advantages to children of having multiple parents through relationships with the mothers' friends and lovers; and multiple grandparents through the involvement of the parents of both the lover and the biological father, where acknowledged. These advantages are felt to far outweigh any disadvantages to children caused by the absence of a father, while the mothers benefit from not having a man permanently present in their lives.

The literature also points out the value of the role model provided for all sorts of people previously thought unsuited to parenthood, for example the disabled. Benefits are also argued to accrue to all women because of the lesbian public advocacy of a man-free, woman-centered approach to childrearing. This will help break down social expectations about what constitutes a "real family," leading to greater acceptance of people who, by choice or necessity, do not live in a regular nuclear family.

There is no evidence that children of lesbian families develop worse than other children. McGuire and Alexander (1985) found that lesbian mothers had higher levels of education and professional training than women in general, scored as more normal on psychological tests, and often had much more support and practical help from their cohabiting partners than wives received from their husbands. Mother–child relationships were reported to be closer than those in two-parent families in general, cognitive and social competence was normal or above average, sex role behavior normal, and daughters "choose more prestigious and masculine careers and report greater popularity than their heterosexual matches" (Green, 1978; McGuire & Alexander, 1985, p. 183). So chosen, father-free parenthood seems to work out where the mothers have good social, economic, and personal resources.

Lesbian women are not of course the only single women who resort to AID to conceive children. Other single women using AID generally give more personal reasons, in particular lack of a suitable partner or distaste for a long-term relationship. The typical heterosexual woman who has conceived via AID is in her 30s, has not married or else has experienced a marriage breakdown, and feels that because of her age time is running out (S. Walker, 1984). A variant is the woman who uses AID in the quest for a particular sort of infant. Plenty of publicity has been received by those who have used the Repository for Germinal Choice in the United States (which draws its stocks from Nobel laureates and other high achievers), in the hope that the sperm sample will contain some of the donor's superior genes. The first single woman (Bacon, 1982) to make use of this facility explained that she did not want the complications of having to "have a relationship with someone with whom you didn't *really* have a relationship," namely the subsequent father-of convenience of any naturally conceived child.

In 1991, the Birmingham branch of the British Pregnancy Advisory Service made headline news by announcing its assistance in enabling one or possibly three "virgin births," via AID to women who did not care for intercourse and thought they probably never would. In the ensuing fever of opining, medical experts pointed out that infertility clinics had been offering AID to single women for many years, and that a number had probably been virgin, because virginity was often hard to ascertain. They also argued that refusal could be unethical, because clinical AID had the advantage over the do-it-yourself version in that at least the sperm was HIV tested. In the light of these arguments, the government announced that it would allow the Birmingham group to continue this practice.

CONCLUSION

This brief summary indicates that we can divide illegitimate births roughly into those born into consensual unions and those born to unpartnered mothers. Consensual unions can be very similar to marriage except that they are more likely to break up than marriages. In Western countries, their prevalence is usually associated with the strength of the Christian church. Unpartnered motherhood has usually been very damaging for women. It has sometimes been very common, sometimes rare. Historically, the incidence has been kept down by religious proscriptions and by the social control of families and communities. It has increased in times of turbulence and change, including change for the better, when expectations rise and pregnancies are incurred in expectation of marriages that do not always eventuate. Women and children have nearly always been the losers in cases of unpartnered motherhood, and the actual numbers of illegitimate children have been kept down by sometimes appalling levels of child mortality. Those most likely to suffer desertion have been women whose initial bargaining position was weak, due to poverty, low status, and the greater power of men able and willing to exploit them. In some families and subgroups a pattern of low prestige, exploitation, and unmarried motherhood has persisted over generations.

However, there have always been some instances of humble but economically independent women who managed quite well as unmarried mothers. Many of these were "interrupted" marriages, in that the women were expecting marriage when the child was conceived. However, a better position in the labor market protected them and their children. Unfortunately, these women's voices have generally gone unrecorded, so we do not know how often they chose this status, or how they felt about it. It is hard to say to what extent their situation contravened Malinowski's principle of legitimacy—that "no child should be brought into the world without a man—and one man at that—assuming the role of sociological father, that is, guardian and protector, the male link between the child and the rest of the community . . ." (p. 13). It may be that most relied on a sociological father in the form of a male relative of protector. In recent decades, however, a group of women have made it clear that they prefer to undertake parenthood without any male partner, or without any of the partners available to them; and it may well be that some women have always done so. In such cases it seems that the principle of legitimacy may not hold.

This short review has suggested many factors that may have contributed to the rise in out-of-wedlock births in the last few decades. It indicated the importance of urbanization, of women's access to paid jobs, and of rises and falls in the dominance of the Christian church. However, international statistics show that the highest and lowest incidence of out-of-wedlock births occur in the non-Western nations where these are less relevant issues. Malinowski believed that the principle of legitimacy held true across all cultures. But are there some issues that emerge outside European culture that we have not considered so far, but that may be relevant for our purposes? In the next chapter we examine whether this is the case.

Chapter 4

Ex-Nuptiality in Non-European Countries

In the last chapter we described some of the factors that have characterized times when out-of-wedlock births have been many or few in European societies. But international statistics show that the greatest extremes are usually found outside Europe. In this chapter, we look first at non-Western countries in which out-of-wedlock births have been particularly high; and then at those in which they have been particularly low. Finally, we consider whether the explanations that were offered in respect to the European countries hold over this wider canvas.

Figure 15 describes the relative percentage of out-of-wedlock births in different countries. Some countries rarely publish figures, so that Fig. 15 makes use of Hartley's (1975) international survey. We can see that the Caribbean and Central American rates are especially high, outranking those of any of the European countries, among whom Iceland, Austria, Sweden, and Denmark are highest. At the foot of the graph, the lowest rates come from the Muslim countries. It is not possible of course to go through these countries one by one, even if information were available in each case. The following discussion, therefore, considers selected countries in which particular features have been considered by observers to be important causes of high or low ex-nuptiality. We then consider whether the factors that seem important in the European nations also emerge as the crucial ones in non-Western countries.

HIGH EX-NUPTIALITY

The Caribbean: Jamaica

Mason (1970) said of the Caribbean, "The region is of wide extent and enormous variety . . . but it remains true that there is something that can be called a Caribbean *style*, something to be found in almost every island and every sec-

Percentage of total births

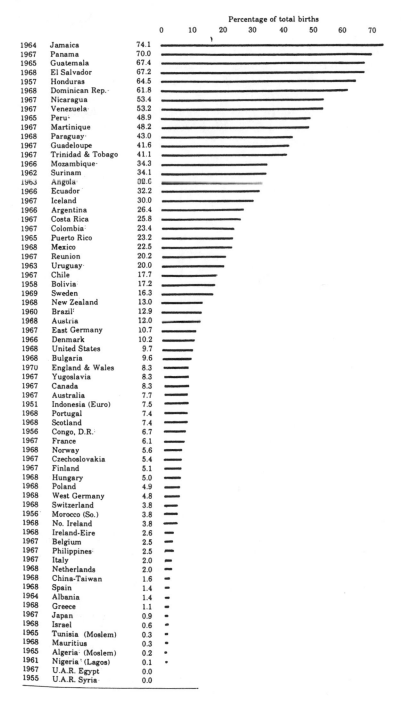

Year	Country	Percentage
1964	Jamaica	74.1
1967	Panama	70.0
1965	Guatemala	67.4
1968	El Salvador	67.2
1957	Honduras	64.5
1968	Dominican Rep.	61.8
1967	Nicaragua	53.4
1967	Venezuela	53.2
1965	Peru	48.9
1967	Martinique	48.2
1968	Paraguay	43.0
1967	Guadeloupe	41.6
1967	Trinidad & Tobago	41.1
1966	Mozambique	34.3
1962	Surinam	34.1
1963	Angola	32.C
1966	Ecuador	32.2
1967	Iceland	30.0
1966	Argentina	26.4
1967	Costa Rica	25.8
1967	Colombia	23.4
1965	Puerto Rico	23.2
1968	Mexico	22.5
1967	Reunion	20.2
1963	Uruguay	20.0
1967	Chile	17.7
1958	Bolivia	17.2
1969	Sweden	16.3
1968	New Zealand	13.0
1960	Brazil	12.9
1968	Austria	12.0
1967	East Germany	10.7
1966	Denmark	10.2
1968	United States	9.7
1968	Bulgaria	9.6
1970	England & Wales	8.3
1967	Yugoslavia	8.3
1967	Canada	8.3
1967	Australia	7.7
1951	Indonesia (Euro)	7.5
1968	Portugal	7.4
1968	Scotland	7.4
1956	Congo, D.R.	6.7
1967	France	6.1
1968	Norway	5.6
1967	Czechoslovakia	5.4
1967	Finland	5.1
1968	Hungary	5.0
1968	Poland	4.9
1968	West Germany	4.8
1968	Switzerland	3.8
1956	Morocco (So.)	3.8
1968	No. Ireland	3.8
1968	Ireland-Eire	2.6
1967	Belgium	2.5
1967	Philippines	2.5
1967	Italy	2.0
1968	Netherlands	2.0
1968	China-Taiwan	1.6
1968	Spain	1.4
1964	Albania	1.4
1968	Greece	1.1
1967	Japan	0.9
1968	Israel	0.6
1965	Tunisia (Moslem)	0.3
1968	Mauritius	0.3
1965	Algeria (Moslem)	0.2
1961	Nigeria (Lagos)	0.1
1967	U.A.R. Egypt	0.0
1955	U.A.R. Syria	0.0

FIG. 15. Illegitimate births of percent of total live births (from Hartley, 1975. Reprinted by permission of University of California Press. Copyright © The Regents of the University of California).

tion of society which is recognizably Caribbean'' (p. 274). Most writings about the Caribbean concentrate on the island of Jamaica, and for this reason we use the two terms fairly interchangeably in this discussion.

Figure 15 shows that in 1974 three quarters of all Jamaican births were recorded as illegitimate. By 1983, this figure had risen to 84.3%. Some neighboring countries recorded similarly high rates—in 1980 there was 87% in St. Lucia, 81% in St. Kitts group, 73.1% in Barbados, and 56.2% in Martinique. This has led many observers to conclude that formal marriage must have little value in Caribbean culture, and that common law unions are equivalent to marriage. On the other hand, many writers point out that ''the ideal of legitimacy prevails even though it is not adhered to in practice'' (Hartley, 1975, p. 4). Observers also point out that a simple explanation in terms of poverty is not adequate. Although the Caribbean nations are poor, they are better off than many others. Jamaica, with a reasonable level of per capital income and an adult literacy rate of 85%, even in the 1950s (Clark, 1957), is ranked at the high end of Third-World countries. The special nature of the Caribbean marriage system is considered a more important influence.

Types of Conjugal Unions

Conjugal relationships have generally been described as taking three forms: (a) visiting unions, (b) consensual unions, and (c) Christian marriage.

Visiting Unions.   In a visiting union, the woman continues to live with her parents or kin in her own home while the man visits, takes her out, and brings gifts. Fidelity is expected, and children are frequently born. Some writers (Mason, 1970) described the family's reaction as depending on their social class, with only the middle class considering illegitimacy to be a serious stain. Others maintain that the real shame lies, regardless of class, in becoming pregnant without the father's acknowledgment of paternity. It is ''maternity without paternal obligation that is heavily sanctioned in Jamaica (a concept quite different from illegitimacy)'' (Kitzinger, 1978, p. 220).

The birth of a first child may cause the end of the relationship, with one or both parties deciding that a long-term relationship is not what they want. In such cases, the resulting child almost always remains with the mother or her family. ''Older women anticipate having a second family consisting of their daughters' firstborn children and other children born outside regular unions to rear when they themselves are in middle age'' (Kitzinger, 1978, p. 20).

If the relationship continues, the man will keep visiting, taking his family on outings and contributing money or goods for the maintenance of his child or children. The woman usually has some form of paid employment and considerable personal independence. She has ''the satisfaction of a relationship with a man but without living with him and being subject to his government'' (Roberts & Sinclair, 1978, p. 65).

Consensual Unions.   After a visiting union has continued for a time, the couple may decide to set up house for themselves; or they may start off this way. Traditionally, the man is now the head of the house and is responsible for its inhabitants, but the woman continues to contribute financially, if only by selling a little produce in the market. This continues to give the woman some independence and power within the relationship; but commitment to the children and commonly held property give the relationship more stability than a visiting union. Consensual unions are none the less regarded as easier to dissolve than marriages. If this happens, the woman nearly always keeps the children. Because she has usually continued in paid employment, she has the means to at least partially support her children, and she also has the option of returning to live with her kin. As they grow older, her children will usually contribute to her support and that of their younger siblings and half siblings.

Christian Marriage.   Marriage is thought to be the ideal state, to confer status and respectability, and not to be entered lightly.

> The fact that marriage is monogamous, is intended to be a lifelong association and that a husband is liable for the support of his wife and their children is fully appreciated. It is often explicitly stated that because of these mutual responsibilities, enforceable at law, marriage is something to be entered into only after the couple have got to know each other thoroughly, in a preliminary period of cohabitation. (Clark, 1957, p. 74)

Marriage is also expensive—another reason why it is frequently delayed. The ceremony itself is expected to be lavish and the couple is expected to be well set up materially with housing and furnishings. A man must also be prepared to support his wife and any of her children even if they are not his. The woman expects not to be in paid employment after marriage and to have at least one servant to help with the housework. Such a financial commitment is beyond the means of the poorest sections of Jamaican society, and often too of younger members of better-off families (Clark, 1957; Roberts & Sinclair, 1978).

A common pattern in Jamaica is for a woman to experience all three types of union during her life, progressing "up" the scale as she grows older. Clark found that with age the percentage of women in visiting and consensual unions declined and the percentage of legally married rose. Children of the better-off or more religious families were more likely to enter marriage directly, and the married were much more likely to have had a single partner. However, even women in visiting and common law unions were unlikely to have had more than two partners (Clark, 1957; Roberts & Sinclair, 1978).

Origin of the Marriage System

Caribbean culture was founded on slavery. The original Spanish invaders wiped out the native Indian population so that when later European (chiefly British) colonists came to establish their sugar plantations they imported African slaves to work them. After emancipation in 1830 the former slaves remained to work the plantations as nominally free people, and formed the basis of the ensuing Caribbean cultures.

The Caribbean system of slavery was particularly cruel and oppressive, due to absentee landownership and the small number of Whites who lived on the islands. "If a landlord never visited his estates, or came only once or twice, there was hardly room for the growth of any personal knowledge of his slaves. He left his affairs to an agent, who reported to his employer in terms of goods produced, regardless of the human cost" (Mason, 1970, p. 276). One consequence of the small number of Whites was a siege mentality that led them to put down any signs of revolt or dissatisfaction with great ruthlessness.

The slaves themselves mostly came from polygynous African societies, where all females were married, and marriage and kinship rules were clear. In the colony, however, the slavers separated the members of different tribal and linguistic groups, so that any one plantation was made up of slaves who could not readily communicate among themselves. In addition, there was a policy of importing more men than women, resulting in a large enough sexual imbalance to discourage the formation of stable relationships. Some *de facto* marriages did develop, and some favored male slaves were "given" one or more wives by their owners; but the more common pattern was one of transient relationships (Fogel & Engerman, 1974).

Role of Religion.   The marriage of slaves was not encouraged by either church or slavers. Pregnant women and mothers were expected to keep up their full workload. From the slave owners' point of view, Mason (1970) said that "It was generally accepted in the Caribbean islands that it did not pay to treat slaves well or breed from them; the best policy was to 'work the slaves out' and trust to more supplies from Africa" (p. 276). Any children born belonged to the owner. The biological father had no part to play, and the children were "neither legitimate nor illegitimate—they were the lawful property of the mother's owner" (Reverend J. Smith, cited in Hartley, 1975). From the Christian missionaries' point of view, the rite of marriage was nowhere near as important as the sacrament of baptism. To be baptized was to be saved, and other behaviors were to some extent irrelevant. The slaves took over this view because they believed that this was the Christian way. Roberts and Sinclair (1978) quoted the case of a slave accused of immoral conduct who maintained that baptism left him free to do anything: "Look yeah, massa . . . don't de Scriptur say, 'Dem who believes and is baptize shall be save'; I want you to know that. . . . I done believe and I done baptize, and I shall be save, suah'' (p. 11).

The belief that baptism is more important than marriage continued after the end of slavery, and today more infants are baptized than adults married.

The Influence of the English Marriage System.   After emancipation, the ex-slaves and their descendants faced the tasks of creating an identity, establishing standards of respectability, and distancing themselves from the deprivations and brutalities of slavery. People who had been free before emancipation were ready-made role models, and the marriage ideology of the plantation owners—mainly English—influenced concepts of what a ''proper'' marriage involved.

Macfarlane (1986) described the English marriage system as a Malthusian system. He believed that at least since the 13th century the usual English pattern has been for marriage to be delayed until the partners could set up an independent household. This meant waiting until training or education was complete, careers established, and material resources accumulated. Marriage was regarded as a contract between independent individuals who were expected to establish an autonomous life for themselves. Marriage was a serious concern: a life-long monogamous partnership between loving companions that was difficult or impossible to dissolve by divorce.

Children under the English marriage system were welcomed and wished for, but were also regarded as something of a burden. They were financially costly because they were supported, educated, and given a start in life, but were not expected to repay these gifts except with respect and gratitude. They were not expected to share their property or income with parents or to support them in their old age. All movement of resources within the family was expected to proceed from parents to children. Children were therefore not such a blessing as to be desired in large numbers and most couples sought to limit the size of their families (Macfarlane, 1986).

The Caribbean stress on the gravity of marriage, its permanence, and the necessity of delaying it until the time is financially right is said to echo these English concerns. Attitudes to fertility on the other hand appear quite different. Children are valued as a resource and a blessing to their families, and the absence of legal marriage is not necessarily a reason for infertility (Kitzinger, 1978).

Aspects of the English system, thus became grafted on to something quite other that arose out of the slaves' African heritage and the experience of slavery itself. The effect for the majority of the population has been to add a ''top story'' of legal marriage onto a different kind of house.

The African Heritage.   In the African cultures from which the Caribbean slaves were taken the view of children was radically different from that of the English plantation owners. In traditional African cultures the extended family or clan group typically held property in common and the resources of individual members were added to the communal pool. Each new member added to the clan potentially increased its power, wealth, and influence, and was thus a valuable addition. Children repaid their parents because their income and property became part of the clan's wealth and contributed to the support of the parents in old age. Lack of heirs was a disaster because it meant dispersal of the clan's wealth. Reflecting this, African religious values stressed sex as a means of procreation and, although sanctions existed against promiscuity, celibacy was not regarded as a virtue (Mair, 1969).

As barrenness was such a curse, provisions were made to overcome childlessness. Sometimes a sister would accompany a bride going to her new home to help her and to substitute for her should she prove barren. If a man was unable to father biological heirs, various means were available to provide him with social heirs. In "ghost" marriages, a woman was married to the "name" of a dead man and any children she bore would be regarded as his. In levirate marriages a widow was married to a brother or other close male kin of her husband who then sired children in the dead man's name. Other arrangements existed whereby an infertile man could have another man sire children for him.

In consequence, social fatherhood was a more important concept than biological fatherhood: What was of supreme importance was providing new members to the clan so as to preserve and increase its property and to guarantee the welfare of dependent members (Mair, 1969). Under this system, men felt their potency and manhood proven if they fathered many children. Women were confirmed as valued members of the group by contributing their fertility as well as their work. Levine (1978) described attending the funeral of a 68-year-old woman of the Gusii, a Kenyan group.

> Many hundred of people attended, and, at the place where male mourners sat with her husband, I was handed a piece of paper on which were written the deceased's name, her dates of birth, marriage and conversion to Christianity, and the numbers of her male and female children, grandchildren and great-grandchildren, which were totalled at the bottom to yield the number of her descendants. This was her epitaph, the final public statement of her worth. In the past, her worth would have been represented by the number of people attending her funeral, for each descendant who married increases the number of kin whose attendance is obligatory; but literacy has added the written, quantitative epitaph.
>
> In my field research of the following two years I discovered how significant that epitaph was, in terms of both the public evaluation of someone whose life is over, and the self-evaluation of adults. . . . (p. 291)

Observers agree that admiration of fertility remains important in Jamaican attitude to childbearing. Men feel their masculinity proven by the children they father and women regard children as a valuable assistance to them and an insurance against deprivation in old age. Smith (1956) stated that "when a woman's children grow up she can always depend on them for help, in the form of money or presents of food, and they will make sure she has a roof over her head'' (p. 65). The social prestige gained by fathering children ensures that most children, legitimate or ex-nuptial, have a father eager to claim them. It has even been said that childless men will claim responsibility for children who cannot possibly be theirs (Clark, 1957).

Migration to Britain

After World War II numbers of Caribbean people migrated to Britain. High unemployment at home, closure of the United States to Caribbean immigrants, plus a feeling, fostered since the days of slavery, that Britain was the home country encouraged this trend.

The pattern of visiting and consensual unions has remained common in Britain (Barrow, 1982), but these often lack the extended family that would have helped support them at home. Barrow reported that

> in Britain . . . there is no extended family network. Even where there are other members of the family living in the neighborhood the pressures of being in a metropolitan society seem to prevent them from forming a supportive network [although] there are . . . some exceptions, especially among the small Black-led churches and some of the parents' groups and other organizations. (p. 227)

As yet, there are no signs of immigrant family structure altering to match the English family system, which has itself moved toward higher levels of ex-nuptiality over the period of African-Caribbean immigration (Barrow, 1982). The ex-nuptial ratio is far higher than among native Britishers or other immigrant groups, and 42.6% of families with dependent children are mother-headed (compared with 4.5% of Asian families; U.K.: *Labor Force Survey*, 1985).

Conclusion

Some of the sources of ex-nuptiality in the Caribbean echo those in Western nations. As slaves, women worked beside the men, working directly for the owner rather than for their husbands and family. After emancipation, they continued to work and to support themselves and their children, at least partially. Thus, women have a long history of self-support rather than dependence on men. Support from kin, especially kinswomen, is also important. This allows a mother to dismiss an unsatisfactory partner, or to survive his dismissal of her, even if no maintenance or state support is available.

The Christian religion also played a part, although a different one from what we have seen in Europe: The version of Christianity that was brought to the Caribbean emphasized baptism rather than legitimacy, so that the pattern of visiting unions and common law marriages was socially and religiously accept-able among much of the population, even if Christian marriage remains the ideal.

The Caribbean example also highlights the importance of the definition of masculinity. The English, or more broadly, the European marriage system has defined masculinity very strongly in terms of being a household head and bread-winner, with a women and her children as dependants. This left little room for children born outside marriage, and gave the father little incentive to sup-port them. The Caribbean system defines masculinity differently, emphasiz-ing the importance of fertility outside and inside marriage, and thus creates a positive role for the unmarried father.

This combination of factors—women's self-support, their support from kin, and absence of social stigma or strong religious proscriptions against unmar-ried unions, and the high value placed on fertility—come together to promote high levels of ex-nuptial births and mother-headed families. The first three are similar to those obtaining in the west, the fourth seems different.

Central America: Nicaragua

The Central American states also have extremely high rates of illegitimate births. Hartley's (1975) survey placed Panama second only to Jamaica with 70% of births illegitimate, followed by Guatemala (67.4%), El Salvador (67.2%), Honduras (65.5%), Dominican Republic (61.8%), and Nicaragua (53%). More recent figures for these states are similar but usually higher. Their proximity to the Caribbean states suggests that the family system of that region is simply being repeated. Are there any other factors that contribute to the high proportion of illegitimate births here, and that we have not yet considered?

Of the Central American states, Nicaragua has been most written about, because of its dramatic political history; and is therefore selected for discus-sion here. One problem is that there is very little relevant information before the Sandinista revolution of 1979, and material written since then is mostly eager to show how the revolution improved people's lives. For this reason, the past may sometimes be painted especially black in order to sharpen the con-trast with the present.

Nicaragua is a small, lightly populated country with plentiful natural resources. Racially it is fairly homogeneous, peopled by ''mestizo'' persons of mixed Spanish and Indian descent. A few African-Caribbeans and Meskita Indians represent racial minorities, both resident on the Atlantic coast. The country is overwhelmingly Catholic in religion and basically Spanish in culture.

Before the revolution, Nicaragua had a low per capita income, low life ex-pectancy, high infant mortality, and a low level of literacy. The Sandinistas introduced literary campaigns, improved social and health services, and redistributed land, but the country remains very poor. During the long war with the Contras, food supplies were often very limited.

Until the Sandinista revolution, Nicaragua was a client state. Claimed by the Spanish in the 16th century it became basically an exporter of resources, in particular timber, beef, gold, and Indian slaves. For a large portion of the 20th century it was under the influence of the United States after direct military intervention the 1920s, 1930s, and 1940s.

According to Gander (1984), the status of Nicaraguan women has typically been very low. Nicaraguan women commonly start sexual activity at an early age: an estimated 40% between the ages of 14 and 16. Common law marriage accounts for at least half of Nicaraguan couples. The tradition of early sexual activity and common law unions thus parallels the Caribbean situation, but the overall pattern is not the same (Gander, 1984; ''Women's Association,'' 1985). It is described as common practice for a man to start a family with one woman, and then leave her for another, and then perhaps move on again. The mother then becomes a single parent, although she may later have children by other men. Alternatively, a man may have several *de facto* wives at the one time, and these too are essentially single-parent families. Poverty and unemployment lead other men to migrate, leaving their families behind.

As a result of these and other practices, nationally 48% of families are headed by women, rising to 60% in urban areas. Most of these women work to support their children and some also receive support from kin. One consequence has been a large prostitution industry, staffed mainly by poor women lacking other job prospects (Women's International Resource Exchange, 1985). Contraception is not popular, and the average woman has five or six children, some many more.

Four influences frequently used to explain the prevalence of ex-nuptiality and mother-headed families are male migration, male mortality, machismo, and motherhood. Unemployed men leave home to seek work elsewhere, and fail to return. They are also likely to die young, through war and other causes. Machismo in this context refers to a male attitude that demands the conquest of women, assumes a double sexual standard to be natural, and takes pride in fathering children unaccompanied by a great sense of responsibility (Sluzki, 1982). The original definition of machismo in Spanish culture was based on the concept of honor: A man must defend his honor and that of his dependants, particularly his female dependants, and any stain on the reputation of his womenfolk is a stain on him. Kerry (cited in Peristiany, 1976) said that ''the ultimate symbol of [Spanish] quality folk is gentle womanhood defended and protected by honorable manhood'' (p. 333).

It has been suggested that the loftier aspects of machismo were undermined in the Central American Spanish colonies by absentee landlordism and in particular the shortage of Spanish women for the male colonists to marry. The native Indian women were less esteemed, and not deemed as worthy of the protectiveness that honor would demand be extended to a women of one's own background. This made common law marriages and the abandonment of common law wives and children more acceptable ("New Legal," 1987; T. Walker, 1986; "Women's Association," 1985).

Another inheritance from Spanish culture has been the stress on motherhood. Motherhood is a sacred concept, and a woman is not considered fulfilled until she has children. Women generally express a desire to have many children, and they do have many children. The Catholic Church has also promoted women's traditional role of stoic wife and mother who bears all as her "cross" (Gander, 1984; T. Walker, 1986). In the late 1970s, the Somoza regime tried to popularize contraception, but only some 5% of fertile women made use of it (T. Walker, 1986). Under the Sandinistas the high birthrate continued. (Sandinista leader Tomas Borge started a famous speech with the words "Nicaragua is a nation of births.") The high fertility results from the traditional high value placed on motherhood, partly from a lack of education and lack of contraceptive supplies, and partly from a felt need to replace population lost in the war between the Sandinistas and the Contras.

Conclusion

Much of the information discussed here seems very different to modern European cultures, but several aspects invite transposition. First, the shortage of men echoes the situation of African Americans in the United States, and to a lesser extent in other countries where women of marriageable age have outnumbered men. Under such circumstances it seems inevitable that a shortage of men will promote ex-nuptial births and mother-headed families, unless motherhood is much devalued. Second, the effect of male migration is itself of interest. Mobility in modern European countries is very different to that in Third-World nations, but it may have somewhat similar effects in freeing the person who moves from the social control of the home community. Many young men and women in Western countries can today relatively easily relocate and establish themselves in another region, country, job, and/or social group. This gives them much more freedom from community oversight. Even an awareness that so many alternatives are feasible may influence commitment to a partner, and hence readiness to enter marriage.

It is worth noting that in recent years a number of legislative changes have been introduced into Nicaragua in order to raise the status of women. The Sandinista government made paternity (rather than legal marriage) the basis for a man's economic responsibility to his children, and gave women equal rights with men in both legal and *de facto* marriages. At the same time, the war allowed women to prove themselves as soldiers, and to move into jobs and professions traditionally closed to them. In 1983, despite the overall much lower literacy level among females, 70% of all students at the Central American University were women. It will be important to see whether these reforms alter the prevalence of ex-nuptiality and mother-headed families; but figures are not yet available.

Sub-Saharan Africa

African societies were traditionally polygynous, with virtually all girls being married at an early age. Hence, illegitimate births were not a concern. However, today a number sub-Saharan countries return quite high illegitimacy rates. Hartley's (1975) international study placed Mozambique highest (except for several islands) among African nations in ex-nuptial births, with a figure of 34.3%. More recent figures are unobtainable due to revolution, invasion, and civil war. As in other countries, a proportion of these registrations were due to conflicting definitions of legitimacy, where the children of traditional but unregistered marriages were officially categorized as illegitimate. But over and above these effects, there are many births outside of marriage and many mother-headed families. The associated conditions show some similarities to and some differences from the other countries that we have examined.

Mozambican culture shares with other sub-Saharan countries the female farming system (Boserup, 1970) under which most agricultural labor is performed by women, who are responsible for feeding and supporting themselves and their children. Women have rights to the land they farm, which provides them with status and security. Polygyny is seen as bringing actual and potential wealth to the husband's clan, but also as helping women because a number of wives share the work.

Male migration and deportation has had an important influence on family structure. In the early 16th century, the Portuguese took control of the main ports, later moving inland, and in 1752 Mozambique was formally declared a colony of Portugal. A million slaves are said to have been deported over the 100 years ending in 1890. During this period, Portuguese control fluctuated and was often tenuous. After that time cash crops became the major economic activity. A system of forced labor (*chibalo*) provided a work force for the tea, sisal, and cotton plantations and also for the construction of road, railways, and ports. Men were press-ganged into performing this work, often a long way from home, while their wives continued to farm the land and support the children. After 1901 men also migrated to work in the South African gold mines and in Southern Rhodesia (later Zimbabwe).

A century of migratory labor combined with traditional marriage patterns to increase illegitimacy. As Hanlan (1984) observed

Men were away for months or years. In the polygamous tradition they would take other wives or have extended relationships with girlfriends in the city. Some abandoned wives are forced to enter other relationships as a means of support. Thus sequential relationships, whether informal or officialised in a traditional ceremony, are common. (p. 152)

Expansion of the cities, which drew many more men than women, exaggerated this effect. Sequential relationships result in many births, due to the high value of fertility and dislike of contraception. Single mothers are unlikely to remarry because children remain the property of their father (even if he is absent). Traditionally, this served the purpose of increasing the power of his clan and providing the father with descendants to care for him and to revere him as an ancestor. In the cities, a partner's children by another man are just an economic burden who will serve no useful function to him, because of owing their allegiance to another man and to his lineage. So even couples in long-term relationships frequently do not marry.

The tradition of the female farming system, along with more recent opportunities for paid work in the cities, allow women to support themselves and their children. So the mother-headed family has access to resources; but "the lot of these abandoned women and children is not easy" (Kilbride & Kilbride, 1990, p. 26). This is particularly the case for women left working at subsistence farming while their men take paid jobs in the city.

In 1975, the Frelimo movement achieved independence from Portugal and formed a national government. Among the reforms which Frelimo introduced were some that inadvertently added to the number of ex-nuptial births. Women were given the right to divorce their husbands and more of them moved to the cities to take paid employment. However, this increased their likelihood of living with a series of men and of bearing children out of wedlock. Extending education for girls also increased the number of illegitimate births. The practice of starting sexual relationships soon after puberty (previously followed by marriage) continued, and many students became pregnant. However, marriage no longer necessarily followed, particularly where the father was also a student.

Kilbride and Kilbride described a similar transition in Kenya and Uganda where there has also been a sharp rise in the birth of illegitimate or "outside" children, many of whom become street children. The Kilbrides described traditional cultures in the region as having kept a fairly tight control over adolescents, which was not too difficult in small towns and villages where everyone knew each other, and families arranged (sometime polygynous) marriages as appropriate. Today, agriculture is less important, and 50% of the new jobs are in the big cities, which draw large numbers of young men. Here too, women and children are commonly left behind, so that an estimated one third of all households in Kenya are headed by women. These women are farmers and traders, which gives them some authority, but farming has become a second-class, under-resourced, and deteriorating industry. Young people stay in school longer, and pregnancy by a fellow student is a common occurrence. However, a family-arranged marriage no longer necessarily follows, as the father has his (expensive) education to complete, and his family is likely to be unwilling to acknowledge the baby. The girl is left to rear the child with the help of her family. Alternatively, the mother too continues with her education, turning the child over to her parents, who may or may not be able to provide the necessary care.

A similar situation occurs among young employees trying to get ahead in their jobs. City life draws them out of the social control of their kin, but they continue to share the culture's disapproval of birth control. When a pregnancy occurs, the community sanctions, which in the village might have forced the father into marriage, are likely to be inoperative. The child is born without a "social father," and the mother is considered shamed. The Kilbrides believe that Western influences play a part in such cases, by way of ideas imported through the Roman Catholic Church and through television—ideas of true love, monogamy, and sexual sin.

Conclusion

These African examples, like the Central American, point up the ways in which migration increases illegitimacy. But in this case it occurs in the context of modernization, city life, and a changeover to wage labor. It recalls Shorter's description of life in the 19th-century European cities, where young immigrants from the villages found themselves outside the social control of kin and community. Thus, it emphasizes the deregulation of behavior that occurs when many people are released from such controls.

Some of the Kilbride's anecdotes also illustrate Shorter's second, 20th-century, sexual revolution. The young people they described are not rich, but they have access to consumer goods and parties. Their city jobs and the people they meet at them introduce all sorts of new possibilities; life can be exciting and full of drama. Although the young still adhere to many of the old values, the abundant alternatives can often lead them into liaisons that go astray, and can result in the birth of children for whom the father and his kin group take no responsibility. The change in a single generation from traditional village life is especially dramatic, but it is quite similar to what Shorter described as occurring in Western countries.

In essence then, these African examples reinforce much of what has been said in the Western literature.

COUNTRIES WITH FEW OUT-OF-WEDLOCK BIRTHS

In marked contrast to the countries just discussed, Japan and the Moslem middle eastern and north African nations report or have reported illegitimacy rates at or approaching zero. How has this been achieved? The following discussion centers on Japan and Egypt, two countries that represent contrasting paths to control of legitimacy.

Japan

In her international study of illegitimacy, Hartley (1975) found the greatest contrast between Japan and Jamaica. For all women ages 15–44, the Japanese illegitimate fertility rate was 1.64, compared to 168.24 in Jamaica. Jamaican 15- to 19-year-olds were 800 times more likely to bear an out-of-wedlock child than Japanese girls of the same age. Most strikingly, illegitimacy in Japan was previously much more common than it is today.

We saw in chapter 1 that divorce was common in 19th-century Japan, but declined when the country modernized. The same holds true for out-of-wedlock births. Under the traditional family system, each member of the *ie* (the family or lineage) was expected to subordinate personal interests to those of the whole, and the needs of parents and even children were to be considered before those of a wife. Love between spouses was not consistent with filial duty ("If you love your wife you spoil your mother's servant"), and marriages were usually arranged so as to further the family's economic and social interests. Among the higher classes, social standing was the crucial factor in partner choice. The lower classes were more concerned with direct economic benefits, like getting a good worker. The compatibility of the partners was not a major issue.

One outcome was the extensive practice of concubinage. The children of concubines could be recognized by the *ie*, but they did not have the status of a wife's children, and they made up the major category of births that were officially registered as illegitimate. The Meiji Restoration began delegalizing concubinage in 1882, but it was not totally outlawed until 1946. In 1900, when figures first became available, 8.8% of all live births in Japan were registered as illegitimate, most of them as "recognized illegitimate" (i.e., by the father from his concubine) as distinct from "strictly illegitimate."

By 1940, however, the proportion of illegitimate births had dropped to 4.1%, by 1950 to 2.5%, and by 1970 to 0.9%. Japan became steadily more industrialized and urbanized over this period, as well as suffering war, nuclear attack, and social reorganization under General MacArthur. Thus, it provides living witness to the fact that modernization does not necessarily result in increased illegitimacy.

One important reason has been the availability of abortion. In 1947–1948 the Japanese Diet passed an Eugenic Protection Law that, with subsequent amendments, provided for virtually unlimited abortion. The purpose was to relieve a population crisis in a difficult economic time. After World War II the real property of Japan was reduced by half, whereas at the same time Japanese residents in other parts of Asia were repatriated. In consequence, population density doubled. The effect of the legislation was the most rapid reduction in illegitimate fertility ever recorded. Between 1940 and 1964 the illegitimate fertility rate declined by 88%, while at the same time legitimate births were halved. In 1957, there were 72 registered abortions for every 100 live births, and a further large number was assumed to occur without being registered (Hartley, 1975).

Some other some influences are important, however, as fertility was already declining before the Eugenic Protection Law. One was the practice of classing children whose parents subsequently marry as legitimate (Hendry, 1981). Another was the system whereby parents contract their daughters for 7–10 years into factory work in sites outside of town. This has been popular with parents because the young women live in a boarding-school atmosphere, and some of their pay is put aside for a dowry. As most of the staff are usually other young women like themselves, pregnancy is unlikely (Hartley, 1975).

However, it is considered that the most important factor is the traditional and hierarchical nature of Japanese society, whereby adult children continue to owe loyalty and duty to their parents, and an unmarried pregnancy shames the family. Hartley pointed out that filial duty also has an economic aspect, as Japan lacks many of the social services that now provide support for unmarried mothers in European countries. The woman who proceeds with an out-of-wedlock pregnancy is in for a hard time, and those who do so are mostly young and uneducated (Wagatsuma & De Vos, 1984). Since the 1960s, abortion has been complemented by contraception as a means of avoiding unwanted births. As births within marriage have also continued to decline, overall fertility, which was well above that of Europe up until the 1940s, is now similar to that of the Western countries.

Conclusion

Just as modernization in Japan reduced rather than increased divorce, so too it reduced the incidence of out-of-wedlock births. The causes include the phasing out of concubinage, a vigorous government population control program after World War II, the maintenance of traditional values despite some apparent westernization, and the expression on these values in social structures that provide little place for the unmarried mother. Taking these together, we can say that Japanese society both strongly disapproves and punishes illegitimacy, and also provides ready means of avoiding it.

A Moslem Society: Egypt

Many of the Moslem countries also report zero or near-zero illegitimacy. Egypt is one such country.

Compared with sub-Saharan Africa, the Egyptian family is more nuclear in type and although extended family ties are important, individual loyalty is more to the immediate family than to the wider lineage. The family is patrilineal and patrilocal and is defined as a man, his male descendants and their dependants (Fernea, 1985).

Traditional Egyptian families are small work groups with a sex-segregated division of labor. Unlike the female farming system of sub-Saharan Africa, agricultural work is mainly done by men. Marriage is not a sacrament but a contract entered into for the procreation of children. Women have inheritance rights, and customs have developed that protect property from leaving family control as would happen if the women married outsiders. The preferred form of marriage is a cross-cousin type, that is one in which the woman marries her father's brother's son. By this means her property is kept under the control of the paternal family. As well as protecting family property from dispersal, such marriages also serve social purposes. It is believed that a woman will be less lonely if she marries back into her own family, and she will also be spared a conflict of loyalties between her own and her husband's family.

Moslem women may not marry outside their faith, although Moslem men may, because children belong to their father's religion. This rejection of outsiders comes out of a long history of invasion. Prevention of intermarriage was one way to preserve cultural identity. Salman (1978) suggested:

> the reaction to colonial and imperialist oppression in the Arab world took the form of attachment to local traditions and beliefs as a response to the cultural pressure of the settlers. . . . The Koranic prohibition of Moslem women marrying non-Moslem men . . . protected Moslem women from delivering their bodies to the oppressors. . . . The women, along with everything connected to private life became a symbol for the men, a concrete refuge from the colonial indignity to which they were subjected. (pp. 27–28)

Dodd (1973) interviewed refugees from the 1967 war who had lost houses, lands, work, and community, and found that for them "[family] honor took precedence over these other considerations. The honor lost by fleeing, the ignoble status of refugee, is compensated by the intact honor of the family" (p. 5).

Under Moslem (Shari'a) law women are under the control of their husbands, who decide where the family will live and what will be the extent of their wives' social and professional activities. A wife is expected to obey her husband's every lawful command and is much more easily divorced by him than he is by her. In return, he must furnish his wife or wives and children with reasonable support, an absolute necessity because of the economic dependence resulting from the restrictions placed on women's activities.

Girls are traditionally married soon after puberty, making premarital conception unlikely. Veiling and seclusion of women further reduce the chances of unsuitable contacts with men. Divorcees and widows are returned to the governance of their fathers if living, or if not, to a brother or other male relative. Men are required by custom to take in and support any female kin left without a male breadwinner. Fernea (1985) observed that "The unmarried woman is perhaps more than any other person felt to be under the protection of community norms. Concomitantly her acts are likely to be subject to the closest possible scrutiny" (p. 39).

As the whole family suffers if a woman is dishonored, they have a good incentive for supervising her behavior.

Conclusion

Egypt's low level of illegitimacy can be seen as due to extensive social control of women resulting from both cultural tradition and a reaction to invasion and occupation. Domination by external powers has made for greater restrictions on women, as a means of asserting cultural identity and moral superiority (Boserup, 1970, 1990). Some writers consider that the consequent reduction of women's productive role to apparently nothing has the effect of emphasizing their sexual and reproductive roles over other aspects of their nature. These aspects, so the argument runs, come in time to be seen as the main characteristics of women, and to loom large and threatening. Women are defined as inherently weak and untrustworthy creatures who must be kept on a very tight rein (Salman, 1978). Thus, restriction breeds restriction.

The comparison with Japan shows that both countries manage to keep illegitimacy down by treating it as shameful and dishonoring of the family, and by providing little or no place for the unmarried mother and her child. However, Japan also provides abortion and birth control, whereas Egyptian society emphasizes seclusion and surveillance.

COMPARING WESTERN AND NON-WESTERN COUNTRIES

This small set of exemplar nations with high or low illegitimacy does not of course describe all possible relevant factors. Other elements that can play a part include, for example, especially savage punishment of nonmarital sexual behavior, or encouragement of it in order to restore a depleted population, or war and widespread rape. We suggest, nevertheless, that although each situation is unique, a quite small number of factors emerge as crucial in both Western and non-Western societies. These are briefly summarized here.

Conflicting Definitions of Legitimacy

Ex-nuptial births resulting from couples' choice of consensual unions over legal marriage occur in many countries. In the non-European countries they are especially significant in populations where colonial powers have imposed their own definitions of legitimacy on the native culture. Many of the indigenous population prefer their traditional form of marriage, or are unable to afford the cost of the imported version, or lack access to the clergy or other officials who are certified to carry out the ceremony. In these cases, official records can give an inflated and misleading picture of the level of "true" ex-nuptiality, and these official figures can change overnight when a new administrative definition is adopted, as in Nicaragua.

Modern Western ex-nuptiality is thus similar to that of other times and places in being inflated by circumstances that lead many people to enter common law marriages rather than those officially defined as legitimate. In Europe it was usually Christianity that imposed a new definition of legitimacy on earlier, pre-Christian traditions. In non-Western countries Christianity has also played a part, but the other aspects of invasion and colonization have also been important.

Patriarchy and Property

In the European countries, legitimacy has been most important where the fate of children and their mothers depends on the status of their fathers. When alternate sources of support and status are available, the need for legitimacy declines. This usually comes from the mother's independent access to resources, or from the support of her kin or community, or from some combination of these. The rather sudden increase in jobs and social supports for women in modern Western societies can thus be seen as promoting an increase in out-of-wedlock births. The literature also suggests that the same effect is brought about by men's lesser access to resources (due to unemployment or other reasons) which makes them less attractive as husbands, and themselves less prepared to marry.

The non-European countries provide further illustrations to this theme. In some regions, experiences such as slavery and labor-indenture have reduced men's capacity to channel status to their families, and have increased women's and children's need to provide for themselves. Increased ex-nuptiality is associated with these conditions. In other regions women are debarred from

gainful employment and have a place in the world only through their menfolk—
and out-of-wedlock births are few.

Religion

We saw in chapter 3 that the Christian church pushed European societies toward
particular family structures involving ideals of virginity, monogamy, and indissolubility; imposed a strict definition of legitimacy; and provided a divine
rationale for the principle of male supremacy and patrilineal descent. The Christian concept of marriage as a sacrament by its nature imposed a zero or very
low official breakdown rate; and the influence of the church has often (although
by no means always) been able to keep the unofficial rate low also.

It follows that, other things being equal, cultures that put less stringent conditions on marriage (regarding it as a contract rather than a sacrament) will
have higher dissolution rates, and consequently more single motherhood. Cohabitors in "post-Christian" modern Western societies commonly espouse the
concept of contract, which they see as providing greater equity and independence than does Christian marriage. In this sense, they are no different from
other groups that view marriage as a contract, and it is no surprise that they
share with them a greater dissolution rate than that of Christian marriage. More
mother-headed families can thus, other things being equal, be expected among
those who are distanced from Christianity (or from any other creed that make
similar stringent demands on marriage).

There are also some special ways in which religion has promoted ex-nuptiality
in colonized non-European countries. In the Caribbean countries the early
Christian missionaries' emphasis on baptism rather than marriages helped de-
emphasize marriage and thus promote out-of-wedlock births; and in the sub-
Saharan countries it is said to have damaged the marriage prospects of young
unmarried mothers by depicting them as sinful. However, these effects do not
appear relevant to ex-nuptiality in modern Western societies.

Community Control

The increase in teenage pregnancies in the United States and some other countries has been partly blamed on loss of parental and community control over
youth behavior. And, as we saw, Shorter argued that the "first sexual revolution" also resulted from young people escaping traditional community control by moving into the European cities of the 18th century. Other historians
have rejected Shorter's view that this constituted a "revolution in eroticism"
but agree that out-of-wedlock births increase when communities reduce their
efforts to divert young people from "intense courtship." (By every means
available, which may include strict socialization, surveillance, chaperonage,

veiling, gossip, stigmatization, bribes, punishment, and threats of eternal damnation.)

Movement to the cities is one way that young people can evade some of these control strategies, but only one. A general increase in prosperity can also make early marriage more of a possibility for many, reducing the community's incentive to control courting, and in consequence causing more births both in and out of wedlock. Migration, war, revolution, and other crises can have similar effects by destroying or reducing the community's capacity to exert control.

The non-European countries provide many extreme examples of lack or loss of community control due to slavery, colonization, labor migration, modernization, and other factors. These seem to be always associated with increased ex-nuptiality, and sometimes also with high infant mortality.

We can conclude that community control can be lost for many different reasons, but the outcome is usually an increase in out-of-wedlock births. The exception is where contraception is so effective that unintended pregnancies rarely occur, as in some European countries today. Ex-nuptiality may still be high in these countries, but has other causes.

The "Bastardy-Prone" Subsociety

In the European countries, out-of-wedlock births have always been the minority, so that the idea of illegitimacy-prone subgroups makes sense. But when practically all births are out of wedlock (as in some of the Caribbean states), the concept no longer makes sense and we have to look to the complex of factors involved. This analysis suggests that the illegitimacy-prone subgroups within larger societies have probably originated out of special sets of conditions such as obtain for the majority of people in the illegitimacy-prone countries. When an illegitimacy-prone subgroup continues to exist over a long period of time within a larger society this is due to nonassimilation and usually stigmatization by the majority culture.

The Value Placed on Women's Labor

Increased work force participation and higher wages for women have been advanced by many as the major reason for today's high ex-nuptiality rates. Marriage is no longer essential for women, even those with children. In consequence, men feel less pressure to "make an honest woman of her," so the argument runs. And even if they do have such motivation, their partners may well reject it.

In European history, those regions where women's agricultural labor was needed and well-paid (e.g., Austria, Scotland, and Denmark) saw many out-of-wedlock births. Smout (1980) noted that "high levels [of ex-nuptial births] follow the lines of turnip cultivation" (p. 215); turnips being a crop that paid well but required a large labor input. The women whose partners left them, or who left their partners, were able to support themselves and their children, and as potential laborers, the children proved to be economic assets.

To some extent, this factor overlaps with the community control factor. As we noted, prosperity generally reduces social control over sexual behavior, as those who can earn good money are better able to withstand community pressures. However, it makes a difference who earns the good money. If it is the potential husband, then marriage is vital for women, and those whose progress toward it is "interrupted" by his departure or death are likely to be left destitute. If it is the woman herself who earns the money, then she can enjoy some independence, even as an unmarried mother; and might prefer this status to an unsatisfactory marriage.

The non-European countries show that factors other than wage labor can provide women with a measure of economic independence, for example land ownership or land rights, market activities, and/or the support of the mother's lineage. Whether or not this results in many out-of-wedlock births, however, depends on other factors such as whether polygyny is practiced, what work the men do, and the nature of women's ties to kin.

This brings us to the conclusion that the relation between the status of women in a society and the amount of illegitimacy is strong but not linear. Where women have relatively high levels of economic independence, ex-nuptiality appears to be high. But it is also high when women's status is low and male dominance strong, as in the Central American nations. Christianity, particularly Roman Catholicism, has played a confusing role here, by importing the concept of sin into pro-sex cultures, while at the same time discouraging birth control.

A final issue is that what is important to women's status is not how hard they work, but what value is placed on their labor. If it is invisible, or devalued, or owned by someone else, no benefit may accrue to the women even though they may work hard and long hours, and even though the group would not survive without their input. Sen (1990a, 1990b) used as a marker of women's status their survival rates compared to those of men. In Western countries, the sex ratio in the population is around 103 women to every 100 men, reflecting the greater longevity of women when men and women have fairly equal access to food and health care. In non-Western countries, access to food and health care is not always gender-neutral, and female survival rates constitute a compelling measure of discrimination against women. They vary hugely, from 86 women per 100 men in parts of India to around 102 women to 100 men in sub-Saharan Africa. Sen suggested that women's status is higher when:

1. they can earn an income outside of home;
2. their work is recognized as productive, which is easier with work done outside the home;
3. they own some economic resources and have some legal or customary rights; and
4. there is a "clear-headed understanding" of the ways in which they are deprived and a recognition of the possibilities of changing this situation (which is influenced by levels of education and by participatory political action).

Sen's four conditions now occur generally in Western countries and it appears that this particular combination or conditions is associated not only with higher status of women but also with higher rates of out-of-wedlock births.

CONCLUSION

It is concluded that the factors encouraging or discouraging out-of-wedlock births are quite similar around the world, so that it is possible for us to discern some general principles. Of course, there are major differences in marriage patterns, notably the practice of monogamy in some countries and polygyny in others; but the similarities apply, nevertheless. Further evidence of the universalities come from those countries that have experienced changes in levels of illegitimacy, and where the associated factors appear similar in the European and non-European instances.

We have discussed the ways in which mother-headed families arise from both divorce/separation and from unmarried motherhood. We turn now to look at a third form of mother-headed family, that formed by widowhood. Widowhood is no longer very common among women with dependent children in Western countries, but it is the most common cause of mother-headed families in much of the rest of the world. Thus, the treatment of widows has much to tell us about such families.

Chapter 5

Widows

For Westerners the word "widow" tends to summon up an image of an elderly and perhaps frail woman. Among heads of single-parent families with dependent children in Western countries, widows today form only a small proportion. Historically, this has not always been the case for when adults died younger, widows formed the bulk of women left with the sole care of children. In many regions of the world, the majority of female-headed single-parent families still result from death rather than illegitimacy or divorce. The early death of many men because of war and other violent acts and the widespread practice of marrying young women to older men have all contributed to the creation of large numbers of widows with young children. For example, in Africa today it is estimated that as many as one quarter of all women are widows. As average life expectancy is 30–35, these women are usually quite young (Potash, 1986).

Societies can outlaw or suppress divorce and illegitimacy, but they cannot do the same with widowhood. Thus, where no other form of mother-headed family is allowed to exist, the widow and her children must still find a place. This means that their situation under varying cultural conditions highlights the factors that can make single parenthood feasible, desirable, or unbearable. As Alteker (1956) said, "The position of the widow in society is one of the most important topics which the historian of woman has to discuss and elucidate. The treatment which she receives is often an index to the attitude of society towards women as a class" (p. 115).

Despite the fact that historically and currently widows have formed and do form a large proportion of the human race, their study has been quite neglected. The indices of books on the family or anthropology texts very often yield no references at all, or at best a page or two. This neglect of the experience of a significant proportion of the human race is intriguing and informative.

It is noteworthy that the term *widow* denotes a female person. Men may be widowers but they are not generally known by that particular strand of their identity. By contrast, women are likely to be categorized by their relationship to a man, in this case that of continuing to live after his death. It has been pointed out by Lopata (1973) that a widow in Western society has only a past, as the wife of a man now dead. She is his *relict*, to use the old-fashioned term. Widowers, being men, are not similarly restricted to being the husbands of dead women. They also have a future in the expression of the other facets of their identity.

The status of widow is complementary to the status of marriage. As Potash (1986) said:

> neglect [of widows] I would argue, relates to the anomalous position of widows in Western societies, which are conjugally structured. Western societies emphasize companionate marriage and common conjugal funds; widows are regarded as somewhat peripheral and hence of little interest. (p. 3)

Alteker (1956) and others have noted that the perception of widows as especially helpless and vulnerable is not universal. It is especially strong in those cultures that are organized conjugally, where women are defined chiefly in terms of their relationships to their husbands, where they are dependent on their menfolk for support, where they lack the means to achieve economic independence, and where they cannot own property. On the death of their husbands, these women become "burdens," vulnerable to the resentment of those who must support them, whether out of family resources, or out of general taxation revenue in public welfare-based societies.

By contrast, when women are economically active individuals or have the capacity to acquire property, the mere fact of being the wife of a man now dead becomes less of a predictor of life circumstances. The widow may be disadvantaged, but she may also be in better circumstances than when her husband was alive.

To understand what it means to be a widow in any given society then, we need to consider how that society organizes marriage, reproduction, and child-rearing and how these fit into the economic system and the wider society. Slater (1986) pointed out that this includes considering "options and restraints [which] vary with such factors as life cycle, demography, marriage systems, residence rules and the division of labor" (p. xix). This looks like an intimidating intellectual prospect. However, as with illegitimacy, a useful shorthand way of understanding the rules that cultures formulate for the conduct of widowhood is through considering some benchmark examples. As we see here, many of the same factors that influence the status of other mother-headed families emerge as important.

WESTERN WIDOWS

Today, women in Western countries have an excellent chance of surviving the childrearing years. Furthermore, increased longevity in developed nations has favored women over men so that the average European woman outlives the average man by 6 to 8 years. As most women marry men a few years older than them, a woman can look forward to a decade or more of late-life widowhood.

How did Western widows fare in the era before state welfare, when they were likely to be young and responsible for dependent children? And what can this tell us about the situation of mother-headed families in general?

The Christian Influence

The influence of the Christian Church again emerges as important. Christianity has been a powerful influence on most aspects of social life in Western countries, including family organization and the rights of widows. It has been argued that Christianity represents a special case in this respect. Although the other great religions have bolstered and justified the secular order, or at least not conflicted with it, Christianity in its early days was a creed very much at odds with the surrounding social order (Goody, 1983). In the case of widows, who were likely to be exploited by men eager for their property, it often provided a welcome alternative.

Christianity started its life as the religion of the dispossessed and powerless. As such, it appealed to women, and particularly to widows, who had no husband to forbid their vows should they choose to convert to the new creed. The first association to appear in the early church was the Order of Widows, which thrived in the first centuries of the Christian era (Boulding, 1976). This and other widows' organizations were given the care of needy members of the church, including other widows and orphans. The property the wealthy widows brought with them was pooled to care for the priests. The first churches in Rome and other cities containing Christian communities were in the homes of wealthy women.

From the start, then, the contribution of women was vital to the survival and growth of the church and they were involved in greater numbers than men. Women were also more likely to leave property to the church than were men, thus increasing its wealth and influence. The church, perceiving this, acted through the medieval period as protector of female property rights, including women's right to inherit and to make wills. In this, particularly the aspect of wills, the church remained in conflict with the common law, which stressed women's incapacity. The church also discouraged the remarriage of widows, because when they remarried their property would be absorbed into their new husbands' estates and thus lost to the ecclesiastical institutions that might otherwise benefit by inheriting it after the widow's death (Goody, 1983).

If the church had a vested interest, so did women. Medieval Europe was a place of considerable risk to single women, whether unmarried or widowed, both to their property and their chastity. The differential age at marriage, with brides as young as 12 or 13 (Guttentag & Secord, 1983), plus the large possibility that husbands would meet early violent deaths meant that the medieval period saw many young widows. Despite the preference given to men as heirs, the differential mortality rate meant that many women inherited substantial property. Plenty of men wished to gain control of this property and sexual exploitation, whether by kin or stranger, was a constant danger. The church offered protection from these risks. Clotild, widow of Clovis, King of the Franks, was among those who took advantage of its offer. She went at the King's death to the church of St. Martin in Tours where she ''remained all the days of her life, distinguished for her great modesty and kindliness. . . . To the churches, the monasteries and other sacred places she gave the lands needful for their welfare'' (cited in Goody, 1983, p. 64).

There has been a modern tendency to see the entering of nunneries by medieval women as some sort of banishment visited on them by families anxious to be rid of them. In fact there were frequently more women wishing to enter orders than there were places for them (Bullough, 1973). Instead of being a dumping ground, religious houses offered upper class women the company of their peers and a congenial refuge from the dangers of the world. A wealthy widow might seek refuge with a clerical relative, in return giving over her property to his see. Or a woman could enter a religious order or found her own, endowing it with her wealth. As Goody (1983) said of medieval noblewomen: ''Retirement into a religious house kept them within their own class but placed them in a protected sphere of social activity. . . . A woman added her portion to the endowment of the house where she could live comfortably under royal patronage'' (pp. 65–66).

Thus, the church and women had an alliance of interest. One result was the passing into the church's possession of massive amounts of land. This occurred by various means, but the bequests of widows played a significant part. It has been estimated that one third of the productive land of France was in the hands of the church by the end of the 7th century. In the German lands, in northern France, and in Italy the church owned twice as much land in the 9th century as in the 8th century. In southern France, too, between the first and second quarter of the 9th century, church property increased from 21% to 40% (Herlihy, 1961). The spectacle of so much of their property passing to the church gave the European nobility a worldly incentive to support the moves for change that culminated in the Reformation. The 12th-century poem "Hervis de Metz" describes sourly how "Today when a man falls ill, and lies down to die, he does not think of his sons or his nephews or cousins; he summons the Black Monks of St. Benedict, and gives them all his lands, his revenues, his ovens, and his mills. The men of this age are impoverished and the clerks are daily becoming richer" (cited in Goody, 1983, p. 105).

It was not only the wealthy who turned to the church. The religious life also appealed to poorer women who were largely barred from entering established orders. Urban-dwelling widows and spinsters banded together for mutual support and protection, forming lay religious houses. The Beguines were one such group, originating in the 13th century.

Beguines lived in group houses or alone and nominally they renounced marriage and took a vow of chastity, although this could be revoked. The Christian duties of prayer and meditation were stressed but the women continued their work in the everyday world. Good works were also encouraged, for example in hospitals, and with the elderly. The Beguines drew on the Christian tradition of allowing women a place outside marriage and family life, but were not a standard religious order. "They had no organization or constitution, promised no benefits, sought no patrons" (Bullough, 1973, p. 161).

The spectacle of women banding together for mutual support did not please everyone. The powerful craft guilds found the Beguines a threat, as did the church. They were accused of heresy and eventually brought under the church's control and integrated into the mainstream religious orders. The church was the ally of women, but on its own terms.

Widow's Property Rights: The Case of England

We saw in the previous chapters that the degree to which women have access to property has an influence on their fate as unmarried mothers. The same is true of widows. In societies in which men have a monopoly on paid employment and ownership of property, losing a husband can be a dire fate. However, when women have property rights, or can hold paid employment, they have some protection from want and the fate of the "useless" members of society. Even so, their claim to property has often been contested, because it has conflicted with the interests of larger groups, usually kin-based, that controlled economic resources. This relationship is very well exemplified by change to women's property rights in England from Anglo-Saxon times onward. As property was originally largely land, and land was a limited resource, propertied widows found themselves in competition with others for this resource. On the one hand, the widow and her children had certain property rights; on the other, plenty of men were eager to take over their property, through marriage or by other means. In England this resulted in extensive litigation, and court records give us an insight into the changing status of widows. Naturally, the records are mostly of those who held property of some value.

In the Anglo-Saxon period, marriage among the common people operated under a community property system. Women had property and inheritance rights, at least in theory. It is from these times that the practice of the dower originated (see later). The Norman conquest saw an end to the relatively egalitarian arrangements of the Anglo-Saxon era. Under the feudal system, land was now owned by virtue of being bestowed by the monarch and in return the holder was to pay both dues and military service. The idea of a woman owning land was thus an anomaly as she could not personally fulfill her duty of rendering armed service and other feudal obligations. However, she could pay men to do this for her, which some propertied women did.

By and large single women had many of the property rights of men. As Kanowitz (1969) noted:

> At common law single women were subject to oppressive sexually discriminating laws principally in the public sphere—as in the denial of the right to vote or to serve on juries on the same basis as men. In the area of contracts and property, however, except for their disqualifications under a system of primogeniture during the time it prevailed in England, single women enjoyed almost equal legal status with the single male. (p. 35)

It was a different matter for married women. When a woman married, the ownership and control of her property passed to her husband. She had no independent access to resources, and no testacy rights as she legally had no property to will. Women and their children deprived by the (very likely early) death of the support and guardianship of a husband and father were thus very vulnerable. Their main protection came through the Anglo-Saxon custom of the dower. This was a gift made by the husband to his wife that had to be bestowed properly, "at the church door," or it could later be challenged. Following a husband's death, it became available to the widow for the support of herself and her children.

The dower amounted to one third of a husband's free tenure land and one third of his personal, nonreal property held at the time of marriage. A man could sell land dowered to his wife, but if he did so his heir was obliged to retrieve it and to give the purchaser suitable land in return. The widow's rights were protected and she could resort to the courts if she had need. However, others could also use the courts to challenge the widow's inheritance, and court records from the 12th century onward contain many examples of such litigation (Loengard, 1985).

By and large, the widow retained the right to her dower if she remarried, the exception being manorial holdings that could be forfeit on remarriage or "loss of chastity." Thus a woman could accumulate considerable amounts of property through judicious and short-lived marriages. Parish records show that widows in favorable circumstances tended to live longer than any other group in the population.

These arrangements suggest that at least wealthy widows were in quite a good position. On the other hand, men were unwilling to allow a rich widow to remain unmarried and once married the woman's property passed under the control of the new husband. The propertied widow could thus find herself beset by suitors with an eye to her dower. A complication arose from the fact that dowered land was only the widow's to enjoy during her lifetime. She could not will it and on her death it passed to her husband's heirs who might not be her children. In consequence, remarriage resulted in much litigation against widows and their new husbands by the warrantors of their previous husbands' estates.

Apart from greedy suitors, other threats to the property of widows existed. In the towns, Orphans' Courts were established to supervise the handling of the estates of fatherless children (classed as orphans even if their mother was still alive). Sometimes the children's portion of the dower was confiscated by the court, nominally to protect it against misuse or dispersal by a new husband, but frequently in the interests of other benefactors of the dead husband's estate, who then held the land, and had the right to its use "in trust" for the orphaned children.

Despite so many hands eager for the property of widows, by the early modern period, the extent to which property was accumulating in the hands of women had become a concern. The feudal system had weakened, commerce had begun to compete with land as a source of wealth, and early capitalism, sometimes called *family capitalism* because of family ownership of the means of production, was growing. To prevent the scattering of family property, men began to make wills instead of relying on the dower and other intestacy provisions. Wills were frequently used to reduce the woman's dower right and her ability to alienate personal (nonreal) property. Men could (and did) also reduce their wives' rights to administer their estates by appointing co-executors, guardians, and overseers (Shammas, 1980).

Shammas commented that "these tactics slowed down rather than reversed an inheritance trend that appears to have been moving in the opposite direction, toward more widow control over estates" (p. 12). From the 18th century the use of anti-wife testatory practices declined. Fewer guardians were appointed to oversee women's use of their inheritances and they were increasingly the sole beneficiaries of their husband's estate. Subsequently, new intestacy provisions recognized the widow as the major beneficiary even when her husband died without making a will. Since the passage of the Married Women's Property Act in the late 19th century, women have maintained control of their own wealth after marriage.

Shammas considered that as the definition of family became more and more restricted to the nuclear family group, men began to see their wives, rather than more distant kin, as the best protectors of family property interests. Thus, the older type of arrangement that sought to protect the rights of various family members against each other was no longer relevant. In addition, as the period of family capitalism declined and corporate capitalism came into its own, the potential economic power women could accumulate via inheritance was significantly reduced. Women as heirs became less of a threat to the economic status quo under postfamily capitalism. As the threat value of widows decreased, they came to be treated more sympathetically. Intestacy laws were subsequently enacted that recognized them as automatically the chief beneficiary of their husband's estate, should he have had any property to will. It is still often possible for a husband to disinherit his wife, should he wish, or to leave all but a fragment of his property away from her. Provisions exist for a widow to contest the contents of her husband's will but statistics are not available on the fate of these court actions.

Laws of inheritance are of course only of interest to those who stand to inherit: They matter little to the poor. In England the poor widow provided for herself and her children as best she could. From Tudor times, the law sought to legislate family obligation by compelling the lineal blood relatives of a poor person unable to work to support that person. If all else failed, poor widows and orphans became the responsibility of the parish and were dependent on charity from the church. Later they came under the enforced welfare measures of the Poor Laws and were prone to incarceration in workhouses. Subsequently, voluntary charitable organizations and then the modern state took over responsibility.

Today

The Western widow of today has other possibilities of support—employment, her husbands' or her own superannuation and/or insurance, her own inherited or earned assets, social security, support from children or relatives, or some combinations of all of these. Relatively few husbands now die young, so that few widows have responsibility for dependent children. By the 1980s, as Fig. 11 showed, they comprised only a minority of single mothers. Their position is similar to that of divorced or unmarried mothers, in that their earning capacity is likely to be modest. However, they usually have greater assets, and their social security rights may be considerably greater. The economic position of older widows has improved markedly over the second half of the 20th century. Poverty surveys taken at different times show that at mid-century elderly widows comprised a major proportion of the poor, but that by the 1980s their position had improved, while younger female lone parents, mostly divorced, separated, or unmarried had become the "new poor" (Kendig & McCallum, 1990).

NON-WESTERN WIDOWS

The view of widows as marginal people has strongly influenced Western accounts of widows in non-Western cultures. The emphasis has tended to be on widows as victims and as charity cases. The victim approach is epitomized by the famous 19th-century text *Das Weib* (Woman; Weideger, 1985), which enumerates examples from many cultures of socially sanctioned ghastliness to widows. Sati is mentioned, as are requirements that widows fast, mutilate themselves, daub their faces and bodies, wear certain clothes or observe long, sometimes life-long, mourning. An example from the Tautin Indians of Oregon describes how

> After the cremation, [the widow] collects the bigger bones in a special container of birch bark which she is obliged to carry on her back for at least a year. She now has to do slave service for all the women and children, and if she is disobedient is severely punished. The ashes of her husband are collected and laid in a grave which she has to keep free from weeds; if weeds appear she has to dig them out with her fingers. In this she is supervised by her husband's relatives and tormented. If she survives the torture for three or four years (often she takes her life instead) she is released from it, and a great feast is given. Her husband's bones are taken off her back and put into a box which is fastened with nails and set up twelve feet high. Her behavior as a faithful widow is praised, and she may marry again. (p. 157)

The implication is that these practices are only forms of victimization. In consequence, there is little explanation of the context or of the social and psychological functions that these rituals may serve; *Das Weib* does, however, make the sharp comment that "the married woman in the period of patriarchy is exactly like the servant [and the widow] is the property of the dead man." It cites the 12th-century Chinese scholar Chu-hi, ". . . Woman is born to serve man with her body, so that the life of a wife comes to an end with that of her husband and she is said to die with him. After the death of her husband she is therefore called 'the woman not yet dead' " (p. 159).

The charity case approach overlooks the fact that the widow may not have been the "property of the dead man." Slater (1986) pointed out that Western descriptions of widow treatment in other cultures overlook the fact that she may have much stronger ties to her own family than to her husband, or may have been herself the principal provider for the family. Although sometimes described as common, enforced welfare measures such as "widow inheritance" (when the dead man's brother or other kinsman marries his widow[s]) are not the rule, and in some cultures, widows have considerable freedom in how they conduct their widowhood. They may not be guaranteed any provision or protection by their society at all, but are frequently able to see to their own welfare.

Slater also contended that Western observers of non-Western cultures are prone to attacks of romanticism. Nostalgia for a lost Golden Age of caring, sharing extended families causes them to overemphasize what are seen as the positive traits of kin-based societies. These societies are seen as providing a safety net of assured subsistence for all their members, including widows. Potash (1986) commented of African societies that "concepts of communal support for widows is more a Rousseauian ideal than an ethnographic reality" (p. 31). At the other extreme to romanticism in Western accounts is astonishment at apparent unfeelingness. *Das Weib* quoted with approval a medieval wife's loving lament for her late husband, and compares it with "Conditions such as Powell has described from New Britain. A chief had carried off a woman from a hostile tribe to take her as his wife, and in so doing her existing husband was killed. At the wedding feast the latter was eaten and his widow calmly shared in the horrible meal" (p. 156)

Many accounts have also overlooked class and caste differences. For instance, in India sati was largely a practice of higher caste families. The prescriptions often encountered in texts for the right behavior of Chinese widows was also largely drawn from the social codes of the upper classes. For women, higher social status is not always a benefit: Lower class widows, although more likely to suffer from material want, have often been much freer to decide the conduct of their lives (Das & Bardis, 1979; Dubois & Beauchamp, 1906).

The Indian Widow

When we think of Indian widows, the first image summoned up is that of the sati (suttee), the woman who was burnt alive on her husband's funeral pyre. The sensational aspects of sati have dominated the literature on Indian widowhood, and the social structures, beliefs, and practices that shaped responses to widowed women are often obscured by sati-related rhetoric. However, it seems that a complex mixture of religious, racial, economic, and psychological factors combined to make self-immolation the solution of choice (and sati was, at least in theory, always voluntary) for some Indian women.

Sati, far from being the fate of most Indian widows, was always the destination of the few. It is estimated that between 1450 and 1824, something between 1 in 1,000 and 1 in 50 widows became sati (Alteker, 1956). Sati was also very much a caste-bound phenomenon with Rajput (warrior caste) widows being those originally burnt. Later Brahmin (priestly caste) widows also started to be sacrificed, although this was originally banned. Very few women from castes beneath these top two become sati.

Apart from variations of frequency among the different castes, the practice also had its ups and downs historically. Sati seems to have originated amongst the Rajputs in the first millenium BC when similar sacrifice of the wives, servants, animals, and possessions of chiefs was also known among other warrior peoples. Whereas in most other warrior cultures such funeral rites disappeared, in India sati became more entrenched and by the early centuries AD it had spread to the Brahmin castes. Religious and scriptural authority having been "found" for it, it became regarded as the highest manifestation of virtuous widowhood (Alteker, 1956; Stein, 1978).

From that time it waxed and waned, becoming more popular, according to Alteker (1956), at times and among segments of the population where it could serve some social function. Ironically, there was an upsurge of widow burning around the time the British came to contemplate banning it. Many observers have noted how, in conquered countries, social customs involving women can become increasingly important as a way of highlighting and affirming cultural identity and resistance to the invaders. There is some justification for seeing the increase in sati during the late 18th and early 19th centuries as a particularly dramatic example of this.

The British ban on sati, which occurred in 1829, may be equally well viewed as an attempt to stress the legitimacy of their conquest by demonstrating their more civilized, and civilizing, culture (Worsoe, 1988). The furor over sati made the Indian widow the most discussed worldwide, with the practice assuring that widows make an appearance in any book on Indian culture or history, which certainly cannot be said of widows from any other part of the world.

Among the widow-burning castes and those that aspired to be like them, the life prescribed for the widow who chose to live was by all accounts grim (Alteker, 1956; Chanduri, 1967; Dubois & Beauchamp, 1906). Widow remarriage was absolutely forbidden and offenders lost caste. All rights to custody of the widow's children belonged to her husband's family as did her husband's estate, although the widow had the life-long right to enjoy his estate even when she did not, as a rule, inherit any of it. An anomaly was Bengali widows, who as well as inheritance rights to their husbands' estates, also had a higher rate of sati, perhaps because of pressure from in-laws who were reluctant to part with their bereaved daughter-in-law's legal share of the estate (Worsoe, 1988).

The widow was expected to shave her head, dress in rough clothing emblematic of her situation, and wear no jewelry. She was to eat frugally, emaciating her body, and was to spend her days in penitence and prayer. She was regarded as inauspicious and the very sight of her was unlucky. Because of this she was banned from festivals and amusements (Dubois & Beauchamp, 1906).

In a classic example of blaming the victim, the pitiful lot inflicted on the Indian widow was seen to be justified as punishment for wrong doings in a former life. It was culturally regarded as natural (despite the relevant demographics) for a woman to predecease her husband. To fail to do so and to be left a widow was a sign that she had committed sins in a previous existence (Alteker, 1956).

An Indian woman was also expected to worship her husband as a god and if she could not bring herself to burn on his funeral pyre with him then she was to remain chaste and to dedicate herself to life-long devotion to his memory. The social reminder of one's former self given by the continued existence of one's faithful widow, would no doubt appeal to many. The virtuous widow becomes a sort of human memorial. The reasons for the prohibition of widow remarriage were not all psychological, however, as we discuss later.

Sati offered some rewards. The sati, her husband, and both their families had their sins wiped out and were guaranteed places in heaven. Instead of being reviled for choosing to survive her husband, the woman became a venerated saint if she died on his funeral pyre.

Perhaps most strange to Westerners is the fate of very young widows. Very young children were often married (not to be married by puberty was thought to be calamitous). The difficulty of securing a suitable mate among the maze of endogamous and constantly proliferating castes plus the absolute insistence on purity in the bride necessitated this. Some of these infant brides became widows before they had even cohabited with their husbands and they, too, were prohibited from remarrying and were expected to live a life of penitence and deprivation. These virgin widows were considered to be paying the price of a particularly grave sin in a previous life, justifying their treatment. Even some of these little girls became sati, children as young as 4 being reported as going onto the funeral pyres of husbands they had never met (Alteker, 1956).

Widows from different castes had quite different sets of options open to them. Remarriage was permitted to lower caste widows. They were able to engage in paid employment such as seasonal farm work. As well, their labor was valuable to their families and they could make a considerable economic contribution to their households.

From time to time a subcaste would attempt to elevate itself within the caste hierarchy and would adopt the ascetic practices of the upper castes (a process called *sanscritization*; Mason, 1970). An example was the adoption of sati and other higher caste practices in the 19th century by some segments of the merchant classes. These groups had become wealthy through their dealings with the British and aspired to social and religious status to match their new economic status (Worsoe, 1988).

Most of what has been written about the Indian family, however, refers to upper caste families. The ideal described is the joint family where a man and his wife and their sons, daughters-in-law, and grandchildren all lived together. Property was held in common and all contributed to the family enterprise, which in turn supported its various members. When an upper caste woman married she ceased to be a member of her own family and was absorbed into her husband's lineage. Her children became the property of his family as did the dowry she brought with her.

Upper caste Indian women could not be involved in any sort of paid work or trade and they were secluded from most social contact. Even domestic work was largely performed by members of the sudra castes rather than by women of the high caste families. Women were also excluded from education and became, for all intents and purposes, useless except as bearers of heirs for their husbands' families. If their husband died they ceased even to be that (Alteker, 1956).

Apart from her dowry, the upper caste widow brought no financial benefit to her husband's family, restricted as she was in her capacity for economically productive activities. She was usually unwelcome to return to her own family's home. The strain on family resources of supporting young economically unproductive members such as young sons and their very young brides added further to the unattractiveness of providing for the widowed or permanently unproductive.

At the same time, the widow was perceived as presenting a severe danger to her husband's family. The constant fear was that a young nubile widow would disgrace the family by introducing bastards into the household. A bastard would throw doubt on the legitimacy of her previous children. In addition, the presence of young unallied women in the household tempted the virtue of the men of the family. Worst of all, the widow might contract an alliance with a lower caste man and threaten the purity of the family. All around, the widow was perceived as a threat to the family's caste membership and social status. The one thing she could do for them was to provide spiritual advancement through sati.

Mazumdar (1978) maintained that "caste endogamy, child marriage and the bar on widow remarriage were manifestations of the anxiety to prevent miscegenation demonstrated by conquering races worldwide" (p. 27). The Indian upper castes derived from the Aryan conquerors of ancient India, whereas the lower castes and outcastes were drawn from the descendants of the original inhabitants. The fear of miscegenation was seen mostly in terms of preserving upper caste women from alliances with lower caste men. Upper caste men could recruit wives from the castes beneath their own, if necessity or gain dictated, as the resulting children were considered to be of their father's caste.

As in other situations where the social group is perceived as approaching the limits of available resources, high fertility was not desired. Uncontrolled increases in numbers strained economic resources and also threatened to undermine caste privileges derived from exclusivity. As it was acceptable for men to marry "down" within the caste system, many upper caste men found their wives among the well-dowried daughters of wealthy lower caste families, who benefited from the increase in status derived from the daughter's upward mobility. Should the high caste son-in-law die the continued existence of his lower caste wife was a constant threat to the ritual purity of his family.

The personal resources that an upper caste widow could muster were few. Her chief resource was her relationship with her sons. Motherhood was revered and the mother–son relationship was particularly idealized. If she could win her son's devotion she, as a widow, had some chance of a reasonably comfortable existence. Otherwise her fate appears unpleasant indeed.

Or at least in theory. It is very difficult to discover how the very many individual women, very frequently so young, who became widows adapted to widowhood. The fixation on the practice of sati makes the discovery of the less sensational facts of Indian widowhood hard to discover (Worsoe, 1988).

Sati was outlawed in 1829 and both the British and, after 1948, the Indian governments legislated to improve all aspects of women's lives. Homes for widows abandoned by their families were established. In the 1950s, the Indian government instituted a Hindu code of law that allows women to enact legitimate civil marriages, and gives widows the right to remarry should they wish. The legal age of marriage has been raised to 18 but this is widely ignored particularly in the rural areas. A marriage between children remains valid unless, on reaching her majority, the girl challenges it. Most widows do not remarry but many abscond, an unpleasant option that sees them resorting to begging, prostitution, or suicide (R. W. Stern, personal communication, October 29, 1987).

Mason (1970) considers that two contrasting and competing forces in Indian society have opposite consequences for the lives of women, widows included. These are westernization and sanscritization.

Westernization and opportunities for upward social mobility have seen an increase in the education level of women, particularly urban women. Longer education that raises the age of marriage, and marrying "up" into a caste where the men have higher life expectancy (a more frequent occurrence today) have meant fewer very young widows in some sections of society. Good education and the access to jobs and careers have given many Indian women personal freedom and resources, such as money and information, with which they are able to protect themselves against the perils of widowhood. Life for the poor rural woman, married young and still subordinate to the extended family is, by Western standards, less attractive (R. W. Stern, personal communication, October 29, 1987).

Sanscritization is the process whereby castes attempt to raise their caste status by adopting the ascetic practices (like bans on widow remarriage) of the upper castes. This has negative implications for the choices available to women of these castes. To it has been added a movement for return to the fundamental values of Hinduism, in reaction to what are perceived as the excesses of westernization and secularism. The advocation of sati for widows is not excluded from the fundamental values being revived and instances of widow burning have occurred, including the much-publicized 1987 case of an 18-year-old Rajasthani widow who went to her death on her husband's funeral pyre before cheering crowds (''A Pagan Sacrifice,'' 1987). The publicity of course signifies the rarity of the event.

Chinese Widows

As with the writings on Indian kin relations, much of what has been written about the Chinese family applies mostly to the upper reaches of pre-revolutionary Chinese society. Thus, one of the main motivations underlying many of these domestic and marital practices was the preservation of property and privilege. The lot of the widow was very much decided by the necessity of containing whatever threat she might have posed to the integrity of family property. However, differing social organizations between the two cultures made the Chinese widow a less potent threat to her families of origin and affiliation. Her fate was accordingly less harsh than the Indian widow's.

Chinese culture is very venerable and it is hard to generalize across time and place, in respect of the treatment of widows as of any other social fact. However, as in India, the status of women was generally low and their personal freedom much restricted; and these features became more marked with the passage of time, up until the modern era. At different periods in both cultures women have fared better only to see their status decline again (Das & Bardis, 1979).

The favored form of the Chinese family also closely paralleled that of the Indian family. The ideal was the joint family with a man, his wife, and their descendants all living together, holding property in common and all contributing to family prosperity. As was true of Indian women, Chinese women left their family of origin and were absorbed into their husband's lineage, to which their children belonged. As in India this family was the prerogative of the upper classes and most people lived in families more approaching the nuclear type (Das & Bardis, 1979).

As in India, the upper class women of China did not inherit property from their husbands as this would have risked the breakup of the family estate. They were also confined to the home and if young, and particularly, without a son, they were thoroughly subordinate to husband and in-laws. They were forbidden outside employment. However, lower class women could and did perform agricultural and other work.

The confinement of higher status women to the house served the usual function of preventing opportunities for sexual misbehavior, thereby preserving the legitimacy of the family's heirs. The family's status was also enhanced by the presence of a cloistered and virtuous wife, her incapacity for hard work sometimes further emphasized by bound feet, so that in all respects she contrasted favorably with the coarse, big-footed women of the laboring classes.

Unlike India, China was not ruled by a rigid caste system with notions of purity and contamination enforcing the divisions between social groups. The incentive existed to consolidate and preserve family property and prestige but fear of the devastating consequences of loss of caste were absent. The Chinese woman also performed more domestic labor than her Indian counterpart as the host of sudra castes did not exist to perform menial labor.

As with upper caste Indian widows, the well-to-do Chinese widow was expected not to remarry. She was to remain with her husband's family and to lead a life of chastity and piety, in the seclusion considered proper. The more severe restrictions on behavior that plagued the Indian widow were absent and although the occasional widow chose suicide upon her husband's death rather than survive him this was regarded, as were all suicides, as inauspicious and something of an accusation against the living, particularly the woman's in-laws (Bullough, 1973).

Although she remained with her in-laws, the widow was supported and if she had borne sons her status was assured. Occasionally, families would arrange a second marriage for their young daughter-in-law if her husband had died childless. The second husband would live with his wife and her first in-laws and their children would belong to the in-laws' lineage. To allow a family to die leaving no one to continue the rites of ancestor worship was considered a grave omission.

Widow remarriage, although frowned on in most instances among the upper classes, was thus not absolutely forbidden. Any woman who remarried on her own account had either to leave her in-laws' house, thus losing her rights to her children and to enjoying her husband's estate, or find some man willing to sacrifice his own independence and come and live with her and her in-laws, should they permit it. Only lower status men were usually willing to do this. Another alternative for the widow was to remarry as the junior wife of a man already married, polygyny being permitted.

These options would usually only appeal to a young childless widow who otherwise faced a dreary future as a lowly member of her in-laws' household. If the widow had children she would generally prefer to remain with her husband's family and become, in her turn, one of the venerated ancestors of his clan. The status of mother of heirs of the family plus the relative freedom the death of her husband afforded her gave the well-to-do widow with children a source of power and influence. This was the most common outcome as the later age of marriage in China compared with India meant fewer very young and childless widows.

Among the lower classes, where preservation of family property and prestige was not an issue, women were usually allowed more liberty. Lower class Chinese women worked and their labor was vital to their families' well being. Hakka women (members of one of China's ethnic minorities) received a sum of money on marriage that was theirs to keep or use. Lower class women were also not as sequestered as their upper class counterparts. That symbol of upper class women's subordination, foot binding, was not common among the lower classes except when a family fancied that they might marry their daughter up. There was a relative shortage of women in the lower classes caused by female infanticide and by women's recruitment by the upper classes as wives, servants, concubines, and courtesans (Guttentag & Secord, 1983). Widow remarriage was thus easier and more common. Elderly widows lived with one or other of their children unless poverty prevented it, in which case they might be abandoned to the streets to beg for a living. As filial piety was a supreme virtue such a solution would not generally occur.

Despite the reticence held to be a feminine virtue, Chinese women were noted for their outspokenness and the anger of women was much feared as an ill omen (Das & Bardis, 1979). A confident woman gifted with a fluent tongue, whether she was a widow or otherwise, could gain a considerable degree of influence over those around her. Thus, the prescriptions for feminine right behavior one encounters in the writings of sages and moralists may not be good indicators of the personal situations of individual women (Das & Bardis, 1979).

While doing no paid work, the upper class Chinese widow had a domestic role to play. If she was young, her in-laws could choose to make use of her fertility to add to their lineage. Her own family might also arrange another marriage for her. As the mother of heirs of her husband's family, the widow with sons could expect to be assured an esteemed place in her husband's family.

If she was young, the widow's fertility did pose a threat to her in-laws but the seclusion of women substantially contained this. Because Chinese women married later than Indian ones (in their mid to late teens) Chinese families were less often faced with containing and supporting very young fertile widows for a prolonged period of time. They could, in any case, arrange a remarriage for them. Chinese families were also not threatened with the dire consequences of loss of caste following sexual misconduct with lower caste persons. The restriction of caste membership to preserve exclusivity and status was not an issue.

As far as the widow's personal resources went, upper class Chinese widows could enjoy their husbands' estates but could not own property or earn money directly themselves. Their chief source of power and prestige was through their children, particularly their sons. The existence or otherwise of sons governed their potential status and the choices open to them. It decided the likelihood and advisability of remarriage and the degree of status, honor, and security a woman could command.

An upper class Chinese widow could pose some danger to her husband's family through unchastity or other actions that threatened loss of face (including her choice to take her own life as an indictment of her in-laws' treatment of her). The seclusion of women plus the standard of conduct expected of a widow diminished this threat. Her own status of ancestor-to-be and the personal loyalty of her sons balanced this threat with esteem and status. The

Chinese widow had thus a valued place in the family and was not, like the upper caste Indian widow, perceived as such an anomaly as to be better off dead.

Sub-Saharan African Widows

All the family systems examined so far have much in common with the West in that women are restricted in their access to resources and expected to be economically dependent on men. We have seen how this influences the choices available to widows. African societies, in contrast, organize the relationship between the sexes differently. This has implications for the conduct of widowhood in these cultures.

As in other regions of the world, the use of the term *African* widows obscures a wealth of variety and detail. But most observers note broad lines of similarity among sub-Saharan African cultures. African families may be patrilineal or matrilineal but they are all characterized by being extended in form. Traditionally, related people live near each other or together, own property in common, and work cooperatively. Private ownership of land has not been the pattern, rather, groups held rights to the utilization of land for grazing or agriculture. Often, larger group size gave access to more land, a powerful incentive to high fertility.

As Boserup (1970) noted, the labor of women is extremely important in shifting agricultural systems. Indeed, women usually do most of the work, although men have specialized tasks to perform such as the felling of large trees. Marketing of produce is often within the domain of women's work as well.

Polygyny was and often still is the norm, with wives traditionally living in their husbands' compound but in separate huts along with their minor children. Women are commonly responsible for the maintenance and support of their own children, the husbands contributing goods such as cloth for making clothes. In return, women have traditionally cooked and provided other services for their husbands.

In most African cultures the husband–wife tie is a fairly loose bond. In fact, Caldwell (1982) maintained that in many African cultures it makes more sense to talk of two cultures, the male and the female, so separate and independent are the spheres of activity of men and women. Rather than having basic allegiance to the members of a Western-style nuclear family "The Yoruba [Nigerian] woman was frequently expected to be the head of an at least partially independent sub-unit of a polygamous family, with strong ties to her own lineage. [She] is often surprisingly independent in terms of what she does and in her finances'' (Caldwell, 1982, p. 85).

Marriage is by and large seen as for the procreation of children, and is rarely for the establishment of a companionable union of man and wife. As well, African marriage may serve other functions such as the forging of links of influence and alliance or the establishment of a large female work force for an individual man or group.

If children are the main purpose of marriage then parent–child ties are among the strongest and most important. It is to their children that people most often turn for comfort, company, and support. A woman can usually expect help and support from her sons and a man may turn more readily to his daughters than to his wife or wives for the performance of feminine tasks, such as sewing or cooking (Potash, 1986). The flow of wealth and resources is not only from parent to child, but also from child to parent. Regardless of the age and condition of their parents, Africans who are earning typically provide them with gifts and support (Caldwell, 1982).

Marriage may terminate in divorce (not uncommon) or death or it may simply fade away, as in "terminal separation" when a woman withdraws her services from her husband because she is "too old," has gone through menopause, or simply wants no more children. The married state may indeed comprise only a brief portion of many African women's life cycles.

If an African woman's experience of marriage is so different from her Western counterpart's, then to view African widowhood through the lens of Western experience is to risk serious distortion. The marital relationship can be such a minor part of her life and her tradition of self-support so strong that widowhood may make little real difference to her day-to-day life (Potash, 1986).

It was once assumed by many Western observers that "widow inheritance" or the levirate (remarriage of widows, usually to some kinsman of their deceased husband who inherits them) was the norm. Instead, Potash (1986) found that only 3 of 10 African cultures she studied practiced the levirate. Even in these cases, the widow usually had the right to refuse the prescribed potential spouse and choose someone else, or even not remarry at all.

Where remarriage is a possibility, as it usually is, a variety of factors help decide the widow's choice. Desire for more children is one compelling reason for remarriage, given children's immense importance. In some societies a woman can choose to have a series of lovers instead of another husband and Slater (1986) said of the Nyika of Tanzania that "A young widow has sexual rights and can demand that a kinsman of her husband 'scratch her back.' " Need of male assistance in farming can necessitate remarriage, although women may prefer to turn to their sons or brothers, or they may have call on the labor of their dead husband's kinsmen. Even in levirate marriages, widows may call on their husbands for assistance but not live with them, or indeed have much contact with them.

The desire to live near children may be a factor in deciding whether to remarry. Of all the societies studied by Potash, only among the Swahili did widows not traditionally live near their sons. To remarry may mean the necessity of moving away from children if they are expected to stay with their father's family. Women may also desire to stay near their husband's family to protect

TABLE 6
Women's Gainful Employment and Survival Rates

Ratio of Women in Gainful Employment Relative to Men	Ratio of Life Expectancy of Women Relative to Men
Sub-Saharan Africa	Sub-Saharan Africa
Southeast and East Asia	Southeast and East Asia
Western Asia	Western Asia
Southern Asia	Northern Africa
Northern Africa	Southern Asia

Source. Sen (1990b).

their children's interests, particularly their inheritance rights. At a later age, the wish to avoid a clash of interests between one's children and grand children is a further reason why an African woman may stop childbearing.

Sen (1990b) noted that "Sub-Saharan Africa, ravaged as it is by extreme poverty, hunger and famine, has a substantial excess rather than deficit of women," the ratio of women to men in the population being as previously noted around 102:100. He attributed this good survival rate to women's relatively high status, which in itself he attributed to their access to "gainful employment" (i.e., work outside the home) either as subsistence or for a wage. Sen ranked five regions in terms first of the proportion of women in gainful employment relative to the proportion of men in such employment, and second in terms of female survival rates (see Table 6).

If the nations involved were to be ranked also for national prosperity, the rank ordering would be very different. For example, Punjab, the richest Indian state, has the lowest female survival rate (the ratio of women to men being 86:100) and also the lowest ratio of women in gainful employment compared to men. Thus, for women—including widows—the sexual division of labor is more important than the level of prosperity. In consequence, sub-Saharan African widows are well-placed relative to their counterparts in some other regions.

CONCLUSIONS: FACTORS INFLUENCING WIDOWS' STATUS

This short review has concentrated mainly on circumstances in the past, as it is there that the lot of the widow is most clearly described. Several aspects of the widow's position emerge as especially relevant to our understanding of mother-headed families in general. First, these are the risk posed by the young widow's potential fertility to those around her; and second, the importance of her direct access to economic and social resources that give her some degree of autonomy and power.

Risk

To begin with risks, the widow can be a danger to those around her because she may be a competitor for resources—for marriageable men, for inherited property, for power and influence, or even, in a subsistence economy, for food itself. A widow's claim to a share of property may threaten the control or integrity of the family estate. Her claim to influence may sow dissent or divide loyalties, for example by causing a rift between her children and their father's family to which they formally belong.

If a widow is young and fertile she may threaten the husband's family, with whom she resides, with the introduction of new, illegitimate mouths to feed. Any unchastity could call into question the legitimacy of her husband's supposed heirs. Any breeches of sexual propriety on her behalf may cause her family to lose face, social status, or ritual purity. In traditional Indian and Chinese societies, terrible dangers of pollution, ill chance, and downright harm, were said to reside in women ungoverned by men, such as widows. The mere sight of an Indian widow was said to be unlucky and Indian and Chinese widows could not attend some festive occasions such as weddings because of the ill luck said to attend such an appearance (Indra, 1955).

Restrictions on the rights of widows to remarry and reproduce tend to arise where there is a perceived need (often disguised or elaborated by religious taboo and ritual) to limit fertility. As an example, Indian ideas on the bad luck said to attend widows and the extreme restrictions placed on their behavior seem designed to make it difficult for a widow to meet men and unlikely that any man she did meet would want to consort with her (Indra, 1955). Where children are a positive economic and social asset such restrictions are less likely to exist.

This emphasis on fertility-related fears in the treatment of widows points up the dramatic disappearance of such fears in Western countries in the last few decades. With them have gone (at least for many people) the concepts of respectability, sexual honor and shame, purity, temptation, stigma, and sin. It seems understandable that when shorn of this powerful backup, traditional marriage should lose some of its edge over the alternative statuses for women.

Access to Resources

When women are involved in farming, when they hold property, or when they work for cash, they are likely to be seen as valuable members of a family or society. Economically productive people who generate a positive flow of resources for their group are unlikely to be disposable, even if predeceased by a husband. A table can be drawn up to describe the likely relationship between wifely and widow status.

TABLE 7
Women's Access to Resources and the Status of Widows

| | | Direct Access to Resources | |
		Yes	No
Husband	Yes	Nondependent wife	Dependent wife
Living	No	Self-supporting widow	Widows are a "burden," vulnerable

Table 7, of course, implies more stasis than is ever the case. Women's access to resources changes with cultural and technological change, for example the development of new industries that differentially employ either sex. Or, division of labor in a society may be so organized that the labor of women is indispensable even if it does not generate income. Nevertheless, Table 7 demonstrates very clearly that the ethos of wifely dependency by its nature puts the unhusbanded woman and her children at tremendous risk.

History shows that even in the most unpromising situations, individual widows have been able to turn events to their own advantage by defying convention, cultivating power in family networks, or gaining indirect control of resources. Various members of royal harems have won favor with their princely consorts, or had their sons made heir and then ruled through them on the death of their husbands. They have usually had a bad press but they also serve as examples of the conversion of powerlessness into personal triumph. The dowager empress of China, mother of the "last emperor," was in the tradition of women who ruled indirectly via their influence over men. In less exalted families, favoritism toward the son likely to become heir also served as an insurance policy for old age or widowhood for women whose access to economic resources was restricted. In such situations, hostility to that potential rival for the son's affection, the daughter-in-law, is commonly reported (Broyelle, 1977), meaning that the system has a built in impetus toward perpetuating itself.

On the other hand, if the widow has access to resources in her own right she should not need to resort to subterfuge, and her achievements are gains that need not be seen as stolen from others. The difference becomes that between the independent citizen and the relict. The grisly examples of relict status described in *Das Weib* dramatize the disadvantages to women of lacking or losing the status of an independent citizen.

Chapter 6

Biosocial and Demographic Theories of Parenting

In previous chapters we have seen that certain conditions are associated with greater or lesser prevalence of mother-headed families, and with the status of such families. With regard to mother-headed families resulting from out-of-wedlock births, we established that the prevalence is least where families are patriarchally organized, where inheritance rights are important, where women have few property rights and/or little access to independent income, and where social controls are strong. The conditions that generate many mother-headed families are more various, including periods of social turbulence when established controls lose their authority, and more stable periods when women have relatively good access to property and income. The status of such families is closely linked to women's access to property and income. When most women lack such access, unmarried mothers are likely to be stigmatized as deviant, sinful, a sign of social ill health, or accursed, depending on the culture. It is only when a significant proportion of single mothers are able to support their children that their status becomes destigmatized.

With respect to mother-headed families initiated by divorce, the role of the law is of course crucial, and the influence of the Christian Church has kept the law very restrictive in most Western countries, until recent decades. Even so, certain predictors can be discerned that overlap with those associated with births out of wedlock. Divorce is low when Christian-patriarchal values hold authority, and when women are economically dependent. It is high when marriage is regarded as a contract rather than a sacrament, when alternatives to the present marriage are available to men and/or women, and in times of social change. However, the status of divorced women is only high when a significant proportion have access to property and income adequate to support the family.

The factors associated with a high incidence of young widowhood are natur-ally more varied. However, the factors associated with their status again over-lap with those that hold for mother-headed families formed by other means. Women's general status, and their access to property and income adequate to support the family again emerges as crucial. Where effective birth control is not normative, social attitudes to fertility are also important. Thus, we can conclude that the factors that govern the prevalence and status of mother-headed families formed by divorce, widowhood, and out-of-wedlock births have much in common.

The salience of these factors is informative in itself, but our understand-ing is likely to be bettered if they can be fitted into some broader under-standing of family and parenting. In this chapter we accordingly look at a selec-tion of family and parenting theories, and consider their relevance to the prevalence and status of mother-headed families. In so doing we bear in mind that although the factors that consistently emerge as associated with the situa-tion of mother-headed families are relatively few—social and religious values and control, women's status and access to independent income and the con-trol of fertility—the relationship is not always a simple linear one. In particu-lar, although the status of women in general is an important predictor of the status of families headed by a divorced or unmarried woman, the incidence of such families can be high when women's status is both unusually high or unusually low.

Which parenting theories are likely to be helpful? A good deal of writing about mother-headed families has been quite narrow and directed to practical ends, concerned for example with welfare dependency and the provisions that might increase or decrease it. General family theories are more expansive, but not usually particularly interested in single parents. The narrower approaches are mostly oriented to issues that are salient in the writer's home country, but not necessarily elsewhere. For this reason, we have favored the more expan-sive approaches and have drawn our own implications for mother-headed fam-ilies, as required.

In so doing we have naturally concentrated on those approaches that seemed to offer the most ideas regarding the prevalence and status of mother-headed families. This means that our choice of approaches is not the usual one offered in family textbooks. We start this chapter with a set of biosocial explanations that address the question of what is "natural" in female–male relations: a ques-tion that attracts different answers. We then move to a series of explanations that concentrate on the influence of demographic factors such as the size of a human community and its relationship to available resources, the ratio of women to men, the role of children and the value placed on them, and the so-called "second demographic transition" of the post-World War II period. In chapter 7 we consider a number of feminist approaches, and then a variety of writings that argue that the complementary nature of gender roles has broken down in recent times—we group these together under the heading of decomplementary theory and discuss some implications and applications.

We do not suggest that these various approaches are mutually exclusive. On the contrary, they overlap at many points, and a number of writers have made contributions to more than one approach. For our purposes, the differentiation between approaches is made on the basis of the organizing ideas they offer regarding female–male and parent–child relations.

BIOSOCIAL THEORIES

Biosocial theories may seem a little remote from the economic, social, legal, and political issues we have looked at so far. But as the reader will have noted, there is often a lurking biological metaphor behind the justification of many gender arrangements—in the last resort, they are justified as being "natural." It seems worthwhile, therefore, to spend a little time setting out these arguments explicitly, and considering their scientific status.

Sociobiological Hypothesis

In the early 1970s, the new science of sociobiology offered an expansion of Darwin's views on sex differences in reproductive and parenting behavior. The original formulation of this explanation, by Harvard biologist Robert Trivers (1972), was not particularly concerned with humans. Rather, it referred to all species in which one sex (usually but not universally the female) makes a much greater investment in reproduction than the other. Writing from a broad Darwinian point of view, Trivers was not concerned with the individual purposes of individual members of a species, but with Nature's purposes—survival and reproduction.

As Trivers explained, sociobiology, and more generally, evolutionary biology puts the ultimate "why" of behavior at the level of the genes carried by the individual. The evolutionary process is such that the genes "want" to reproduce themselves in a new generation, and the instincts and behaviors—courting, mating, parenting—that will best achieve this result get built into individuals through natural selection. Trivers proposed that in those species in which one sex invests a great deal of time and energy in bearing and rearing the young, the reproductive strategies of the males and females will differ. In mammalian species each conception subjects the female to the heavy energy costs of pregnancy, lactation, and infant care, and may even put her life at risk. In consequence, she will be selective in partner choice, preferring at the very least a healthy individual who will be likely to father similarly healthy offspring. Depending on the species, she may also prefer a mate who can offer protection, or some assistance in infant care and feeding, or both. Whatever direction her choice goes, its ultimate purpose will be to maximize the likelihood of rearing offspring to adulthood (in technical terms *maximizing inclusive fitness*).

For the male, the situation is different. Because his only physical commitment is the provision of sperm, his best strategy will involve some degree of promiscuity, in the hope that at least some of the ensuing offspring may be reared to adulthood by the mother. In some species, this results in a single dominant male capturing and defending a large harem, while the majority of males die without a single descendant. This makes for intense competition among the males, with the result that large body size, strength, and aggression are selected, and the males may be much larger than females. In other species, a season of competitive display or fighting among the males ends with most attracting a partner, or there may be an amicable pairing off. Some degree of promiscuity will still, however, be advantageous, because devotion of energy to a single partner and her offspring always entails the risk that the offspring are not his own.

Although Trivers' paper was not very concerned with humans (his main emphasis was in fact on birds), others have extended the concept of differential parental investment to humans. Hinde (1984), for example, in an article entitled *Why do the Sexes Behave Differently in Close Relationships?*, uses the concept of the *environment of evolutionary adaptedness*. For humans, this is the environment in which present day characteristics were shaped by natural selection, at the time when homo sapiens first appeared on the planet, living in small groups assumed to be somewhat similar to those of modern hunter–gatherers.

Hinde proposed that in the human environment of evolutionary adaptedness, relatively long-lasting bonds between a man and one or two women would have emerged as the species pattern, with the bonds strengthened by the evolution of a non-estrus pattern of sexuality, such that mating became possible at all times. The bond was advantageous to females (read: gene-derived female instincts) because it brought a protector and helpmeet to the task of infant rearing. It was also advantageous to men (read: gene-derived male instincts), as human infants required much tending, and if the task was left to the mother alone many infants would succumb, reducing the man's reproductive success.

On the other hand, philandering would also be to men's advantage, as it could augment their reproductive success, would not detract from that of their mates (assuming the men provided no assistance to the offspring of their casual partners), and thus would not provide the mates with "a biological reason to desert." Philandering would, however, be very dangerous for women because if a partner found out he would fear he had been cuckolded, and might transfer his allegiance to a more faithful wife.

The outcome would be that different considerations would be selected into males and females in respect of which members of the opposite sex they were prepared to bond to. Men would be likely to bond to women who appeared receptive, fertile, and faithful; and averse to bonding with those seen as sexually promiscuous because any investment in the offspring of a promiscuous woman could be rendered biologically useless by her infidelity. Women would bond to men who looked like good protectors and providers, would make efforts to convince a partner that he was the father of her children, and would be tolerant of his infidelity so long as he showed no concern for the resulting "illegitimate" offspring.

Human sociobiology holds that these functionally evolved characteristics have not changed much over the intervening millenia. Their expression varies across cultures, but the same evolutionarily defined themes manifest in such diverse practices as polygyny and haremage, chaperonage, claustration, chastity belts, and infibulation, and male contempt for "unvirtuous" women and even for the victims of rape. Hinde argued that they manifest also in the attitudes of contemporary tertiary students. He cited a range of surveys that have found that these young people, who could be expected to be most freed from "traditional" attitudes, could more accurately be described as having modernized them. Virginity might no longer be required of women, but both males and females surveyed considered that women's sexual activities should occur within a loving relationship, whereas promiscuity was acceptable and even admired in men. The men's ideal was for an attractive woman who was easy to get for him, but hard to get for all other men (Hinde, 1984). This forced adolescent girls in particular to walk a tightrope between appearing too fast or too slow in self-presentation.

Sociobiological theory has not had much to say about single mothers, but the deductions are easy to make. Plainly, the woman who accepts a man without some evidence of bonding is putting herself at risk of unaided parenthood. Men can never be trusted to show responsibility to such a woman or her children, and their bond-partners can be expected to encourage their men in this irresponsibility. Where a father has died or departed, other men have nothing to gain (biologically speaking) by increasing his reproductive success (i.e., looking after his children), unless perhaps they are close relatives and share some of his genes. In addition, anything that could taint a woman's reputation for fidelity would reduce her value, including the mere fact of a previous marriage, or the opportunity for sexual activity provided by the husband's absence. Thus, on evolutionary grounds, single mothers can expect to be treated shabbily. As we have seen, this has often been the case.

As might be expected, sociobiological theorizing has not been popular among people with some optimism about human nature. It has also been attacked for providing a pseudoscientific justification for the sexual double standard and for dated and dispiriting sexual stereotypes, notably those of philandering husband and ball-and-chain wife. In addition, the argument has been accused of disregarding all the historical, economic, religious, and social forces than shape human behavior. There is also the problem of the counterfacts: Many men and women choose to be childless (i.e., reduce their reproductive fitness to zero), many become devoted stepparents and adoptive parents, some men leave faithful women and become besotted with less faithful ones, some women abandon good providers for feckless charmers, and some prefer their own sex as partners.

We come back to these criticisms. First, however, we look at the way that the evolutionary explanation has developed in the years since Trivers published his famous 1972 paper.

Revisionist Sociobiology

The Primatologists.   Much of this development has come from a small group of scientists who have observed the life of various primate troops in their natural habitats. The logic is clear. If human reproductive behavior has developed out of an evolutionary stream that inevitably dictated certain adaptations, then we should be able to see the direction of this stream by observing our nearest relatives. The fact that they have little culture to overlay their natural dispositions is seen as an added advantage.

The first primatologists were mostly men, and described male-centered primate groups that appeared to be following the reproductive strategies favored by sociobiology. In these groups, the females were *coy* (to use the popular term) and did little of interest except mothering. In the 1970s, however, the primatologists were joined by a group of women who paid particular attention to what the females were doing. These new observers wore different conceptual spectacles, and some of the women considered that it was only natural that an observer would have more empathy with their own sex. In the words of one, "Of course I identify with them. I sometimes identify with female baboons more than I do with males of my own species" (Hrdy, 1986, p. 139).

Whatever the reasons, the new studies produced new findings. An outstanding figure has been Sara Hrdy, a primatologist who has spent long periods of time studying the langurs of Rajasthan. She described how her experiences changed the ideas she had been taught at Harvard (Hrdy, 1981, 1986). Three sets of facts seemed to fly in the face of the traditional sociobiological wisdom that male–male competition and female coyness explained the evolution of breeding systems. She gradually came to see that when considered together they presented an alternative picture to the traditional one.

The first set of facts concerned the comparative reproductive success rates of females. A major sociobiological tenet was that a female does not need to do much more than copulate once a season in order to breed at a near maximum level. Thus, natural selection was seen to exert its main effect on males, whose descendants might be multitudinous or none, whereas females produced a more or less equivalent number of infants over a lifetime.

Hrdy found this to be quite untrue. She observed that the higher status and larger females of a troop were more successful than the less advantaged as mothers. This came about through a variety of mechanisms. In some cases, the presence of a more dominant female was enough to suppress ovulation in subordinates. In other cases, the dominants harassed the subordinates into miscarrying. In still others, they cornered the good feeding grounds, and the low-status infants died of starvation. Yet again, the infant might be snatched, killed, or "aunted" to death through a combination of rough handling and failure to feed.

As though that were not bad enough, the infants were also at risk from adult males. In the langur troops that Hrdy observed, the typical practice for a new male who successfully invaded a breeding troop was to kill the infants, thus terminating the mothers' lactation and bringing them back into estrus. As a result of all these hazards, some low-status females never raised a single offspring to adulthood.

Second, Hrdy quickly discovered that instead of being coy, her female langurs would sometimes leave their home troop to travel and mate with all-male bands; or they would solicit and mate with new arrivals joining their own troop, or with members of nearby troops, even when pregnant or lactating. This put them at considerable risk of attack and of retaliation by their own troop leader. She asked why they should risk so much for so little apparent reproductive gain.

A third discovery was that the males contributed far more to the welfare of infants than generally allowed. Only around 10% of all mammalian species provide some form of direct paternal care, but the rate for primates is closer to half. In some species, the females have frequent pregnancies and the fathers assume almost total responsibility for infants once they are born. In others, the brother or father of an orphaned infant may adopt and mother it, and in still others, the fathers may help their maturing sons to set up and defend territories.

Of greatest theoretical interest, however, is the phenomenon of godfathering among troop-living primates. Here, the mother and her new baby spend regular time close to her special male friends, usually past consorts. As a result, the infants come to know these males, to seek them out, and to spend much of their time playing close by a godfather, sometimes in the company of the offspring of his other previous consorts. The godfathers don't give the infants much in the way of direct care, but their presence greatly improves survival chances by discouraging attacks by other males and by rival females. The mother's social connections thus provide a safety net for her infant.

For Hrdy, a pattern underlying all these phenomena emerged when she put herself in the position of the female langurs she was observing and asked herself how she would cope with a world in which a new would-be patriarch turned up every 27 months on average and attempted to slaughter all infants. Her answer was that she would try to manipulate the system by forming alliances (in the langur's cases, heterosexual alliances) and that natural selection would favor those who did so. Suddenly the evolutionary model of parental behavior shifted from patriarchy to sexual politics.

Hrdy's writings have been extremely influential in overthrowing what prima-tologists now regard as the male bias of earlier studies. Not all accept her in-terpretations, and a number of others have been offered: But the kinds of evidence described here is no longer ignored. Hrdy's picture continues to be one in which male and female nature are very different, for evolutionary rea-sons. However, the theoretical "universal female" has been restored from vic-timhood to agency. This is a critical achievement, as it underscores the message that what is "natural" in gender relations is adaptability, rather than any fixed set of behaviors.

Hrdy did not take up the issue of single mothers, but her model of male and female nature can be readily applied, particularly because most monkey and ape mothers can justifiably be regarded as "single mothers." The model is one in which the female pursues her own ends by means that allow for the generally greater size and aggression of males, their shorter life-span and their potential for interest in infants. Hrdy called it the "manipulation hypothesis," and deemed that the actual strategies used will vary with the subspecies and the ecology. Whatever the variant, the female is a player in a shifting game in which long-term partnering may sometimes be advantageous, sometimes not. Plainly, this is a much more positive evolutionary scenario for single motherhood than that offered by Hinde.

The Sexual Division of Labor.   Many quite lowly species divide up the labor of parenting, for example, those fish whose females concentrate on laying large numbers of eggs that the male hatches and fans. In some primate species also, the females concentrate on gestation and lactation, and the males on day-to-day infant care. The term *sexual division of labor* is not, however, usually used to describe these specializations, but reserved for those situations where sex segregation goes beyond the tasks of infant care. In effect, this restricts the use of the term to human beings.

Some writers in this area (e.g., J. Lancaster & C. Lancaster, 1987) describe the elaboration of the sexual division of labor as one of the major strategies responsible for the reproductive success of homo sapiens. As they see it, the human reproduction pattern, with its very extended juvenile period was, in evolutionary terms, a gamble. There is at the least a 15- to 20-year gap be-tween generations, the young are vulnerable for a long time, and heavy de-mands are made on the mother. But it was a gamble that paid off, and one very important reason for this was the evolution of "the most unusual behavioral pattern" of continuing to feed the young after weaning.

To do this, early humans evolved a system whereby the males specialized in hunting and the females in gathering. This allowed for a varied diet for children and adults, and also instigated reciprocal food sharing, and, subsequently, other forms of sharing and exchange. Because of the mixed economy input from the two sexes, even preindustrial human societies have been able to raise to adulthood an average one of every two children born, compared with only 10%–30% among other primates and group-hunting carnivores (J. Lancaster, 1984; J. Lancaster & C. Lancaster, 1987).

Thus, through multiadult involvement and the sexual division of labor, the human species was able to achieve a reproduction rate up to fivefold that of competing species. It went on to take over the world. Reproductive success was achieved with a variety of family forms, including polygyny and polyandry, so long as most children obtained support from more than a single adult. The actual biological father need not be involved. Sociobiological theory suggests that only he can be trusted with his children, but this formulation overlooks the high mortality among many peoples. If biological fathers were always needed to see their children into adulthood, human reproduction would be less of a success story. What counts is that human parenting is a shared and social enterprise. Fathers can be dispensed with, but they need to be replaced by other adults. Single parenthood is only a disadvantage when no alternative adult compeers are available, and this in itself is a matter of social arrangements.

Conclusion

Intriguing though they are, biosocial explanations of human parenting involve dizzying imaginative leaps. Furthermore, the extended speculative reconstruction of evolutionary history that they offer often fails to account for some of what we do know of human behavior. For example, the approach that puts all its motivational eggs in the "continuing one's genes" basket plainly has a problem with the multitude of human behaviors that have the opposite effect—abortion, homosexuality, and vasectomy, for a start.

Where these approaches are very helpful, however, is that they do try to define the idea of biological "naturalness" in human reproductive behavior. Theories of parenting behavior are wont to resort to belief in the natural when other concepts fail, and although the natural remains undefined, it readily takes on a mystic significance. The sociobiological approach has therefore been very valuable in spelling out a mechanism that could operate, and thus opening up the natural to rational analysis. Revisionist sociobiology has added new and complicating observations and highlighted the fact that even among infrahuman primates what is natural is constant adaptation to circumstances rather than the playing out of immutable reproductive motivations. Modern biosocial theory thus provides a comfortable basis from which to explore family theories that explain particular kinds of parenting behaviors in terms of particular adaptations to particular circumstances. On this basis, we turn now to a group of theories that emphasize the importance of demographic factors.

DEMOGRAPHIC THEORIES

Low- and High-Density Population Hypothesis

It is generally agreed that overpopulation does not usually emerge as a problem
with hunter–gatherer societies, because the migratory, foraging lifestyle means
that luggage, including infant luggage, must be kept to a minimum. It is not
possible to forage many miles a day and to bring much of the take home while
carrying more than one baby. As a result, hunter–gatherer societies have generally been found to observe a 4-year rule in spacing births, relying for birth
control mostly on extended lactation, but using other means, including infanticide, when necessary. Given high mortality, late menarche, and early
menopause, it has been estimated that the typical hunter–gatherer woman would
produce only five surviving offspring over a lifetime (Short, 1978).

   J. Lancaster and C. Lancaster (1987) argued that to understand human social life we need to understand the crucial difference between life in low- and
high-density populations. The following discussion is based on their description of this distinction.

   In low-density populations like hunter–gatherer groups the material resources
necessary for life and reproduction have generally been free for the taking, and
except in periods of famine or drought, anyone who reached adulthood could
readily obtain the necessities of life. Land (migrated through rather than tilled)
is held in common, and the luggage problem discourages the acquisition of
personal goods. Thus, there is little in the way of material property for children to inherit, and children born out of marriage are accordingly not
bastardized and disinherited. Groups are generally small and adult fatalities
common, so any fit adult is a valuable asset, who will be expected to replace
a same-sex relative as and when the occasion arises. Marriage is universal,
and for women generally occurs at puberty or earlier. Virginity is not highly
valued and women may be allowed a degree of sexual freedom, particularly
before children are born. As a consequence of all these features, status and
role differences between members of the group typically remain low, and the
child who loses a father or a mother will quickly be allocated to another. The
dangers of life make orphanhood a common experience, but single parenthood
does not really exist as a status.

   According to Lancaster and Lancaster, the low-density pattern can be maintained in village life as well as among migratory groups, so long as the land
available is greater than the capacity of the population to make use of it. So
long as this remains the case, prosperity and power accrue to those families
who are most fertile. With the luggage problem no longer an issue, births are
more closely spaced, and the labor of rearing these additional children is reduced
by giving even quite small children various horticultural and domestic tasks,
including the care of younger siblings. Parents who lose a spouse still belong

to the larger family, and the labor of both parent and children remains of value.

The critical change in family life comes when the available land has all been claimed, and wealth and power are measured primarily in terms of the family estate, rather than by the number of family members. Keeping the family estate intact, and if possible increasing it, now becomes an overriding concern. Because it is the women who bear babies who may or may not be wanted by the family, control of female sexuality becomes crucial. Bridal virginity and wifely fidelity become central to the honor of the family, and a variety of main tenance strategies are developed including claustration of women, veiling, purdah, and genital armor and/or mutilation. Marriage may be postponed until some kind of resource base is available, and some people never marry, either because they are not permitted to, or because they are so poor that even two parents will be unable to provide for children.

In this situation, each child that is born is potentially in competition for limited resources with each of its peers. At the same time, a high and unpredictable mortality rate requires a substantial reserve labor and reproduction force. Thus, couples of some substance may produce large families, of whom the firstborn or another son is the designated heir. Nonheirs may have to make their own way in the world, usually with a ''portion'' to get them started. However, they also act as first reserves in case the heir should die prematurely. Members of cadet branches of the family may act as second reserves, and illegitimate children perhaps as third reserves. It is even suggested (Johansson, 1984) that parental neglect of less-favored children acts as a form of subinfanticide or ''deferred infanticide,'' which keeps excess children alive at a low investment cost, in case they should subsequently be needed.

In high-density societies, family alliances forged through marriage are important, and sharp status differences emerge. Among those of higher status, dowry and bride price arrangements emerge as a means of obtaining good quality husbands and valuable wives. The need to dower daughters, however, puts a special pressure on higher status families and may result in only some daughters being allowed to marry, and sometimes in female infanticide. If adult male life is particularly dangerous, female infanticide may also serve the purpose of keeping sex ratios roughly equal. The details vary from one culture to another, but practices aimed at keeping down the numbers of marriageable women have been widespread throughout feudal Japan, China, Southeast Asia, India, the Middle East, and Europe, with the highest status families (i.e., those with most property to protect), always in the vanguard. As we have seen, cousin marriage has often been popular as a means of keeping property within the family, and has the added advantage of reducing the need for dowry and bride price.

In high-density cultures, ''legitimate'' children become sharply discriminated from the ''illegitimate,'' who lack inheritance rights (although they may gain them if the legitimate heirs die, or if some other means of gaining legitimacy is available). The mother of an illegitimate child typically loses market value, and may be considered dishonored, or even to have forfeited the right to live. In some cases, the whole family may lose caste from the birth of a child out of wedlock, so that all family members are highly motivated to maintain the virginity of unmarried daughters. Illegitimate births occur, of course, but typically to low status women, and to those who support themselves through wage labor. Prospects for these children are poor except when labor is scarce and well rewarded.

Along with, and because of these various practices, high-density cultures typically develop beliefs about human nature that stress the innate chastity and purity of "good" women, and the naturalness of a double standard of male and female sexuality. Hrdy (1986) described the higher classes of Darwin's England as representing one such culture, and noted that Darwin's writings on infrahuman species reflect his acculturation, by regularly describing a "coy" female and a male who is "almost always the wooer." This orientation could be said to have lingered on in sociobiological theorizing.

High-density societies in this description sound like classic cases of patriarchal oppression. However, Lancaster and Lancaster followed Hrdy in seeing women as agents as well as victims of reproductive strategies. As they viewed it, whatever the particular cultural or historical set up, the women as well as the men will attempt to use it to their own advantage. If families are nuclear in form, and only men have access to economic resources, then women will try to get husbands able and willing to support them. In a different kinship arrangement, they will seek to embed themselves within an extended group of relatives. Where virginity is socially demanded, women will generally be just as active as men in discriminating against "dishonored" women and illegitimate children, and if at all possible, they will make use of the ideology of female purity to their own advantage. Thus, the way in which female "nature" is expressed will vary quite a bit with circumstances. What is common is the use of strategies that compensate for the fact that their reproductive makeup renders them generally less physically powerful and aggressive than men.

What happens in that densest of environments, the modern industrialized city? Lancaster and Lancaster viewed a further stage in human reproductive strategies as emerging when industry displaces agriculture as a population's major means of support. When this happens, property inheritance diminishes in importance, and what counts is the education and skills necessary for obtaining a good job. A whole new "parental investment calculus" has to be evolved, and this is being worked out in industrialized countries today. The heavy parental investment required for competitive success presumably handicaps the single-parented child, unless other adult support is available.

Conclusion. The distinction between low- and high-density populations is valuable for our purposes, as it spotlights the importance of the family estate as a factor discouraging the formation of mother-headed families. We came across many relevant examples in our discussion of divorce, ex-nuptiality, and widowhood. One example was the practice of cross-cousin marriage. Another was that of remarrying widows to the late husband's brother or cousin, thus keeping her part of the estate within the family. Yet another was the regularly noted low incidence of illegitimate births among daughters of higher class families, in some cases associated with close chaperonage, but not in others, such as the European Alpine areas. In these latter cases, the value of family honor had presumably been well internalized, so that young women protected their own virginity when no chaperones were present. Most dramatically, there was the example of the widow-burning castes of India, for whom the widow's very existence presented a threat to family integrity. All of these examples seem to fit the density explanation very well.

The density hypothesis implies that once the family estate loses importance in favor of personally earned income, unhusbanded mothers become less of a threat to their lineages, and their incidence should therefore increase—as they have. The density hypothesis also sees values—in this case the values of virginity, purity, and honor—as derived from material causes. It thus predicts that these values will snuff out rather quickly once the material cause disappears. This certainly fits with the remarkably swift devaluation of sexual purity in Western cultures after the 1950s.

Despite these features, the density hypothesis is for our own purposes rather limited. It does not, for example, propose any mechanism to explain why some poorer groups have many out-of-wedlock births, and others—like the Irish—have traditionally had very few. Nor does it have much to say about recent Western trends in marriage, births and divorces. Accordingly, we now turn to a different approach.

Neo-Malthusian Hypothesis

The popular image of Malthus is of someone who believed that human populations would inevitably expand to outstrip the globe's resources unless regularly checked by war and pestilence; and who was proved wrong by the invention of effective contraception and the green revolution. But Malthus' ideas were a good deal more sophisticated than this, and have been developed further by modern followers (Macfarlane, 1986).

In the first edition of his famous *Essay on Population* (1798, cited in James, 1990), Malthus did indeed propose that the capacity of humans to reproduce themselves geometrically (many children for each two parents, many children from each of those children) meant that any increase in prosperity would easily be negated by the encouragement it gave to earlier marriage and reproduction.

"Such is the disposition to marry, particularly in very young people, that if the difficulties of providing for a family were entirely removed, very few would remain single at twenty-two" (p. 52).

Under these conditions, populations would expand until controlled by the checks of "misery"—war, famine, and disease.

In his 1803 revision of the *Essay*, however, Malthus noted that in parts of Europe other population checks existed, including that provided by "vice"— contraception and infanticide—and the desirable "preventive check" of late marriage and selective nonmarriage. He observed that the preventive check was particularly strong in England, where the general view was that marriage was a costly undertaking that was likely to reduce one's standard of living (by producing more mouths to feed on the same income) and associated position. It should, therefore, be postponed until enough assets had been garnered to afford it, or even foregone.

If this was the case in England, asked Malthus, why was it not so in those countries where people were a good deal poorer but nevertheless married and parented early? In discussing why this might be, he concluded that English society had four especially relevant factors, each of which encouraged the delay or abandonment of marriage. The factors were relevant for all social classes, although they impacted in different ways, which he described in some detail.

The first and most important factor was an acquisitive ethic that encouraged and rewarded the pursuit of gain. The second was a stratified but open social structure that motivated people to attempt to climb to higher levels, and to avoid falling below their present one. The third was the institution of private property, protected by a strong government and strong laws, that enabled people to keep their gains. The fourth was a relatively high standard of living, which gave people a taste for comforts and disinclined them to sacrifice these in favor of a hasty marriage. In a word, the Englishman saw the possibility of a good life if only he were prudent. (The Englishwoman does not get a great deal of mention in the *Essay*.)

> [A man] cannot look around him and see the distress which frequently presses upon those who have large families; he cannot contemplate his present posses-sions or earnings, which he now nearly consumes himself, and calculate the amount of each share, when with very little addition they must be divided, perhaps, among seven or eight—without feeling a doubt whether, if he follow the bent of his incli-nations, he may be able to support the offspring which he will probably bring into the world. (Malthus, 1970, Vol. I, p. 12)

By contrast, among those peoples who could never hope to rise above sub-sistence level (here Malthus made unfavorable reference to other nations), prudence brings no reward, and there is accordingly no reason to delay marriage.

One of the most salutary and least pernicious checks to the frequency of early
marriages in this country is the difficulty of procuring a cottage, and the laud-
able habits which prompt a laborer rather to defer his marriage some years in
the expectation of a vacancy than to content himself with a wretched mud cabin,
like those in Ireland. (Vol. II, p. 50)

Later writers pointed out that the "English marriage system" was not restricted to England, but rather common in northwestern Europe. Hajnal (1965)
described an imaginary line that could be drawn from Trieste to Leningrad,
west of which women typically married some 10 years later than they reached
sexual maturity, some 15% or more never married at all, and given early
menopause and considerable mortality, the numbers of surviving children were
quite small.

The fact that the pattern was strongest in England has been attributed in
part to the fact that the setting up of a separate household was an important
part of the late marriage pattern. England developed a monetarized wage economy earlier than other countries, making it easier to plan and save to acquire
a home, whereas in Europe it was necessary to wait until a farm holding became available through a farmer's death or retirement, events less under the
waiting couple's control.

Macfarlane (1986) considered that some other aspects of English attitudes
to marriage and children were also crucial. The first was the doctrine that mutual consent of husband and wife is the heart of marriage, and the wishes of other
family members less important. He saw this as a longstanding belief, originating from the Germanic tribes who settled in England, and who even in the
first century AD were known for their late marriage and relatively egalitarian
relations between men and women.

The second feature was Christianity's downgrading of marriage to second
best to celibacy, which undercut any belief that marriage should be universal,
and consequently made for a relatively low identification of personal worth
with success in fathering or bearing children. The third was the belief that
husband–wife loyalties overrode obligations to kin, and the marriages should
therefore be companionate, and between partners similar in age. The fourth
feature was a belief in married love. Macfarlane pointed out that celebrations
of marital love are found in much Anglo-Saxon and Celtic poetry, and rejects
as not fitting the dates the popular theory that it originated in Provençal courtly
love.

A fifth feature was the legal position of children, who had protected rights
to their own property and earnings, including against their parents. Even before the children's marriage, and certainly after, English parents had no automatic rights to their earnings or inheritances—a situation quite different from
that under Roman law. A final feature was the dilution of parent–child loyalties that resulted from the English habit of sending children away early to live

with another family as servant, apprentice, page or maid, depending on sex and social class.

Taken together with the aspects of English society described by Malthus, Macfarlane saw a very special concept of family as having been developed: One that emphasized independence, self-help, and individual responsibility, and made children something of luxury items, who were not expected to do too much for their parents in return. The fact that it was in England that the pattern bloomed most vigorously was viewed as a historical accident by Macfarlane, because its component features were widespread in northwestern Europe up until the 11th century. However, after that time, much of Europe was reconquered by "a renovated Roman Law and a renovated Roman Catholicism," leaving England in the strongest position to develop the old Germanic tradition into modern form. The viability of the product is attested by its subsequent export to many parts of the world, including back into Europe.

Conclusion. Macfarlane's account emphasizes the relative gender egalitarianism of the English/European marriage system. Other writers emphasize the much greater power it gave to men (Pateman, 1986). The discrepancy may not be so important if the system is seen as providing the framework and the potential for assertion of individualist demands by both spouses. The value of individualism is a key concept. The pro-male bias of society—for example in access to property and paid employment—will always favor the individualist demands of the husband. But the framework and potential for wives' individualist demands also exists, and this can be actualized when external circumstances permit.

For example, if it is believed that marriage decisions are basically those of the couple alone, then no one else has the right to demand or forbid a dissolution. Other considerations may lead the state and the church to oppose such dissolutions, but when these other considerations grow weaker, they must eventually agree to what the spouses want. If love is believed to be the essential ingredient, then its absence provides grounds for dissolution to both partners, grounds that can override other duties, for example to kin, society, or God. Lack of alternatives may keep both spouses at home; or lack of alternatives for women but not for men may lead to various arrangements to keep men at home supporting their families. But once alternatives emerge, both wife and husband are likely to prefer them to marriage without love. If children are largely a costly luxury item, then there is reason for abandoning them when the marriage is no longer appealing (although mothers do not seem to do this much). Whenever an attractive set of alternatives to marriage are present (as for many people today), partners can be expected to turn rather readily to cost–benefit analysis regarding their own options. And given the difficulties of marriage, many will perceive better value elsewhere.

The English/European family system can accordingly be seen as providing a system of values that, when mixed with prosperity and the presence of alternatives, inevitably generates a high level of movement in and out of unions. As we have seen, a proportion of fathers have always deserted their families: Increased alternatives can be expected to increase the proportion. The place given to marital love in the system is important, as it follows that affectional values will be given an important weighting in marital cost–benefit analyses (whereas in other cultures, duty to kin may play a more important role). One implication is that mothers who are not happy in their marriages will be rather ready to exchange them for different arrangements (including single parenthood) once social changes render this a not-too-costly option. One could conclude, therefore, that the increase in single-parent families in the 1970s and 1980s is a natural development of the English/European marriage system.

National variations in divorce, separation, and single motherhood can then be seen as resulting from the mix of the English/European system with the local culture, which may accentuate its effects (as in the Scandinavian countries) or limit them (as in the Catholic European countries). Japan represents an especially interesting example: Although "love marriages" have become steadily more popular through the 20th century, the incidence of divorce, out-of-wedlock births, and mother-headed families remains very low. Observers such as Kumagai (1983) consider that this is because the Japanese traditions of family obligation and male supremacy remain so strong as to render the apparent westernization fairly superficial: The English/European marriage system has not really been adopted.

We conclude that neo-Malthusian theory provides valuable insights into the family structures and values influencing the prevalence of mother-headed families. However, being like the population density theory, basically historical, it too makes rather limited reference to the present. For example, it does not offer much explanation for the high rate of mother-headed families among African Americans. We turn now to a group of approaches that put more emphasis on recent family changes.

Sex Ratio Hypothesis

Guttentag and Secord's (1983) book, *Too Many Women*, put forward an intriguing hypothesis about the effect of sex ratios on male–female relationships. Guttentag argued that when men exceed women in the population (high masculinity ratio), the women become valued as a scarce resource, and men make efforts to obtain, and keep, wives of their own. This generally involves the women (but not necessarily the men) being married at an early age, and subsequently being kept firmly within a monogamous wife-mother role. Long-term commitment becomes the norm, as the men wish to keep hold of their personal "scarce resource," and the women have little experience of other men. Men are also motivated to promote "morality" for women so that they can maintain exclusive possession of their own wife, and virginity comes to be prized in potential wives. If the women have some say in choosing their spouses, romantic love is likely to become a cultural value; but if the society is very patriarchal, the women may be little more than chattels.

If on the other hand, women exceed men (low masculinity), a situation of market oversupply exists. Aware of the many options open to them, men are no longer motivated to seek out and commit themselves to a single partner. Sexual relationships become more varied and more transient, and attitudes more libertarian. Singleness, separation, divorce, and out-of-wedlock birthrates will be high. Women will react to the situation in various ways, depending especially on the status of women in the particular society. If the society is very male-dominated, they may have to play out the roles allotted to them by the men. If, however, women have more structural power—through access to gainful employment, voting rights, and the like—many will refuse to play a game in which the odds are so stacked against them, and will direct their energies instead into seeking economic, political, and/or sexual independence. A feminist movement may develop.

Guttentag documented this argument with a number of case studies of societies with unbalanced sex ratios, but she drew particular attention to the change that occurred in the United States in the 1970s, when for the first time in U.S. history women in the main marrying ages came to outnumber men. The *permissive society*, the *sexual revolution*, and the *flight from the breadwinner role* (Bernard, 1981)—terms used to describe this period—are in Guttentag's view just the most recent variant of low-masculinity culture. The increase in mother-headed families forms part of this total package.

Many Western countries experienced low masculinity in the 1970s, due to the long-term effects of the post-1945 baby boom, which saw yearly increases in the number of children born. As women typically marry men 2–3 years older than themselves, this meant that each year's cohort of girls, when adult, were looking for partners within the smaller cohort born several years earlier. Thus, a low-masculinity culture came into being when these young people entered adulthood. According to the sex ratio hypothesis, things should change back toward greater "traditionality" when the post-baby boom cohorts in which males slightly outnumber females arrive on the marriage scene—which should take place in the 1990s.

Various forms of evidence have been adduced for and against the sex ratio hypothesis. Guttentag and Secord (1983) cited the fact that the masculinity ratio was particularly low among African Americans for various reasons (see chapter 5), and the incidence of out-of-wedlock births and mother-headed families particularly high. In essence, there were not enough men to go around; many of the men were not interested in permanent commitments; and many of the women learned to manage and raise children in nonmarriage arrangements.

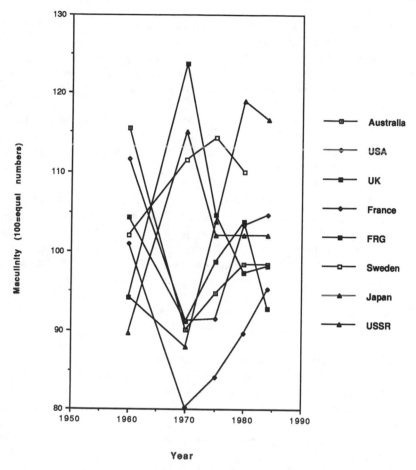

FIG. 16.   Masculinity ratios for selected countries (above 100 = masculine;
from U.N. Demographic Yearbook, various editions).

Figure 16 illustrates masculinity ratios (numbers of men for each 100 wom-
en) for eight countries, calculated as the ratio of slightly older men to slightly
younger women within the 20–35 age bracket.

Figure 16 supports Guttentag's thesis for five of the countries. There is a
sharp fall in the masculinity ratio in the early 1970s and a rise after that,
although four countries were still below 100 in 1984. The drop is most striking
in the United States, where the figure went down to 80 in 1970, and was still
just over 95 in 1984. West Germany and the former Soviet Union show quite
a reverse pattern, however. Sweden, a noncombatant nation in World War
II, registered only a brief baby boom, which ended by 1948. As a result, its
masculinity ratio was consistently high after 1960. The youngest of the Swedish baby-boomers reached age 40 in 1988, so that according to the sex ratio

hypothesis, marital disruption and mother-headed families should already be on the decline. On the contrary, as we have seen, they increased spectacularly over this period. In most of the other countries also, the ratio had reached or overtaken parity by 1984, while single-parent families continued to rise. There is only mixed support for sex ratio theory here, then, and some serious counter-evidence.

In a large international survey, South and Trent (1987) found significant relationships between the sex ratio and rates of female marriage, fertility, divorce, illegitimacy, and literacy. In a later study using data from 111 countries, South (1988) included measures of national socioeconomic development and women's labor force participation in his analysis. He found that the most powerful influence of all was national development level, which brought later marriage, lower fertility, and greater literacy for women. However, when development level was controlled for, the sex ratio hypothesis was to some extent supported, in that countries with a relative undersupply of women were more likely to restrict them to narrow domestic roles: The women were less likely to be literate, and more likely to marry young and to have large families. These effects were less marked when women were gainfully employed.

Divorce rate, however, behaved in an unpredicted manner. The Guttentag hypothesis assumes that husbands are the main initiators of divorce, and thus predicts that divorce will rise when there are more women than men, and fall when there are more men than women. This is indeed the case in lesser developed countries. But development brings a large increase in divorce regardless of sex ratio. South and Trent interpreted this to mean that once women have a certain degree of structural power, they become divorce initiators as frequently or more frequently than are men and could conceivably be more likely to do so when men are relatively plentiful. We have already seen that in modern Western countries divorce is more commonly initiated by women. South and Trent's findings thus go some way to explaining the strong but nonlinear relationship between status of women and single motherhood. In summary, divorce is common when the status of women is low, because men initiate it; but it is also common when the status of women is high, because then many women initiate it. However, the sex ratio can play a part, by providing more or fewer alternatives (in this case alternative partners) to the marriage. This explanation, of course, suggests that divorce and mother-headed families will continue high in Western countries, regardless of changes in the sex ratio.

Conclusion. The potential availability of new partners increases or decreases the alternatives to the present marriage, but modern life reduces the need for an opposite-sex life partner, and other alternatives may be relatively more important to the decision of whether or not to stay in a relationship. It seems, therefore, that although the sex ratio may influence family formation and dissolution, its effects can be moderated or even overcome by other factors.

There is also the complication that the sex ratio may itself be the effect rather than the cause, when for example daughters are killed or let die because they are seen as burdensome, or their potential fertility as a threat, and their early marriage and claustration represents just another means of containing the threat. This was the case for example among some of the upper castes of the 19th-century Indian society, which not only practiced child marriage and sati, but also female infanticide; the latter to such an extent that the 1854 census of 50 plains villages inhabited by the Munhas Rajputs of Lahore (the highest ranking subcaste on the plains) discovered only five living Munhas females born before 1846 (Guttentag & Secord, 1983).

At the same time, a shortage of adult males in a community can hardly help but make it more difficult for women who separate from one partner to find another. In this way at least, low masculinity can be seen as a contributory factor to the increase in mother-headed families. In addition, we have seen that where the shortage of men is severe, as in the Soviet Union during and after World War II, and currently in urban African-American populations, high rates of ex-nuptiality are well documented. In our experience, also, many women comment on their different experiences in living in high and low sex ratio places—for example mining towns with few women—and feel that sex ratio hypothesis makes intuitive good sense. It may be then that the kinds of analyses described here may have failed to capture the power of sex ratios to influence behavior, and that finer measures are required.

Value of Children Hypothesis

Many social scientists have wrestled with the problems of understanding how people make fertility choices, with the aim of discovering what motivates some to limit family size but not others. The hope has been that this knowledge could then be used to persuade people in the world's overpopulated regions to restrict their fertility. It could also throw light on why some fathers lose contact with the children they have created.

A central concept here is the fertility transition—from higher to lower reproduction rates—that occurs when counties reach a certain point of development. One line of research has explored the "cultural props" that underpin continuing commitment to large families and a consequently delayed fertility transition. An example is the research reported by Bulatao (1979). Bulatao and his associates set out to explore childbearing motives in a cross-national study carried out in the United States, the Philippines, Indonesia, Thailand, Korea, Taiwan, Singapore, Turkey, and Germany. Questionnaires were administered to a large sample of mainly married women in their childbearing years and a smaller sample of husbands.

The research measured a variety of "values" and "disvalues" of children and how these related to childbearing decisions. The influence of modernization on fertility decisions was particularly of interest. The researchers found that, as fertility transition theory would predict, families were smaller in countries and social groups where parents had come to see children as costly. However, there did not seem to be a linear relationship between the values and disvalues of children and decisions about family size. The researchers proposed that perhaps there may be two fertility transitions, first from high to moderate fertility, and later from moderate to low fertility, caused by different economics obtaining at different stages of modernization.

This type of research has not been without its critics. Zelizer (1985) remarked that studies of this sort ''remain limited by a primarily individualistic and utilitarian framework and an ahistorical perspective. They produce organized lists of children's costs and benefits but ignore the cultural and social determinants of such inventories'' (p. 5).

Another prominent critic is Caldwell (1982), who also approached the question of declining fertility from an economic perspective, but who offered a different interpretation of findings such as Bulatao's. He suggested that the methodologies chosen, the types of questions asked, and the interpretation placed on the results have been meaningful to the researchers but not necessarily to the respondents. As an example, he pointed out that the value of children as a posed question depends for its existence on a degree of introspection that may be typical only of populations already in fertility transition. Stable traditional societies are a ''seamless cloth'' in which the various contributions made by each of the separate members and classes of members is difficult to discern. Members of such societies may have difficulty answering questions about the discrete contributions of children although out of politeness they may try anyway.

In addition, the Western assumption that a couple's fertility decisions are their own property is also likely to distort the attempt to understand what motivates the choice to bear children in societies where this is not the case. Frequently, it is other people, such as parents or in-laws who have the greatest say in whether a couple should commence or continue having children. Again, responses to questions based on the assumption that the decision is the couple's alone to make will be of doubtful value.

Caldwell, dissatisfied with earlier demographic thinking, proposed a different model of fertility. He used evidence gathered from field studies of African cultures to show that high fertility does not necessarily impoverish families, but can instead enrich them. The critical factor is the direction of the flow of resources. Where the flow of wealth, in cash, kind and services, is from child to parent or more generally from the young to the old, then the larger the number of descendants an individual or family has, the wealthier they will be. Where the unit of ownership is not the individual but the communal group and property, goods and services are freely shared, sheer numbers are a lineage's guarantee of power, influence, and access to resources. This in turn guarantees individual members aid and support whenever it is necessary. The economically rational choice becomes to bear large numbers of children and to encourage one's kin to do similarly.

Where on the other hand, as happened relatively early in European societies, the flow of wealth is from parent to child, and ownership of resources is an individual prerogative, the rational way to economic advantage is to restrict the size of one's family. These changes can occur with modernization, but Caldwell was cautious about attributing causality. He contended that it is westernization (and particularly the spread of the Western nuclear family) rather than modernization that will bring about falling fertility in the rest of the world.

He also gave an important place to the advent of mass schooling as the factor that may tip the balance. Children become costly—they need fees, books, and equipment—and their psychological position also changes. Children attending school take on a new status. They know things their parents may not, their futures look brighter, aspirations rise, plans need to be made. They become more equal, and it no longer seems so reasonable that they should live more frugally than their parents, eat cheaper food, and not expect the same consumption rights as their elders, fathers in particular. As aspirations for children rise, the parents begin to think in terms of spending money on all sorts of enhancing experiences. The result is that children become a cost and are perceived as a cost.

As Caldwell viewed it, education becomes a self-sustaining process. As more educated adults become available, employers come to demand them, putting up work entry qualifications. At the same time, other forces feed into the effect. The economy moves in the direction of providing more consumer goods for "the family"—all of which require cash. The health industries expand, bringing medical and other health costs. As girls become educated, the status of women improves, making it more possible for husbands and wives to relate as equals in planning family limitation. The grown-up generation of educated children wants at least as much education for its children, and the educated girls demand and get more say in family decisions. As employment opportunities and higher wages become available to women, the opportunity costs of childbearing increase. Technology provides the means of effective family limitation.

Caldwell commented that from the viewpoint of economic rationality there are only two types of societies—those where rationality dictates unlimited reproduction and those where it leads to childlessness. That neither completely unlimited fertility nor utter barrenness is typical of any culture points to the operation of factors other than the purely economic. He pointed out that even in rural societies, too large a number of children becomes a stress because of worry, noise, and discipline problems. In high-cost modern urban settings, children still have special nonsubstitutable value, as sources of affection and as giving life meaning. In consequence, most people continue to want and to have children. What results in each culture is a range of desirable family sizes, with cultural norms about what is too few children and what is too many. The range may be wide or narrow. In modern Western societies, where the flow of wealth, aid, and support is down from parent to child, the accepted range is fairly narrow, coming to approximate more and more the two-child family. However, a significant minority will find the rewards provided by children are substitutable, and will remain childless.

This line of thinking suggests that the fertility transition may be somewhat different for men and women. Fathering in particular is likely to lose appeal, because it is very costly, has lost much of its prestige, patriarchal, and religious value, and is easily avoided. The emotional value remains, but as affectional values are generally found to be more important for women (Gilligan, 1982), this may be insufficient to keep many fathers involved. Women by contrast did less well out of the old system (where the economic value of children went mostly to adult men), and because of their greater interest in relationships find children's nonsubstitutable qualities more rewarding. The theory thus offers a powerful explanation for paternal withdrawal from children and the resulting mother-headed families. However, it is not so good at explaining woman-initiated separations, because these place the sole mother in the situation where the costs of the children relative to her likely income are quite exceptionally high.

A somewhat different approach is taken by Zelizer (1985), who documented the evolution of the economically valuable child of the 19th century into the emotionally priceless one of the 20th. Zelizer's basic thesis is that from the 19th century to the 20th a change occurred in the value placed on children—a "profound transformation in the economic and sentimental value of children" (p. 3). She too viewed children as originally an economic asset because of the labor they performed or the income they earned. Starting with the children of the middle classes and extending to the working classes, children then changed from involved and productive members into useless but sacred guests in their own home. This prohibition of child labor extended even to the home and household work was frowned on unless it could be justified as "good" for the child.

Zelizer traced the evolution of the economically valuable child to one that is a priceless emotional asset through the rise of laws prohibiting child labor and studies of changing attitudes to the accidental death of children, child life insurance, and the selling of babies for adoption. She showed how consideration of the monetary worth of children came to be seen as profaning something sacred. She suggested that separation of the notion of value from that of monetary worth was a deliberate attempt to keep the operation of the market out of domestic life.

> While in the nineteenth century, the market value of children was culturally acceptable, later the new normative ideal of the child as an exclusively emotional

and affective asset precluded instrumental or fiscal considerations. In an increasingly commercialized world, children were reserved a separate noncommercial place, extracommercium. (p. 11)

Zelizer tied the sacralization of the children to the rise of the family. Childhood was discovered as the family itself became of increased emotional importance, and as its instrumental value declined. The conception of children as precious also served women's interests because it inflated the status of the domestic realm, to that of equal to but different from their husbands' world of work (Degler, 1980).

Thus, into the equation that decides family size comes a factor often overlooked by economic theorists—that of the quality child. Good parenting now requires great time and effort. Furthermore, by demanding its own share of these finite resources, each new child threatens to reduce the quality of his or her older sibs. Parents are thus motivated to limit their families; while at the same time the fear of raising a spoiled only child militates against the decision to stop at one. In this variant of the value-of-children explanation, then, the well-being of the existing children rather than that of the parents dictates reproductive decisions.

Zelizer's explanation suggests still more reasons for relationship breakup than does that of Caldwell. From the father's point of view, the demands of parenting a sacred child are even greater than those of a nonproductive one, and the flow of resources even more one-way. From the mother's point of view, her commitment and duty to the sacred child(ren) may be felt as greater than that to an unsatisfactory husband.

Conclusion. The value-of-children theory presents an interesting complement to Macfarlane's neo-Malthusian approach. The two theories differ in that Macfarlane sees children as always something of a luxury item under the English/European family system, whereas the value-of-children theory sees this as a recent development. Both, however, agree that children are costly now. In addition, Caldwell concluded from his African studies that even when children require expensive education, it is possible for them to enrich, rather than impoverish the family. He did not find that the English/European family system works in this way, and Macfarlane's propositions regarding this fit very well with his observations.

The two approaches thus appear quite complementary. Both suggest that the modern Western father is expected to invest a great deal in his children, for mainly affectional rewards. If the affectional rewards he receives from the mother dwindle, or lose value, those available from the children may appear hardly worth the outlay. Cost–benefit analysis would therefore predict that both out-of-wedlock fathering, with its lesser commitment than marriage, and separation/divorce, would become increasingly attractive options for men. Zelizer's

approach makes fathering appear particularly onerous, if potentially more emotionally enriching. Thus, the value-of-children theory suggests that by somewhat reversing the position of fathers and children, modern Western societies
have tended to cast men as tributaries to their children, a role that many are
willing to forego. Insofar as mother-headed families are the creations of men,
then, the value-of-children theory has much to offer. However, it is less helpful in explaining woman-initiated separations, which place the single mother
in an even costlier situation than does marriage. The theory can do so, but
this requires the importation of a set of propositions about the psychology of
gender relations (see chapter 7), which the theory does not itself include. We
conclude, therefore, that the value-of-children theory makes a useful but limited
contribution to our understanding.

The Second Demographic Transition

The Dutch demographer Hendrik van de Kaa (1987) described himself driving in 1986 through Belgium, a country he had always considered rather stuffy
in its values, and being astounded at a giant roadside hoarding on which an
attractive young woman announced that ''Driving fast is as stupid as making
love fast.'' He asked himself what had happened to the world, and concluded
that Europe was experiencing a ''second demographic transition'' that had rendered the old values obsolete. The ''first demographic transition'' had occurred
in the 19th century, when death rates gradually declined, followed by a fertility decline starting around 1880 in most countries. In van de Kaa's views, the
second had started in the mid-1960s and comprised a sequence of events in
family formation, each of which triggered off the next.

The first of these was the postwar decline in the age of marriage. The next
was an extension of the period between marriage and first birth, brought about
by improved contraception and young couples' desire to get a home together
before starting a family. Once it became socially accepted that sexual relations
in marriage were not primarily aimed at procreation, the next value shift was
inevitable. If it was acceptable to live together for some years with no intention of childbearing, why was it necessary to have society's seal of approval
(marriage) for this period? Why not start to just live together and postpone
marriage until children arrive? When that step was taken by enough people,
societal pressure to marry was undermined to such an extent that the point
of marrying just because of a birth was lost. And as the individual's right to
happiness and fulfillment was important, why prolong any of these relationships beyond the point where they are gratifying?

van de Kaa saw this sequence of changes in retrospect as so logical and understandable he wondered why no one had predicted them. He went on to divide
the European nations into four groups, in terms of how far they had progressed

along the sequence. Group 1 comprised Denmark, Sweden, and the northern and western European countries that "appear to be following close on their tracks—Finland, Norway, the United Kingdom, Austria, Belgium, France, the former West Germany, the Netherlands, Switzerland, and Italy. Group 2 included Greece, Malta, and Portugal, where "the second transition is late, but there is little doubt that it has begun and will be completed." Group 3 comprised six eastern European countries—Bulgaria, Czechoslovakia, East Germany, Hungary, Poland, and Rumania—where political developments after World War II gave the second demographic transition a different shape, involving less sexual freedom, and a reactive clinging to traditional mores among people resentful of forcible attempts to change the structure and norms of their society. Group 4 comprised a miscellany of countries that for a variety of cultural and historical reasons were all "late in completing the first demographic transition"—including Ireland, Iceland, Albania, Turkey, and parts of the Soviet Union. Birthrates in these countries remain high by European standards. van de Kaa did not discuss the non-European Western nations—for example the United States and Australia—but presumably these would be included in the first group.

van de Kaa saw four features as central to these changes. The first was the shift from the "golden age of marriage" toward social acceptance of unmarried cohabitation; the second was the shift from children to the adult couple as the focus of the family; and the third was the development of reliable contraception and acceptance of its use as normal practice. But underlying all of these, at the heart of the matter, was the growing popular belief in the rights of the individual, in particular the right to personal and career fulfillment through the development of one's talents and interests. This holds for both men and women, but the women inevitably pay more costs because of their reproductive status and public life's greater hospitality toward men. Extrapolating from van de Kaa's argument, one could also propose that as children have less ability than adults to demand their individual rights, they are likely to be at risk of underwriting their parents' personal fulfillment.

Looking to the future, van de Kaa cited United Nations projections that the population of Europe will decrease by the year 2025 to about two thirds that of Latin America and only one third that of Africa. He saw this reduced population as inevitably including more children born out of wedlock, who may or may not be assisted by generous social security provisions, or by increased solicitousness among fathers toward their needs.

Conclusion. Unlike most of the other researchers discussed in this chapter, van der Kaa derived his ideas from the population statistics of the last several decades, rather than from more historical sources. His ideas are in many ways a continuation of those we have already considered. In particular, they apply to recent history the concept of individualism that is emphasized within neo-

Mathusian theory. In other ways there are differences. For example, whereas the value-of-children theory sees children as having become more central to the family, van de Kaa saw them as having retreated to the periphery. This discrepancy highlights the dangers of drawing broad speculative conclusions from historical and demographic data. At a speculative level, it is as easy to argue that accentuating the importance of children undermines family stability as it is to argue that focusing on adults' rights does. In the former case, it can be proposed that the children have become too costly for many to tolerate; in the latter, that their interests no longer count so much in adults' calculations about how to obtain the best possible life for themselves.

Despite such difficulties, van der Kaa's cross-national data, and his emphasis on the increased significance of individualist values in modern family life, add important components to the other demographic approaches we have examined.

SUMMARY

In this chapter we looked at some of the major biosocial and demographic theories of parenting and the family, and considered how they may help us understand the reasons behind the rise in mother-headed families. We have given less space to the biosocial, but we nevertheless consider these approaches very important in offering a means of exploring the operation of the "natural" in human parenting behavior. In particular, we saw that revisionist sociobiology has highlighted the fact that even among the infrahuman primates, what is natural is constant adaptation to circumstances rather than the playing out of immutable reproductive motivations. Thus, modern biosocial theory provided a comfortable basis from which to explore approaches that explain parenting behaviors as adaptations to particular contexts and circumstances. On this basis, we considered a selection of demographically oriented theories.

The demographically oriented theories sometimes refer to particular historical periods, sometimes not. Some are strongly materialist, with the focus being on how parenting (and other) behaviors are influenced by the fit between population size and natural resources. We found the distinction made by Lancaster and Lancaster (1987) between low- and high-density populations especially interesting, as it spotlights the importance of the family estate as a factor discouraging the formation of mother-headed families in high-density populations. The reader will recall that we came across many examples of this in our discussion of divorce, illegitimacy, and widowhood, including widow inheritance, voluntary spinsterhood, and most dramatically, widow burning.

The density hypothesis implies that once the family estate loses importance in favor of personally earned income, unhusbanded mothers become less of a threat, and their incidence should therefore increase—as they have. The density hypothesis also sees values, in this case the values of virginity, purity, and honor, as likely to change once the underlying material causes disappear. This certainly fits with the remarkably swift devaluation of sexual purity in Western cultures after the 1950s. Despite these features, the density hypothesis is, for our own purposes, rather underdeveloped. It does not, for example, propose any mechanism to explain why some asset-poor groups have many out-of-wedlock births, and others very few. Nor does it have much to say about recent Western trends in marriage, births, and divorces.

Macfarlane's neo-Malthusian approach puts more emphasis on culture, in that it locates the development of the English/European family system is a set of beliefs about private property, self-help, man–woman relations and parent–child relations. We drew the conclusion that the resultant family system, when mixed with prosperity and the consequently increased alternatives, inevitably generates a high level of movement—by men and women—in and out of unions. We concluded that neo-Malthusian theory provides valuable insights into the family structures and values influencing the prevalence mother-headed families. However, being basically historical, like the population density theory, it too makes rather limited reference to the present, and we acknowledged that our extrapolations were rather speculative.

Sex ratio theory, like density theory, is materialist in approach, and makes bold claims for the influence of resource availability—in this case the resource of potential opposite-sex partners—on sexual and relationship behavior. The evidence gives only ambiguous support for the full sex ratio argument, but the availability of new partners is certainly relevant to whether a single parent will remain single or repartner. The value-of children theory and the second demographic transition hypothesis both make a further useful contribution to our understanding of the factors influencing the prevalence and status of mother-headed families.

The major weakness of all these approaches, however, is that they emphasize single causes, and pay limited attention to the ways in which sets of influences are processed psychologically by individuals as they struggle to deal effectively with their lives. In the next chapter we accordingly turn to several approaches that include consideration of such processes.

Chapter 7

Feminist and Decomplementary Theories of Parenting

FEMINIST THEORY

The Feminist Critique of the Family

Feminist theory differs in many ways from the demographic approaches discussed in chapter 6, principally through its emphasis on the fact that practically nothing is ever the same for women and men. From the feminist point of view, approaches that talk about what "people" do fudge the fact that people come in two kinds—male and female—and have different kinds of experiences. Furthermore, the "people" in such theoretical explanations usually turn out to be largely male people, whose experiences are taken to represent those of both sexes. Thus, the explanations of recent changes in family structure that see "individualism" as the prime mover are hopelessly flawed by their failure to appreciate that individualism affects women and men very differently. Similarly, an approach such as Shorter's theory of the two sexual revolutions overlooks the fact that sexual revolutions have devastatingly different outcomes for males and females.

Critical analyses of the family, and efforts to change traditional family arrangements, have been central to feminist writings (Barrett & MacIntosh, 1982; Thorne & Yalom, 1982). Commencing in the late 1960s, feminist writers set out to debunk the belief that the contemporary Western nuclear family constituted "the family" as ordained by nature. A particular concern has been exposure of the "myth of the dependent wife." Feminist scholars pointed out the absurdity of the implicit biological metaphor that lurks behind many traditional formulations of male and female roles. As they saw it, the working metaphor is of a primal male who (with cultural variants) ventures out daily into the jungle (literal, industrial, or commercial) to bring home the catch (physical or metaphorical) to his women and children. The woman, for her part, rewards and succours him by developing the home into a "haven in a heartless world," and by preparing the children for their future gender-driven roles. The feminist writers pointed out that the myth of the dependent wife had been well developed by male politicians, philosophers, and professionals. It places the single mother in an especially unattractive position—weak, nonproductive, deprived of her natural provider and protector, and vulnerable to the depradations of various jungle beasts.

Feminists have pointed out that when the family is subjected to critical analysis and decomposed into its constituent members, things begin to look rather different. It becomes apparent that the interests of certain family members, in particular husbands/fathers, are much better served than the interests of other members, in particular wives/mothers; and that the "dependent" wife provides large amounts of essential but unpaid and devalued service to others. The feminist critique has been applied to family arrangements in many different cultures and periods. It has made explicit the fact that what has been described by many people as the traditional family is just one of many variants that human societies have developed. For this reason, the word "traditional," when used in this context, is often presented between inverted commas.

As applied to Western nations, the essentials of the feminist critique can be briefly summarized as follows:

1. Western marriage and family life involve an assumption of male authority and supremacy. This proposition has been supported by a wealth of studies demonstrating the pervasiveness of male domestic dominance. They have documented, for example, that a considerable proportion of men are violent toward their wives, and consider this violence justified; and that husbands are far more likely than their wives to drink heavily, to be unfaithful, and to renege on agreements and promises they have made. Other studies have shown that wives deprecate their own abilities where these equal or outdo those of their partner; pay far more attention to his moods than vice versa; move the conversation toward the topics he wishes to talk about; justify his actions to the children even when they consider these unacceptable; interrupt less, and tolerate being interrupted more; occupy less private space within the house; and even occupy a smaller territory within the matrimonial bed, at times no more than a narrow border strip (Bernard, 1973; Ferree, 1991; Pleck, 1977).

2. Family life involves a set of cultural assumptions and a sexual division of labor under which housework and child care are relegated to the wife/mother, classed as nonwork and accordingly devalued and unwaged, despite the fact that they may consume 80 or more hours per week, and if costed at market rates would be beyond the husband's capacity to purchase. In fact, these

unpaid reproductive, productive, and person-maintenance activities are socially essential, and they are work (Waring, 1988). Therefore, a distinction can be drawn between privileged work, which is paid, and unprivileged work, which is unpaid, undervalued, and mostly done by women. Because of the demands on time, commitment, and energy of this unprivileged work, it is assumed that women's paid employment, even if full time, will be secondary to that of their men.

3. The family work done free by women makes it possible for men to pursue careers and interests unencumbered by the need to provide care for their children. Because of being allocated the provider role, the man has the family income paid to him, greatly strengthening his power over his wife, especially when she has no paid work of her own. In industrialized societies, the men's power is backed up by elaborate work force and career structures organized around the life cycle and interests of men.

4. Because of this organization of work around men's life cycles, the processes of reproduction and the existence of children are not "recognized" in work force arrangements. Parenting responsibilities in an employee are defined as illegitimate and those people bearing such responsibilities (women) are seen as unreliable and lacking in commitment to the job. As a result, the job slots left vacant for women generally continue to be those deemed appropriate for such uncommitted people: lower status, lower paid, less secure, less interesting, and involving little or no possibility for advancement. No injustice is considered to be involved, because the woman's job is conceptualized as secondary to her main life career of motherhood.

5. Because of the attitudes and arrangements just discussed, it continues to be the case that when the wife/mother is in the paid work force (the majority case today), she will continue to perform her normal unpaid labor at home, whereas her husband will at most make a modest contribution to "help her out."

6. In consequence of all these forces, there is an early assumption by many girls growing up within families that for them too the family rather than the work force will be their major life commitment. This results in a lack of interest in acquiring the attitudes and job skills that might open up a "male" career. Thus, the effect is transmitted from one generation to another.

7. Taken together with other social conditions, these arrangements give men much more power than women. Whether a particular man does or does not exercise the power given to him by the marriage institution is up to him. There are plenty who do, in ways ranging from shirking chores to violence.

8. If a wife in consequence finds her marriage too unpleasant to continue (or if her husband leaves her), she (and her children) are likely to reap the consequences of her specialization in the domestic role—poverty.

9. Even if a wife ends up in poverty, she may be better off. Leaving an oppressive relationship can bring personal growth and increased self-esteem.

Although for men the home may be a haven in a heartless world, for women the extrafamilial world can often prove to be a haven against a heartless husband. The great merit of modern societies is that they allow women the freedom to decide whether or not to live with men. Deciding not to live with a man may bring a substantial drop in the standard of living, but today it is financially and otherwise possible for most women, and can provide a vastly improved quality of life.

The feminist critique was developed in the 1970s and was immediately considered by so many people as "right" that its influence spread rapidly. In consequence, most Western countries introduced some forms of equal opportunity or antidiscrimination legislation aimed at improving women's position. More women entered the work force, and some of these achieved senior professional and executive positions. In some countries, women's welfare and family support services were also improved. All of these developments made it easier (although not usually easy) for women to support themselves (and their children) outside of marriage.

By the 1990s, however, 20 years of feminist activism and research had revealed the intransigeance of the old ways. It has become clear that most employed women have remained in the traditionally "female" work force sectors, and mostly in the lower ranks; and even the high achievers have often ended up in sideline areas of their professions, due to gender-linked factors such as glass ceilings and outright discrimination, unnecessarily rigid career timetables that make no allowances for motherhood, and exclusion from old boy networks (Burton, 1986; Hewlett, 1987; Pringle, 1993). At home, the evidence is that women continue to do most of the unprivileged work, even when their partners profess egalitarian attitudes (Bittman & Lovejoy, 1991).

Furthermore, difficult economic times and work force changes through the 1980s left many women and men unemployed. In many countries, this has been associated with government enthusiasm for rewarding the "productive" members of society, and declining patience with the "unproductive," such as single mothers and the unemployed. In consequence, in many Western countries, the rich got richer and the poor got poorer through the 1980s. As the poor are predominantly women and children, their situation actually worsened over this period. For example, figures from the U.S. Census (1992) show that the proportion of children under 6 years of age who were living below the poverty line increased from 17.7% in 1976 (the first year for which figures are available) to 24.6% in 1991.

Herstory. Feminist writers have responded to these developments by offering many further analyses of the issues. One approach has been through the exploration of women's history (*herstory*), in order to explain the "long delay" (over 3,500 years) in women's coming to consciousness of their own subordinate position in society (Lerner, 1986, p. 6). As Lerner asked:

> What could explain women's historical "complicity" in upholding the patriarchal system that subordinated them and in transmitting that system, generation after generation, to their children of both sexes . . .
>
> I began with the conviction shared by most feminist thinkers, that patriarchy as a system is historical: it has a beginning in history. If that is so, it can be ended by historical process. . . . What is important to my analysis is the insight that the relation of men and women to the knowledge of their past is in itself a shaping force in the making of history. (pp. 6–7)

Lerner's question then is "How did patriarchy come about in the first place?" To answer it, she drew on the ideas of Engels, Levi-Strauss, and others and chose a far distant period—Mesopotamia in the period 8000–2000 BC— as exemplifying the forces that shaped up humankind's tradition of male dominance and female subordination. According to Lerner, the central factor is men's conceptualization of women as property, indeed as the very first (and rewarding) form of private property. As property, women could be exchanged with other families or clans to cement alliances and to provide workers "by hand and by womb." As social groups became more settled and more militaristic, the women of conquered tribes were taken as slaves, whose sexual services were considered part of their labor and whose children were the property of their masters. Later still, as societies became more socially stratified, the daughters of the poor could be sold into marriage or prostitution to the profit of the family (read: father); and better-off men who got into debt could trade out by presenting their wives and children to the creditors as debt slaves.

Lerner's sources certainly make her point that women were treated very explicitly in past societies as the possessions of men. For example, Hammurabic law decreed that if a man raped a virgin who lived in her father's house

> Whether it was within the city or in the open country or at night in the street . . . or at a festival of the city, the father of the virgin shall take the wife of the ravisher of the virgin [and] give her to be dishonored; he shall not give her [back] to her husband [but] shall take her. The father shall give his daughter who has been ravished as a spouse to the ravisher;

If the rapist has no wife, he must pay the price of a virgin to the father, marry the girl, and know that he can never divorce her. As Lerner pointed out, here we see the property concept of women carried to devastating conclusions. The logic is that rape damages the owner of the woman (father or husband), not the victim herself (who is property, not a person). Thus, a just solution is that the rape victim (whose value to the father has been lowered by the rape) gets indissolubly married to the rapist, and the totally innocent wife of the rapist will be turned into a prostitute.

Lerner described all societies as commodifying women, but as more or less extreme in this respect, and as varying in the emphasis they place on men's control of women's sexuality, labor, and/or submissiveness to male authority. In addition, women's social class is important to their status: Upper class women have privileges that the lower classes do not. On the other hand, social class is not the same for women as it is for men. For women, class has always been mediated through their ties to a man, and has been at risk if they violated the rules for their behavior set by men. This has been true throughout history and is still true in most of the world today.

As Lerner saw it, the system of patriarchy can function only with the cooperation of women. This has been secured through history by various means: gender socialization; educational deprivation; by dividing and ruling women through the definition of some as respectable and others as not; by various constraints and outright coercion; by discrimination in access to economic resources and political power; and by privatizing women within individual families, making the development of female solidarity and group cohesiveness extremely problematic. Most significant of all, however, has been men's dominance over the cultural tradition. Within these traditions, women have no history, no philosophy, no religion, no law of their own; they are marginalized, second-class figures in the grand sweep of male history. Particularly outrageous forms of this marginalization are found in those religions whereby reproduction itself has been claimed for men; for example in the Judeo-Christian creation story, wherein rather than woman giving birth to new life, it is man (via Adam's rib) who gives birth to woman.

In Lerner's view, modern Western women have seen great improvements in their own status, but they remain subordinated in countless ways. Piecemeal reforms will not basically change patriarchy. What is needed is a "vast cultural revolution" that will overthrow the androcentric fallacy that is built into all the institutions and mental constructs of Western civilization, and replace it by ways of thinking and acting that give equal value to the experiences of both sexes. Fortunately, the conditions necessary for such a revolution have now arrived, in at least some Western countries. For women in these countries, the patriarchal scales have increasingly fallen from the eyes, allowing them to see the profundity of their subordination.

Lerner is only one of many feminists who have used historical and cross-cultural material to illustrate how women have been oppressed by male assumptions of superiority and male concepts of "the family." Different writers emphasize different motivations. For example, whereas Lerner stressed the geopolitical and economic forces that create and maintain patriarchy, French's (1992) *War Against Women* emphasizes men's hatred of women and their readiness to scapegoat them for any difficulties that arise; and Waring (1988) described how men systematically devalue and sequester women's labor. They agreed, however, that the time for liberation is now.

These analyses clearly foresee a great deal of turbulence in female–male relationships as women struggle to reorder society and men respond with incomprehension and hostility. These researchers make the point that this turbulence is likely to be greatest when the conditions are most propitious, that is, when women's status is already relatively high, and when the most alternatives are open to women. They also underline the point made by earlier feminist writings that divorce will often be a liberating experience for women, because marriage is by its history an oppressive institution. In French's words "After millenia of male war against them, women are fighting back on every front." Disruption of older concepts of marriage seems an inevitable consequence of this revolt, especially in those countries where women have developed high expectations. In consequence, the incidence of mother-headed families can be expected to remain high, and probably to increase.

Developmental Approaches.   From a more here-and-now psychological viewpoint, feminist writers have tried to describe the differences between women and men that undermine heterosexual relationships. They have usually started from the well-documented fact that from the preschool years onward, girls show more interest than boys in personal relationships (Duck, 1986/1992). In consequence, women spend more time and energy monitoring their relationships, maintaining them, and attempting to iron out problems. In marriage, they are quicker to understand problems, and to try to deal with them. If their efforts continue to fail, they may reach the conclusion that there is no future before their partners have even noticed any kind of problem.

This formulation certainly fits with what men and women have to say about failed relationships. P. Jordan (1985), for example, found that men whose wives had initiated a separation were often incredulous and angry ("We were perfectly alright. How could she do this to me?"). This occurred despite the fact the wives had often been trying to discuss the problem for years, but had been unable to get a hearing. Five years later, a substantial proportion of men still did not understand what had gone wrong. The wives by contrast made remarks like "For me it was all over long over. I had done all my grieving before we even discussed separating."

Given a changed social climate that offers more alternatives to a poor marriage, and sees less virtue in "working at" it, this would certainly encourage women to cut their losses, and thus promote an increase in one-parent families. McGoldrick, Anderson, and Walsh (1991) also made the point that being highly invested in relationships brings both supports and stresses, because it involves identification with the joys and setbacks of a band of other people. If the partner is untouched by all these occurrences, then the two may be living in worlds with quite limited overlap; and there may not be all that much of a relationship to dissolve. This approach also then foresees continuing disruptions in woman–man relationships.

Taking a somewhat different direction, some psychoanalytically oriented feminists have seen heterosexual relationships as shaped in infancy. Dinnerstein (1977) described women's monopoly of childrearing as the critical factor, which leads males to develop largely unconscious internal images of their mothers (and by extension, all women) as dangerously powerful and frustrating, but also infantile. Men, generally encountered when the child is older and more cognitively mature, are perceived as more adult, and the boy constructs a masculine identity for himself of which being not-woman is an important component. In adulthood, men experience an overwhelming need to control these threatening fantasy figures, and in consequence seek to dominate women in personal life and to exclude them from areas of life outside the family. Women acquiesce in this because their own identity formation has led them to "become" the mother who nurtures and applauds, and if she does it right, holds the devotion of her man.

Another psychoanalytically oriented feminist, Nancy Chodorow (1978), also emphasized the importance of women's monopoly of childrearing. She asked why mothers continue to do mothering, given the availability of birth control and the fact that men can mother equally well. She saw the answer as lying in the fact that mothers treat sons and daughters differently. Sons are from early on treated as separate and other, and their autonomy encouraged. Daughters are more likely to be perceived as one with the mother's self, and their period of close attachment prolonged. In consequence:

> growing girls come to define and experience themselves as continuous with others; their experience of self contains more flexible or permeable ego boundaries. Boys come to define themselves as more separate and distinct, with a greater sense of rigid ego boundaries and differentiation. The basic feminine sense of self is connected to the world, the basic masculine sense of self as separate. (p. 169)

Because women's basic self is to tied up in relating and in the experiences of infancy, and men's in separation and autonomy, for adult women a relationship with just a man is inadequate. Women feel impelled to recreate their early experience through motherhood, which allows them to recapture (from the side of the adult) the intense experience that was theirs as a child. And so on to the next generation.

These kinds of formulation see change as only occurring when fathers accept a far greater part of the childrearing job. They do not immediately suggest any explanation for the increase in dissolutions and mother-headed families as it is not suggested that those birth cohorts who have had high dissolution rates (since the early 1970s) have had different infantile experiences from their predecessors whose dissolution rates were low. Indeed, both Dinnerstein and Chodorow proffered their explanations because they felt so little had changed in male–female relationships that profound and irrational unconscious motivations must be involved. However, it can be argued that public discussion of gender issues in the last decades, along with the increase in economic alternatives for women, may to some extent have freed Western women, and perhaps men also, from the tyranny of their archaic drives, and led them to abjure relationships driven by infantile needs. In this case, the penetration of feminist thinking into the culture would itself be a causal factor.

Divorce.   Feminists have also written specifically about divorce, unmarried motherhood, and their sequelae. Some of this material has already been presented in earlier chapters. The literature on divorce offers particular insights into our topic, and some further aspects are accordingly discussed here.

Weitzman, in her 1985 evaluation of the pioneer Californian no-fault legislation, pointed out that it was greeted with optimism by feminists (including Weitzman herself) who saw the old fault legislation as grounded in the anachronistic legal concept of the wife as her husband's property. They believed that the new law would get rid of the adversarial attacks, hypocrisy, and collusion involved in "fault" litigation. Thus, it would reduce hostility and bitterness, and would facilitate cooperative postdivorce parenting. Feminists also looked with favor on the concept that maintenance payments under the new law would become gender neutral rather than, as previously, an acknowledgment of the "old sex-based assumption" of women's continuing dependency on men.

After reviewing the first decade of the new legislation's operation, however, Weitzman concluded that it had weakened the position of women, particularly in those cases in which the husband sought the divorce. Under the old legislation, such wives could use the fault provisions as leverage to obtain a better financial settlement. Because she was innocent of marital fault, a man could not divorce an unwilling wife. Therefore, she could refuse to "give" him a divorce (by charging him with fault), unless he met her terms, which could provide an income for the family after he had left. Under the new law, wives had no such leverage, and the knowledge that they had been freed from the old gender-based assumptions regarding maintenance provided cold comfort.

Weitzman also interviewed a number of judges (mostly men). She found that they often had difficulty understanding the situation of the women who came before them, and were particularly concerned not to make decisions that would damage the husband's ability to get on with his job. In consequence of all this, many ex-wives and their children were thrown into poverty, whereas the husbands made a quick financial recovery from the divorce. In fact, husbands were, on average, substantially better off than before the divorce, because they now made minimal contributions toward their children's upkeep.

The problem of course is that traditional marriage by its nature gives all the property and potential property to the man. As breadwinner, he is the one who is paid the wage, and the one who also acquires skills, knowledge, connections, assets, superannuation, and pension rights. By taking on the homemaker role, his wife is likely to write herself out of all of these benefits. This may work all right while the marriage goes well, but when marriage terminates, the inequality of the marriage system becomes explicit: The husband gets the income and the wife gets the children. Weitzman pointed out that those who suffer the greatest deterioration in living standards are those who have invested most in traditional marriage (i.e., women who have given up their own occupations and devoted themselves full time to the family, including in some cases unpaid work for the husband's business). Those who do best are those who have invested least in the family and most in their own career development. In essence, marriage rewards the more selfish.

An Australian study (P. McDonald, 1986) reports similar outcomes. At 1–3 years after divorce, men were substantially better off than before the separation, and women and children were substantially worse off. Those women who had remarried were best off financially, whereas single mothers and older women living alone were worst off. Reflecting Lerner's point that higher social class is not the same for women as for men, it was found that women who had been married to men in the highest income category were most likely to have no independent earnings at separation and least likely to re-partner. In consequence, of all women, they were the most likely to be dependent on social security, despite their husband's continuing high income. Housing was a particular problem. Despite the Australian court's emphasis on keeping children in the family home, 3–5 years after the original separation, 75% of children had moved out of the home. However, husbands with custody remained in the home in 87% in cases.

In a follow-up study 3 years later (5–8 years after the separation), the men had continued to improve their financial situation. Unpartnered wives previously married to low- and medium-income men had slightly improved their position, but the ex-wives of the wealthy men had not, and they were now worse off than the ex-wives of lower income men. Their husbands were still doing well, and the cost of their child maintenance payments—initially low—had been further trivialized by inflation (Funder, Harrison, & Weston, 1993).

These findings underline the point that the marriage system disadvantages women. However, although Weitzman stressed the injustice to wives whose husbands seek divorce, the Australian study emphasized that it is mostly wives who are the divorce initiators. For example, of those women whose incomes had dropped most severely after separation, 55% had themselves made the decision to separate (P. McDonald, 1986). Voegeli (1993), writing of Germany, noted that there too women have become increasingly willing to abandon marriages they perceive as low quality, despite the associated risk of poverty.

Asked to explain why they initiated the divorce despite the economic risks, the majority of women make the point that "my standard of living has dropped but my quality of life is way ahead," because of release from tensions, conflicts, and sometimes fear, and the gaining of freedom and independence.

One divorcee explained that her "present flat is the size of my old kitchen, and I do not have any furniture, radio, music, books or TV. I have to watch every penny in case I become ill. However I do have peace of mind" (Burns, 1980, p. 171).

Similarly, Weitzman noted that "It's only money" was a favorite response of the divorced women she interviewed when asked how they coped with their changed circumstances.

However, within the family even "standard of living" is a tricky concept. Other divorcees report that despite a lower family income, their standard of living has risen, because they now have control of their own money, and are no longer dependent on a husband who was frequently unemployed, spent most of his money on himself, or ran up large debts.

From the feminist point of view, women's difficulties with marriage are predictable, because marriage is a male-designed institution that gives men tremendous power over their wives. Difficulties are not inevitable, because individual men may choose not to exercise this power, and make charming husbands. But there are always plenty who do exercise it, and in these cases it is an act of self-liberation to leave the marriage.

There is nothing new in all this, because marriage has always been a high risk enterprise for women. However, in past times, the cost of not marrying has usually been even greater because no alternatives were available. Today, in Western countries, alternatives are available in the form of social acceptance, jobs, and social security. These latter may be low-income, but the gain in terms of happiness may be well worth it, as increasing numbers of women are coming to realize. In line with Lerner's point about the importance of cultural tradition, feminist writers give weight to cultural as well as economic changes as facilitators of women's lesser attachment to unsatisfactory marriages. They point out that a great advantage for women has been the fading (although by no means disappearance) of the patriarchal philosophy that sees the divorcee as sinful or tainted, and her children as inevitably disadvantaged. Because of its powerful impact on popular culture, feminism itself has played an important part here. This is true even for women who do not see themselves as feminists, but who have come to expect more for themselves.

However, a continuing acceptance of patriarchal values is relevant for the poverty of mother-headed families. P. McDonald (1986) found that both ex-husbands and ex-wives believed that direct financial contributions to the family were more important than other inputs. As men had contributed more in dollar terms, the women saw the men's input as more valuable, and denigrated the worth of their own labor. They were in consequence prepared to accept inadequate property and income settlements that underestimated the value of their years of unpaid child care and domestic work ("It's his money after all"). Weitzman's women interviewees similarly devalued their own inputs, and were likely to drop property claims if the husband countered by announcing that he would contest custody. The Swedish concept of children as citizens entitled to adequate support by both state and father was not strongly established in their thinking.

In summary, feminist writers emphasize three aspects of divorce law changes as sources of mother-headed families. First, no-fault law has made it easier and more socially and legally acceptable for men to shake off responsibility for wives and children, and many have seized the opportunity. (One study found that after divorce ex-husbands were more likely to keep up the payments on their cars than on their children; Funder, Harrison, & Weston, 1993.) Second, the new laws, along with other social changes, have made it possible for wives to escape marriages they find unsatisfactory, and many have seized this opportunity, usually taking their children with them. Disappointment with the relationship is the main reason, and is likely to continue to be the main reason because women put a high value on good intimate relationships. Third, divorce affects more than one generation. Children observe what happens to their parents and draw their own conclusions. In the case of Californian family law, this was in Weitzman's view that one should be wary of both marriage and divorce. It is not of course necessary to be the child of divorced parents to come to this conclusion. It is a rare child today who does not have at least one friend in this situation.

There is no reason to expect any decline in divorce in the near future, but other things certainly need to change. Voegeli (1993), for example, pointed out that the German taxation system awards the highest benefits to the status of being married, while giving little relief to parents. In consequence, the growing number of employed single mothers are actually subsidizing childless married couples, while themselves raising the future generation of taxpayers with relatively little assistance.

Conclusion. Feminist writings offer a host of insights into the family changes this book has described. A weakness is the dominance of White Anglo-American writing, which has "felt too secure in the belief that it is international when it is so only in the narrowest sense" (Kaplan, 1992, p. xxii). This criticism has been made extensively in recent years, by feminists as well as others. They have pointed out that the anti-male flavor of much feminist writing, and its critique of the family, indicate the particular concerns of White Anglo-American women, and have little to offer to, for example, depressed minority groups for whom the family is the main source of support; or those for whom oppressive social conditions rather than men in general are the main enemy (Bottomley, de Lepervanche, & Martin, 1992). It can be said then that feminist writings offer a better explanation of the rise of mother-headed families in the majority populations of the English-speaking countries than elsewhere.

A second critique for our purposes is feminism's relative lack of interest in the motivations of men in family formation and dissolution. For this reason, we turn now to an approach that incorporates many of the insights that have already been described, but within a different framework.

DECOMPLEMENTARY THEORY

As we have seen, many explanations of changes in the roles of women have highlighted the importance of their vastly increased work force participation in modern Western societies. From this point of view, the economic independence of women is the central cause of the move away from traditional family roles, and the increase in divorce, out-of-wedlock births, and mother-headed families.

We have noted that the status of women in a culture does indeed influence the incidence and status of mother-headed families, but that the association is a U-shaped rather than a simple linear one. South and Trent's (1987) study shows that when women are plentiful and have little structural power, divorce initiated by husbands is likely to be common. However, when women have a fairly high degree of status and power, they are likely to be the initiators, and the divorce rate is again high. A similar phenomenon was seen with out-of-wedlock births. When women's position is weak, and marriage is essential for acquiring some status and security, illegitimate births following the father's desertion may be quite common. However, when the status of women is relatively high, it may be they who prefer ex-nuptial to nuptial childbearing, so that the rate may again be high.

As South and Trent showed, the picture is complicated by other factors. These include a country's level of development, the degree to which women have access to visible and valued employment, and the sex ratio, all of which interact in complex ways. A higher level of development generally increases women's status, but as Sen (1990b) noted, some parts of the world that have become quite prosperous have continued to discriminate against women in the most basic way—restricting them to unpaid domestic tasks and providing less nutrition and health care than that given to men. Similarly, access to gainful employment normally results in less traditional family roles for women and more divorce, but this is not always the case. The largely agricultural countries of sub-Saharan Africa that practice the female farming system report high rates of female work force participation but also high marriage rates (Pampel & Tanaka, 1986).

Because of these and other complications, a new kind of explanation has become popular, one that is centered around the premise that the interests of men and women have become less interdependent in modern societies. This interdependence has not always been a happy one. Historical and cross-cultural writings have shown us that the interests of men and women often diverge, and that different societies stitch them together in various ways, generally if not universally to the benefit of men. We have already described many examples of how women have been subordinated in this way. Some authors (Bernard, 1981; Glick, 1988; Goode, 1984; Harris, 1980; Illich, 1983; Rossi, 1987), now suggest that the way in which the two sexes no longer rely heavily on each other is new and is an important feature of our times.

We call this approach *decomplementary theory*, because it emphasizes how the interests of women and men have lost much of their complementary nature. An interesting feature is the fact that this type of explanation has been advanced by writers from across the political spectrum, often with little or no reference to one another. The solutions they propose are also often radically different; and none of them, to our knowledge, uses the term *decomplementary theory*. We think it is fair enough to group them together under this title, however, because their arguments converge on the central premise of loss of complementarity. We present the argument here because it strikes us as combining in a valuable form many of the insights of other approaches. In presenting it we bring together strands from a range of different writings. We also draw quite heavily on the concept of gender ''role,'' which has often been criticized for implying an overdeterministic view of human development. We use it here because many of the relevant authors use it, as a shorthand way of describing the typical expectations of men and women at a particular time and place.

In times past, so the argument goes, man–woman relations were not always good, but the two sexes did need each other. Men needed women's labor and reproductive capacity; women needed men's strength and protection. Economic necessity threw up religious and/or cultural values that further encouraged conformity. However, recent social and economic changes have been so great that this interdependence no longer holds. Prosperity, technology, education, contraception, and social services have ushered in a new era. Most women are able to earn wages, efficient contraception has reduced their vulnerability, virginity is no longer prized, unmarried motherhood is socially tolerated, and welfare services provide a safety net against catastrophe.

For men, good wages and domestic technology have reduced their need for a homemaker-wife, women are sexually available outside marriage, and marriage is no longer a sign of virility and maturity. Traditional moral and religious values have lost their power to exact conformity. The days are long gone when a single person over 30 is regarded as ''a pervert, a person with severe emotional problems, or a poor created fettered to mother'' (Harris, 1980, p. 97).

Many people continue to find marriage the best way of meeting their needs, but the alternatives have become steadily more attractive. In essence, marriage has become deregulated. Until the 1970s, marriage was clearly the favored marital status. Legal, economic, social, and religious arrangements all placed the nonmarried at relative disadvantage. Then, quite suddenly, changes in the law, the job market, welfare policy, and popular attitudes combined to erode marriage's elite status. Previously stigmatized alternatives—unmarried cohabitation, serial partnerships, single parenthood, gay/lesbian households, noncoresidential partnership and plain singlehood—offered new forms of freedom, and developed a new popularity. Compared with the alternatives, marriage of course retains the advantage of being traditional, respectable, a sign of commitment, and hopefully, a source of emotional security for both partners. However, it has the disadvantage of being seen as the arrangement most likely to push spouses into the old inegalitarian domestic roles. The picture is compounded by an echo effect among younger generations who observe their parents' dissatisfaction with traditional roles, and to whom modern life offers the opportunity to try other arrangements. Consequently, in future marriage in Western countries may have trouble in retaining even its present market share.

Anthropologist Marvin Harris (1980), writing of the United States, argued that the crucial element has been the shift in Western nations from an industrial to a postindustrial finance and marketing economy. This change wrenched women out of the home and into the job market. The jobs created needed women, but married women also needed the jobs as inflation reduced their husbands' wages and family life became more money expensive, due to increased service costs, lengthier education for children, higher standards of consumerism, and other factors. At the same time, blue-collar male jobs, the economic base of the traditional working-class family, went into decline. As women entered the work force and men left it, the traditional family became well and truly de-mystified, and the

> entire edifice of the marital and procreative imperative with its Victorian double standards and its patriarchal prudery began to crumble. Down came the fertility and first-time marriage rates. Up went the divorce rate, consensual liaisons, delayed marriages, childless and one-child families, and a whole new anti-procreationist and libertine sexual consciousness. (p. 171)

As Harris saw it, whereas for previous generations "traditional" family life presented the best guarantee of security for both men and women, it now became a high-cost choice. The market produced an infinity of alternative enjoyable ways for adults to spend their time and money, and increasing numbers of people came to perceive two incomes and few or no children as the best path to the good life. At the other end of the financial spectrum, marriage to an unemployed or precariously employed man could prove an expensive choice for a woman who could find herself supporting the entire family as well as servicing her man's domestic needs.

Taking in a further aspect of contemporary Western life, Harris argued that the gay revolution forms part of the total picture, as gay lifestyles simply exaggerate the advantages of the childfree heterosexual couple (two male incomes, no children, sexual freedom). Consequently, the breadwinner/homemaker family now stands "hollow and near collapse." The traditional family required the cooperation of both sexes, but postindustrial relationships do not. As women nevertheless, do often have children, their chances of being left to rear them alone, and in poverty, are high, especially among working-class women, whose menfolk's economic position has declined. The men are likely to find family commitments too burdensome, and the women are likely to find the men and their requirements a burden. Where mother-headed families have social security rights that two-parent families do not, a resident male can doubly reduce the family's income.

As Harris described it, the prime force in these changes is capitalism, which has been carried by its own momentum away from the manufacturing industries that supported traditional gender roles and toward industries that often find women to be more suitable employees. According to Harris (1980):

> The dormant white American housewife was the service-and-information employer's sleeping beauty. Her qualifications were superb. She was available in vast numbers. She had been trained for her entire life to be unaggressive and to take orders from men. Her husband earned more than she did so she would take a job that was neither permanent nor secure. She had little interest in joining a union and still less in struggling to form one. She would accept temporary jobs, part-time jobs, jobs that let her go home to cook or take care of the children, jobs that were boring, jobs that had no future. And she could read and write. All she needed was . . . some service- and information-boss charming to kiss her into life.
>
> The timing of the feminist outburst of the 1960s marks the moment of collective realization that women, married or not, would have to continue to work as a consequence of inflation and the growing dearth of males who held genuine breadwinner jobs, and that unless they rebelled they would continue to get the worst of all possible worlds: dull, boring dead-end jobs at work, and cooking, cleaning, child care and chauvinist males at home. (p. 93)

Although Harris was unsympathetic to the traditional family system that he saw as crumbling, he was also unsympathetic to the changes he described, which he saw as demoralizing the men whose jobs have disappeared and as overburdening women. As we see here, this is rather typical of decomplementary theorists, although some, like Illich, are enthusiastically in favor of the past.

Bernard (1981), in an interesting version of the decomplementary approach, argued that male–female roles are always changing. She quoted historical and cross-cultural evidence showing that women are often the main providers for the family, whereas the male role is that of warrior, or supervisor of his wives' and children's labor, or whatever might be. Again, writing of the United States, she argued that the so-called traditional family with its male provider and female homemaker roles was a particular variant that arose around the 1830s when the nation shifted from a subsistence economy to a market economy.

It lasted until 1980, when the U.S. Census of 1980 declared that a man was no longer automatically assumed to be head of the household. This variant of the family put the husband/father into the paid work force as family breadwinner, and tied his sense of self-worth and his public status to his success in this role. This brought stresses because failure to provide adequately meant failure as a person. In addition, being a good provider was often defined as being a better provider than others, so that the man could become a player in an endlessly competitive game. In consequence, there were always some defectors, who deserted or refused their responsibilities, or who took to drink. By and large, however, the breadwinner role was a good deal for men, who were provided by their jobs with a passport to masculinity and family power.

It was nowhere near such a good deal for women who, when young, were forced to concentrate on winning a good provider for themselves, and once married, were condemned to housewifely dependency. Consequently, they fled into the work force in large numbers once economic changes made jobs available to them. This diluted the powers and prerogatives once conferred by the sole-provider role and left men to struggle toward new definitions of masculinity. The struggle, and the lack of fit between male–female roles, continues. "The good-provider role may be on its way out, but its legitimate successor has not yet appeared on the scene" (Bernard, 1981, p. 12).

Bernard's paper is especially valuable in its emphasis on the fact that marital roles are not only shaped up differently by different cultures, but go through periods of decline and transition when the incumbents are uncertain as to what they should be doing, and are forced to make up the rules for themselves, often in conflict with their partners and significant others. It raises the thought that there are and have been many circumstances where gender roles have been noncomplementary, the present being only a close-at-hand example.

Ehrenreich, another feminist writer with a decomplementary approach, emphasized the importance of the breadwinner ethic for *women* over that long period when they had little independent access to bread themselves. Like Bernard, she viewed the breadwinner ethic as having been supported by a great weight of public opinion, religious prescription, legal obligations and sanctions, and expert opinions of various kinds. Like Harris, she believed the ethic collapsed in the period after 1950, and she charted this collapse through a series of cultural developments. Unlike Harris and Bernard, however, she emphasized the value to men of escape from the ethical requirement to work for the support of others. For this reason she concluded: "I feel justified in using a more active construction than the 'collapse of the breadwinner ethic' and talking about a male revolt—though hardly organized and seldom conscious of its goals—against the breadwinner ethic" (Ehrenreich, 1983, p. 13).

As Ehrenreich viewed it, this revolt was fueled by a male resentment of female economic dependency that was every bit as deep as women's. She made the interesting point that the right-wing antifeminist women's groups that emerged in the United States in the 1970s were not so much a backlash against feminism as against the male revolt from the breadwinner ethic.

Although Harris saw changes in capitalism as the motive force in gender-role change, Bernard and Ehrenreich did not go into the forces that first created and then destroyed the breadwinner and homemaker roles. Other writers on this topic seem to agree, however, that the 19th and earlier 20th century saw a relative exclusion of married women from the expanding paid work force in many countries, due to some combination of employer preference for male workers; state policy; trade union concern to establish a family wage that would keep cheap female labor out of the marketplace; women's domestic responsibilities; the differential education of girls and boys; male workers' desire and ability to keep good jobs for themselves; and the apprenticeship system that excluded women from entry to many skilled trades (Curthoys, 1986; Hartmann, 1981; Humphries, 1977). As such, men and women were forced into complementary roles that made women (and children) extremely dependent on their man's continuing support, and pressured men to provide that support.

As Harris pointed out, these pressures have now weakened, along with the associated pressures for sexual conformity. Married women increasingly found jobs. Although these were often part time and the income secondary to the husband's wage, the size and range of women's work force contribution meant that something else happened. Women were increasingly stratified into the social class structure in their own right, as paid workers, rather than as appendages of their menfolk (Bryson, 1993). Although this process has been supported by the women's movement, the driving forces have been economic. These have included capitalism's need for more workers through the 1970s and 1980s and latterly its desire for a more "flexible" work force that can readily be taken up or shed as circumstances require—an arrangement to which women workers have long been accustomed. International labor force statistics show that decreasing numbers of women in European countries are now totally financially dependent on their partners (from as few as 11.2% in Sweden to a high of 68.2% in Holland in the early 1980s) and increasing numbers have achieved complete economic equality with them (a high of 11.6% in Sweden and a low of 2.6% in Switzerland in the early 1980s). This trend has been paralleled in some countries by a movement toward treating women more like men, as workers rather than dependants, in family, taxation, and social security law (Bryson, 1993). This is particularly relevant for single mothers, who are expected to become the family breadwinner as soon as possible, rather than being classed as a permanent or temporary ex-wife.

As yet, women are mostly at the bottom of this class structure, in the lowest paid and least secure jobs, but even so their access to paid employment has generally increased their well-being, status, and freedom. This is true of Third-World countries as well, as the research of Sen and of South and Trent have shown. Better education among younger women should further improve their occupational prospects, other things being equal.

Another force increasing women's direct involvement in the class structure is greater unemployment among men, particularly young men, and industry's enthusiasm for "rationalizing" and feminizing men's jobs by rendering them short term and/or part time as required. All of these forces move women out of the status of being complementary to their partners, and men out of sole responsibility for the family's economic welfare. Male roles have become feminized and female roles masculinized. Thus, decomplementarity creates the context for more individual, rather than family-constrained choices. This, in its turn, brings more rationalist evaluations of relationships and more termination of unsatisfactory ones. It comes as no surprise then that Sweden, with high opportunities for personal choice underwritten by high levels of female employment and social security support, should have high rates of relationship dissolution and many mother-headed families. The reader will perceive that decomplementary theory includes a good many of the concepts that we have already looked at in other contexts—a strong emphasis on individualism, economic conditions, and women's work force participation—and incorporates many concepts and arguments that we have already come across. It also gets support from some unexpected quarters. For example, Illich (1983) presented an extreme version of the decomplementary argument, for the purpose of opposing it. Illich argued that sexual freedom (including access to contraception) reduces responsibility, particularly men's sense of responsibility, and thus results in worsening the position of the majority of women. What is needed, according to Illich, is a return to the situation where intercourse is likely to cause pregnancy, where virginity is accordingly prized, marriage enforced, and "men and women collectively depend on each other: their mutual dependence sets limits to struggle, exploitation and defeat" (p. 93). Some right-wing women's groups opposed to abortion offer a rather similar argument (Ehrenreich, 1983), although they do not usually go so far as to oppose all forms of contraception, as does Illich.

Applications

How well does the decomplementary approach explain the family changes of recent decades? It certainly offers many reasons why mainstream populations in Western nations should be abjuring family goals in favor of individualist ones. It provides an explanation for various behaviors we have described— late marriage and nonmarriage; the popularity of cohabitation, which allows for relatively easy exit should one partner become dissatisfied; high rates of divorce when one party is dissatisfied; and a growth in mother-headed families and single-person households. It also predicts that relationship dissolutions will be highest when the state provides adequate support for women and children, because the benefit to be gained from "keeping the family together" will be reduced. This is borne out by figures from the Scandinavian countries, where both state support and mother-headed families are above the European average.

The decomplementary approach differs from many feminist writings by emphasizing that these changes are likely to be attractive to men as well as to women. This aspect is neatly summed up in Glick's (1988) opinion that many young U.S. men and women may be reaching the conclusion that several years of marital experience are enough for them. One spinoff has been an interest in behavioral and attitudinal changes among young people. We saw earlier that Hoem and Hoem (1988) were able to show clear differences between the marriage-related behavior of Swedish cohorts born only 5 years apart. Findings in other countries echo these findings. Writing of the United States, Goering (1992) listed a series of factors that discourage today's young U.S. men and women from marriage. These include the sight of so many failed marriages around them; the range of attractive alternatives available; the demands of many modern careers and the associated tendency to become a workaholic; women's greater expectations of men and unwillingness to settle for someone who expects his partner to do all the housework and child care; the economic insecurity of the times; and the "inertia of being alone." One man described how "Once you're used to being alone, it develops an energy of its own. You begin to see others as encroaching on your own space. . . . My biggest fear is that someone would always be there" (p. 9). Writing of Sweden, Popenoe (1988) described a similar enthusiasm for single life.

Glezer (1993) presented some interesting findings from a sample of 1,536 18- to 34-year-old Australians interviewed in 1982 and again in 1991 at ages 27–43. Some attitudes showed a change over this period. Whereas in 1981 65% of women and 73% of men believed that "children are an attraction of marriage," by 1981 44% of the women and only 56% of men did so. The number who believed that "Marriage gives you economic security" had dropped, particularly among women (from 59% to 36%) but also among men (from 42% to 33%). Less than 25% of women now believed that "The needs of one's spouse and kids come first," compared with more than 50% in 1981 (77% of the men agreed that this was so in 1981, but only 45% did in 1991). Of the sample, 33% thought that a person should not stay in a marriage if he or she was not continuing to grow as a person, and women were more likely to take this view than men.

A comparison of the reasons for leaving home given by older (born 1948–1955) and younger cohorts (born 1957–1964) showed that marriage, employment, and study were more common reasons among the older and the need for independence more common among the younger. The married among the older group had married at earlier ages than those in the younger cohort, whereas the younger group were more frequent cohabitors. One in five of the unmarried did not expect to marry, and 50% of the women and around 33% of the men were uncertain. This was despite the fact that more than 50% had cohabited at some time. The unmarried were generally positive about single life, the women more so than the men. Of the never married, around 50% were prepared to consider having a child outside of marriage.

What about the situation in other populations? The experience of the former Soviet Union is especially interesting here, as it did not embrace the breadwinner ethic in the way the Western nations did. Consequently, there have been no traditional provider/homemaker roles for men and women to liberate themselves from. Nevertheless, divorce and mother-headed families have been and are common. Interestingly, a viewpoint quite similar to that of Harris and Bernard has appeared in Soviet writings, although expressed in different terminology (e.g., Kharchev & Matskovskii, 1981; Sonin, 1981). In these writings, the emphasis is again on the poor fit between men and women's lives and family values. However, the Russian writers do not see female employment and technological developments as having turned people from family to individualist values. Rather, they emphasize how the combination of work and family demands without adequate support can render marriage and motherhood such a costly option for women that once the means (divorce and birth control) become accessible, many withdraw from both. This certainly suggests a failure of female and male roles to complement one another. Interestingly the (ex-)Soviet writers pointed out that this did not occur in the Central Asian regions, where patriarchal and religious values and rural living have kept families large and divorce very low.

Similar arguments can be made regarding populations with high mobility among young people and consequent weakening of social control over their behavior. We referred earlier to some examples such as France in the late 18th- to mid-19th century, when large numbers of young people moved from the villages into the expanding cities, and out of the control of their elders. As we saw, illegitimate births at such times were very common. However, the harsh conditions of the time meant that the outcome was often child abandonment rather than a mother-headed family.

We can also extend the argument to populations with high male unemployment. As Staples (1982) said of the African-American population, "if the minimum criterion for a husband is that he be regularly and gainfully employed" than almost half the men of working age fail to qualify. In such cases, female and male roles again fail to complement one another—marriage is a risky option for women and the taking on of family responsibilities is beyond the reach of many men. This situation, however, is likely to be different from the revolt against the breadwinner/homemaker roles described by Bernard and Ehrenreich as occurring in more prosperous sectors of the same populations. In high unemployment and/or minority populations, traditional family roles may be highly regarded by women and men, but may be impossible to obtain because of the conditions of life (Huggins & Blake, 1992).

CONCLUSION

We have coined the term *decomplementary theory* to describe a variety of writings, from differing ideological contexts, that present a remarkably similar set of ideas. The attraction of decomplementary theory is that it manages to synthesize within its own framework much that is most interesting in other approaches. Of all the theories discussed, it is also the one that takes cognizance of the broadest range of evidence and uses a broad socioeconomic framework. For these reasons, our greatest sympathy lies with this approach. We consider that decomplementary theory has much to offer as a means of understanding the family changes of recent decades. It has been mainly presented as an interpretation of the movement in the Anglo-American countries away from the breadwinner/homemaker model of the family and toward a more individualist model; and this is where it has the clearest explanatory power. However, the notion of ''fit'' between male and female roles and family values is a valuable one that can be extended to a variety of other situations and other cultures and we have suggested some further applications.

We emphasize that fit is not considered by decomplementary theory to be necessarily a good thing. Bernard (1981) emphasized the disadvantages to women of the breadwinner/homemaker ethic, and Ehrenreich (1983) pointed out its disadvantages for men. Harris (1980) seemed to view it as a generally unattractive arrangement. Some of the woman-enslaving societies described by Lerner (1986) could also be described as having a good fit between gender roles and the family values of the time, in the sense that both suited the interests of the dominant groups. A poor fit may be an advantage, in that it provides greater freedom for many. However, it is likely to promote greater levels of relationship dissolution, mother-headed families, and in some cases child abandonment. To overcome the costs of freedom, strong social supports for one-parent families are required, from government, kin group, or some other source. If these are unavailable, it seems inevitable that this growing group of families will suffer multiple disadvantages.

We have already described some of the economic hardships experienced by mother-headed families in many countries. There is now also evidence of second-generation effects. For example, McLanahan and Bumpass (1988) argued that although the prevailing wisdom in the United States has been that family disruption has few and relatively small negative effects on the subsequent lives of offspring, very recent studies indicate that negative effects have become stronger and that the female-headed family is an important link in the intergenerational transmission of marital dissolution and poverty. In a large national sample, these authors found parental separation/divorce was significantly related to daughters' teenage marriages and births, premarital births, divorce and single motherhood. Compared to the offspring of continuing marriages, women who had spent time in a single-parent family formed through separation of ex-nuptial birth were 53% more likely to marry as a teenager, 111% more likely to have a teenage birth, 164% more likely to have a premarital birth, and 92% more likely to separate from their own partner. The effects were the same, although weaker, for daughters of widowed parents.

An important linkage was through educational attainment. Daughters of one-parent families had less schooling, and less schooling brought about early fertility. In a second study using another large national sample, McLanahan (1985) showed that offspring who lived in mother-headed families were less likely to finish high school than those living with two parents, the effect being greatest among those who separated during the children's adolescence. Economic hardship among the mother-headed families was an important factor. McLanahan concluded that policies aimed at equalizing the incomes of one-parent families may be quite successful in reducing much of the intergenerational disadvantage associated with divorce.

However, McLanahan and Bumpass noted that even with amount of schooling controlled for, the effects of single parenthood persist. They saw this as best explained by the effects of a single mother as role model and as source of supervision. As role model, the mother presents single motherhood as a legitimate lifestyle and a viable alternative to an unsatisfactory marriage. As the single authority, she has more difficulty in maintaining control over daughters' dating, which is in turn related to early family formation. The mothers' influence as role models may be desirable, but their inability to protect their daughters from early pregnancy clearly is not. This suggests that not only income equalization but also adequate social support is required. Taking things as they stand, the results of their analysis suggest to McLanahan and Bumpass the existence of a "dynamic in current family changes that may well further weaken the prevalence of simple nuclear families" (p. 148). In essence, they proposed an augmentive model, wherein each cohort of divorcing parents strengthens the trend toward nontraditional family behavior among its children.

Concentrating on the effects of parental divorce, Amato and Keith (1991) pointed out that U.S. national survey studies such as those of McLanahan have found that adult children of divorce, compared to the nondivorced, are more likely to have less education, earn less income, be dependent on welfare, bear an ex-nuptial child, get divorced themselves, and become the head of a single-parent family. They undertook a meta-analyses of the effects of divorce on children as adults, using a technique whereby all the studies on a particular topic are located and their findings added together. They found 37 studies involving

81,678 individuals and 169 comparisons on various measures. Although differences between the two groups tended to be small, the majority of comparisons favored the intact family group. The strongest effects were for becoming oneself a single parent and for psychological adjustment; and behavior disorders, separation/divorce, use of mental health services, educational achievement, and material quality of life also showed differences between the groups.

As in McLanahan's studies, many of these effects were mediated through children's lowered educational achievement. In this case, however, it was found that daughters of divorced parents dropped out of school earlier than sons, as well as earlier than daughters of two-parent families. The explanation seems to be that nonresident fathers are more likely to maintain contact with sons and more likely to provide child support payments for them; and are less willing to finance the education of daughters than sons. Thus, it seems that the long-term disadvantages of growing up in a mother-headed family may be greater for girls than boys, and that mothers with daughters need especially strong social and income supports, including mandatory and realistic financial contributions from fathers, such as already required in some countries.

Another implication of present Western trends has been drawn by Alice Rossi (1987). Rossi argued that the family has been a universal social unit in all societies, and the bond between a man and woman and their children is the most treasured relationship of people everywhere. Hence, the decline in the proportion of adults who are embedded in marriage and childrearing may trigger a lack of concern for child welfare in domestic politics, and even less for the children of poor countries facing famine and misery. This is a neat inversion of Malthus' belief that finer feelings toward children are only possible among those nations who have controlled their own fertility in order to achieve a better standard of life. The increased level of family services and aid given by the low birthrate northwestern European societies seems to support Malthus rather than Rossi so far.

We conclude that it is useful to think in terms of a chain of developments that runs like this. The social and economic changes in Western countries have inevitably undermined traditional marriage. The social forces impelling women and men to complement one another within marriage have declined: Personal fulfillment within relationships has become more important, and loyalty to the institution of marriage less. This has been in general a popular development, as it increases personal freedom. However, it results in an increasing number of mother-headed families. There seems every likelihood that the number will continue high, or even increase. This is not necessarily a bad thing, but it requires arrangements that will equalize the situation of one- and two-parent families. Children can get by with one parent, but not so successfully with only one adult supporter. If fathers are not available, then other supports have to be provided.

Chapter 8

Final Conclusions

THE GOALS

This volume was commenced with two goals. The first was to bring together information on the past and present incidence of mother-headed families in different countries, and to explore the conditions under which such families have been many or few, and better or worse treated by their communities.

We looked first at the experience of divorce in selected countries, and explored some of the legal, religious, social, and economic issues that have been associated with greater and less divorce, and consequently more or fewer mother-headed families originating in divorce. We noted that divorce was a major source of mother-headed families in the Western countries in the 1970s, and we concluded that the increase was due not to any decline in the quality of marriage, but rather to a lowering of the barriers to leaving marriage, and an increase in the alternatives, in particular the alternatives open to women.

We noted next that although divorce remained the major source of mother-headed families through the 1980s, its proportional contribution declined, whereas that of births outside of marriage increased. The majority of these were not births to truly "lone" mothers, but to couples living in consensual unions. However, such unions have a breakup rate well above that of marriage, explaining the 1980s increase in mother-headed families originating in an ex-nuptial birth. Given the apparent fragility of consensual unions, we went on to explore the conditions under which large numbers of women bear children within such unions. We did this first within the Western nations, but as the most striking figures come from other regions of the world, we then considered whether the same kinds of explanations hold across widely different cultures. We concluded that

194

on the whole they did. We also noted a U-shaped relation between ex-nuptial births and the status of women: Ex-nuptial births are high when women's status is low, but also when their access to gainful employment provides them with relatively high status.

The historical and cross-cultural material explored made it clear that until very recently the great majority of single mothers have been young widows, and that the status and treatment of widows has much in common with that of other single mothers. We accordingly considered the situation of widows in more depth, and proposed a model linking the status of women in general and of widows in particular to the nature of their access to economic resources and to the value or threat associated with female fertility. We noted that these latter two factors—nature of access to resources, and value or threat of fertility—dominate descriptions of the prevalence and status of all forms of mother-headed families in all cultures. This of course takes different forms: for example, access to resources sometimes centers on the issue of property rights, in other cases on availability of paid employment.

Our second goal was to explore theories of the family and of parenting that might offer a larger context within which to place the facts that we had gathered, and to consider what they may imply for the future. Is the number of mother-headed families likely to increase, stabilize, or decrease? We found that much of the writing about mother-headed families has been quite narrow and oriented to practical ends, for example, those concerned with welfare dependency and the provisions that might increase or decrease it. General theories of parenting proved more expansive, but not usually especially interested in single parents. Accordingly, we found it necessary to extrapolate quite a bit from these theories and to draw our own implications for mother-headed families.

We first considered some biosocial theories of the family, on the grounds that although these may seem a little remote from the economic, social, legal, and political issues we had been exploring, there are often biological assumptions behind the explanations that have been offered of many family arrangements—in the last resort, they are explained as being "natural." It seemed worthwhile, therefore, to spend a little time setting out some of the major biosocial explanations that have been offered. We found that modern biosocial theory and research has highlighted that what is natural is constant adaptation to circumstances rather than the playing out of immutable reproductive motivations. This then provided a comfortable basis from which to explore approaches that explain parenting behaviors as adaptations to particular contexts and circumstances.

We considered first a selection of demographically oriented theories. We felt that each of these provided valuable insights into the family structures and values influencing the prevalence of mother-headed families. The major weakness of these approaches was their emphasis on structural arrangements, and the limited attention they pay to the ways in which sets of influences are processed psychologically by individuals as they struggle to deal effectively with their lives.

In our final chapter we accordingly turned to several more psychologically oriented approaches—that of feminism and decomplementary theory. We concluded that of all approaches discussed, our sympathy lies particularly with decomplementary theory, which manages to incorporate much of the other approaches within its own framework.

What are the implications for the future? The various explanations we have looked at agree in many ways about what influences are involved, but differ in which they emphasize. With the exception of sex ratio theory, however, they all predict more of the same: continuing high levels of relationship dissolution between men and women, leaving many of the women and children (at least in the immediate future) to get by in a high-cost world with a poverty-line income.

What is to be done? This question is outside the scope of the present work. However, a number of recent writings have given interesting descriptions of the social policies that different countries have adopted, and the extent to which these have made life better or worse for mother-headed families. Wolfe (1989) offered an interesting comparison of policies in two regions with a high incidence of mother-headed families—the United States and Scandinavia—which he saw as standing at the extreme poles, with the other Western nations ranged within.

Wolfe described the strong tradition of "civil society" in the United States, which traditionally meant that families were seen as entities that should be at least partly protected from the reach of pure market forces, through moral and religious norms, women's relative exclusion from the work force, restrictive divorce law, and by other means. In the 1970s, however, something new happened: The family was invaded by the doctrine of economic rationality. The new thinking held that market forces were as good for family and personal relations as they were for the economy: "invisible hands, self-interested behaviours and unanticipated consequences [would] do for society as a whole what they once seemed to do for markets, that is, coordinate diverse behaviour into harmonious wholes" (Wolfe, 1989, p. 49).

The result was a general deregulation of sexual and family behavior. The further result was that the number of mother-headed families tripled between 1960 and 1980; by 1983 40% of all poor people in the United States were children, and 13.8 million children were living in poor families. However, adult Americans remained and remain reluctant to tax themselves in order to provide for these children, and continued to believe that the market, by rewarding effort and efficiency, will "eventually" solve all problems.

In Scandinavia, by contrast, taxes are very high, and the increasing numbers of mother-headed families receive considerable state support. Not only has the state made divorce and separation easier, it has also been active in providing solutions to the problems that this creates: in particular jobs for women, but also housing and other woman-friendly supports. As a result "in Scandinavia something is emerging that can be called a public family" (p. 141).

A dramatic increase in the percentage of women entering the labour force has occurred in Scandinavia . . . in Norway, whereas in 1965 14% of women with small children were in the workforce, by 1986 that figure stood at 69%. The great bulk of this new work involves civil service jobs that carry out the functions once performed by private families. In Norway, 66% of social workers, 93% of nurses and 98% of home helpers are women. Of the growth in the labour force that took place in Denmark between 1960 and 1982 owing to the entrance of women, 25% was in day-care institutions and old-age homes, 12% hospitals, and 27% in schools.

Socialising the young and caring for the sick, viewed traditionally as women's work, are still women's work, *but now they are carried out for a government wage rather than within a family setting.* Within a twenty-five year period, women have jumped from the family sector over the market sector to a direct, and often difficult relationship with the state sector—as dramatic, if not more dramatic, a development as the transformation of men from peasants to workers two hundred years ago. It is in this sense that we can speak of the public family in Scandinavia. The distribution of sex roles has not greatly changed (gender-defined work has probably been more thoroughly transformed in the United States) but their character has changed greatly: they have become 'nationalised' in the sense that the Scandinavian welfare states organise through taxation and public services activities for all of society that were once undertaken more intimately and privately. . . .

What is taking place, in short, is the replacement of the *welfare* state by the welfare *state.* Instead of familial and community relations creating a sense of responsibility for the welfare of others, which the state enforces as a matter of last resort, the state is becoming the primary moral agent in society. (pp. 141–143, 152)

Wolfe's analysis is complemented by many other international surveys that have compared the supports to mother-headed families provided by the various Western nations and come up with a rank ordering that puts the Scandinavian countries at the top and the United States at the bottom (Kamerman, 1984; Katz, 1989; Roll, 1989). They all point out, however, that although the "public family" solution provides a far superior outcome for mother-headed families than the laissez-faire, it needs constant rethinking as economic and social conditions change. For example, 1993 saw publication of the report by the economic commission appointed by the Swedish government to consider possible changes to the social security system in the light of economic recession since 1990. The report recommended that benefits be drastically cut and the entire social security system be privatized (McIvor, 1993). Integrating such changes in thinking with the concept of the public family obviously represents a formidable challenge. On a more positive note, measures are already well advanced in a number of European countries to restructure family policies so as to equalize the opportunities for parents and children regardless of the family form (Voegeli, 1993).

References

Aldous, J., & Dumon, W. (1990). Family policy. *Journal of Marriage and the Family, 52*(4), 1136–1151.

Alexander, F. (1982). *"Those poor unfortunate mothers. . . ." A social history of the single mothers of N.S.W. and the institutions which cared for them.* Unpublished masters thesis, Macquarie University, New South Wales, Australia.

Allott, S. (1985). Soviet rural women: Employment and family life. In B. Holland (Ed.), *Soviet sisterhood* (pp. 179–206). Bloomington: Indiana University Press.

Alteker, A. S. (1956). *The position of women in India* (2nd ed.). Delhi: Motil Banarsidass.

Amato, P., & Keith, B. (1991). Parental divorce and adult wellbeing: A meta-analysis. *Journal of Marriage and the Family, 53*, 43–58.

Archbishop of Canterbury's Group. (1966). *Putting asunder: A divorce law for contemporary society: The report of a group appointed by the Archbishop of Canterbury in January 1964.* London: Society for the Propagation of Christian Knowledge.

Arditti, R., Klein, R. D., & Minden, S. (1984). *Test-tube women: What future motherhood?* London: Pandora Press.

Australian Bureau of Statistics. (1984). *Social indicators No. 4* (Catalogue No. 4101.0). Canberra: Author.

Australian Bureau of Statistics. (1985). *Family formation and dissolution 1982* (Catalogue No. 4411.0). Canberra: Author.

Australian Bureau of Statistics. (1987). *Births Australia 1986* (Catalogue No. 3301.0). Canberra: Author.

Australian Bureau of Statistics. (1991). *Australia's one parent families* (Catalogue No. 2511.0). Canberra: Author.

Bacon, D. K. (1982, October 18). When unmarried Afton Blake wanted a baby she made a withdrawal from her friendly sperm bank. *People Weekly*, pp. 63–64.

Balakrishnan, T. R., Rao, K., Lapierre-Adamcyk, E., & Krotki, K. (1987). A hazard model analysis of the covariates of marriage dissolution in Canada. *Demography, 24*, 396–406.

Barrett, M., & MacIntosh, M. (1982). *The antisocial family.* London: Verso.

Barrow, J., (1982). West Indian families: An insider's perspective. In R. Rapaport, M. Fogarty, & R. Rapaport (Eds.), *Families in Britain* (pp. 220–232). London: Routledge Kegan Paul.

Barry, W. (1970). Marriage research and conflict: An integrative review. *Psychological Bulletin, 73*, 41–54.

Bergmann, B. (1986). *The economic emergence of women.* New York: Basic Books.

Bernard, J. (1973). *The future of marriage.* New York: Bantam.

Bernard, J. (1981). The good provider role. *American Psychologist, 36*, 1–12.

Bernard, J. (1985). No fault—Whose fault? *Women's Review of Books, 3*, 1–4.

Bernhardt, E. M. (1988). *Changing family ties, women's position and low fertility* (Stockholm Research Reports in Demography No. 46). Stockholm: Stockholm University.

Bittman, M., & Lovejoy, F. (1991, December). *Domestic power: Negotiating an unequal division of labour within a framework of equality.* Paper presented to TASA '91 Sociology Conference, Perth, Western Australia.

Bjornsson, B. (1971). *The Lutheran doctrine of marriage in modern Icelandic society.* Oslo: Universitets-forlaget.

Blanc, A. K. (1987). Marriage and conhabitation in Sweden and Norway. *Journal of Marriage and the Family, 49*, 391–400.

Boserup, E. (1970). *Women's role in economic development.* London: George Allen & Unwin.

Boserup, E. (1990). Economic change and the role of women. In I. Tinker (Ed.), *Persistent inequalities: Women and world development* (pp. 14–24). Oxford: Oxford University Press.

Bottomley, G., de Lepervanche, M., & Martin, J. (Eds.). (1992). *Intersexions: Gender/class culture/ethnicity.* Sydney: Allen & Unwin.

Boulding, E. (1976). *The underside of history: A view of women through time.* Boulder, CO: Westview Press.

Broyelle, C. (1977). *Women's liberation in China.* Atlantic Highlands, NJ: Humanities Press.

Bryson, L. (1993). Women, paid work and social policy. In N. Grieve & A. Burns (Eds.), *Australian women: Issues in the '90s.* Melbourne: Oxford University Press.

Buckley, M. (1985). Soviet interpretations of the woman question. In B. Holland (Ed.), *Soviet sisterhood* (pp. 24–53). Bloomington: Indiana University Press.

Bulatao, R. A. (1979). *On the nature of the transition in the value of children* (Current Studies in the Value of Children. Papers of the East-West Population Institute, no 60-A). Honolulu, HI: East-West Population Institute.

Bullough, V. (1973). *The subordinate sex: A history of attitudes to women.* Urbana: University of Illinois Press.

Bumpass, L., & Sweet, G. (1987). *Families and households in America.* New York: Russell Sage.

Burguiere, A. (1975). The formation of the couple. *Journal of Family History, 12*, 1-3, 39–53.

Burns, A. (1980). *Breaking up.* Melbourne: Nelson.

Burns, A. (1984). Perceived causes of marriage breakdown and conditions of life. *Journal of Marriage and the Family, 46*, 551–565.

Burton, C. (1986). Equal employment opportunity programmes: Issues in implementation. In N. Grieve & A. Burns (Eds.), *Australian women: New feminist perspectives* (pp. 292–304). Melbourne: Oxford University Press.

Caesar-Wolf, B., Eidmann, D., & Willenbacher-Zahlmann, B. (1983, September). *Divorce proceedings under the West German Reform Law.* Paper presented to the Committee on Sociology of Law of the International Sociological Association, Antwerp.

Caldwell, J. C. (1982). *Theory of fertility decline.* London: Academic Press.

Chanduri, N. C. (1967). *The continent of Circe: Being an essay on the people of India.* Delhi: Chatto & Windus.

Chodorow, N. (1978). *The reproduction of mothering: psychoanalysis and the sociology of gender.* Berkeley: University of California Press.

Clark, E. (1957). *My mother who fathered me.* London: Simon Shand.

Cotton, S., Antill, J., & Cunningham, J. (1983). Living together: Before, instead of, or after marriage? In A. Burns, G. Bottomley, & P. Jools (Eds.), *The family in the modern world* (pp. 167–183). Sydney: Allen & Unwin.

Cunningham, J., & Antill, J. K. (1979). *Cohabitation: Marriage of the future?* Paper presented at the ANZAAS Congress, Auckland, New Zealand.

Curthoys, A. (1986). The sexual division of labour: Theoretical perspective. In N. Grieve & A. Burns (Eds.), *Australian women: New feminist perspectives* (pp. 319–339). Melbourne: Oxford University Press.

Darity, W. A., & Myers, S. L. (1984). Does welfare dependency cause female headship? The case of the black family. *Journal of Marriage and the Family, 46*, 765-780.

Das, M. S., & Bardis, P. E. (1979). *The family in Asia*. London: Allen & Unwin.

Degler, C. (1980). *At odds: Women and the family in America from the revolution to the present*. New York: Oxford University Press.

Demaris, A. (1984). A comparison of remarriages with first marriages on satisfaction in marriage and its relationship to prior cohabitation. *Family Relations, 33*, 443-449.

Dinnerstein, D. (1977). *The mermaid and the minotaur*. New York: Harper & Row.

Dodd, P. (1973). Family honour and forces of change in contemporary Arab society. *International Journal of Middle East Studies, 4*, 40-54.

Dubois, A. J., & Beauchamp, H. K. (1906). *Hindu manners, customs and ceremonies*. Oxford: Clarendon Press.

Duck, S. (1992). *Human relationships*. London: Sage. (Original work published 1986)

Durrett, M., Richards, P., Otaki, M., Penebaker, J., & Nyquist, L. (1986). Mothers in Japan and America. *Journal of Marriage and the Family, 48*, 187-194.

Edelman, M. W. (1987). *Families in peril: An agenda for social change*. Cambridge, MA: Harvard University Press.

Ehrenreich, B. (1983). *The hearts of men*. New York: Pluto Press.

Engels, F. (1985). *The origin of the family, private property and the state*. Harmondsworth Middlesex: Penguin Classics. (Original work published 1884)

Ermisch, J. (1987, December). *Demographic aspects of the growing number of lone parent families*. Paper presented to the Conference of National Experts on Lone Parents: The Economic Challenge of Changing Family Structures, Brussels.

Fairchilds, C. (1978). Female sexual attitudes and the rise of illegitimacy: A case study. *Journal of Interdisciplinary History, 8*, 627-667.

Fernea, E. W. (1985). *Women and the family in the Middle East: New voices of change*. Austin: University of Texas Press.

Ferree, M. (1991). Feminism and family research. In A. Booth (Ed.), *Contemporary families: Looking forward, looking back* (pp. 103-121). Minneapolis: National Council on Family Relations.

Fogel, R. W., & Engerman, S. L. (1974). *Time on the cross*. Boston: Little Brown.

French, M. (1992). *The war against women*. London: Hamish Hamilton.

Funder, K. (1989). International perspectives on the economics of divorce. *Family Matters, 24*, 18-22.

Funder, K., Harrison, M., & Weston, R. (1993). *Settling down*. Melbourne: Australian Institute of Family Studies.

Gander, C. (1984). *Nicaraguan women at war*. Washington, DC: Central American Historical Institute.

Garfinkel, I., & McLanahan, S. (1989). *Single mothers and their children: A new American dilemma*. Washington, DC: Urban Institute Press.

Gaunt, D. (1980). Illegitimacy in 17th and 18th century east Sweden. In P. Laslett, K. Oosterveen, & R. M. Smith (Eds.), *Bastardy and its comparative history* (pp. 313-326). London: Edward Arnold.

Geiger, H. K. (1968). *The family in Soviet Russia*. Cambridge, MA: Harvard University Press.

Geronimus, A. T. (1987). On teenage childbearing and neonatal mortality in the United States. *Population and Development Review, 13*, 245-279.

Gilder, G. (1974). *Naked nomads*. New York: Times Books.

Gilligan, C. (1982). *In a different voice: Psychological theory and women's development*. Cambridge, MA: Harvard University Press.

Glendon, M. A. (1987). *Abortion and divorce in western law: American failures, European challenges*. Cambridge, MA: Harvard University Press.

Glezer, H. (1984a). Antecedents and correlates of marriage and family attitudes in young Australian men and women. In *Social change and family policies. Proceedings of the XXth International Committee on Family Research Seminar* (pp. 81-107). Melbourne: Australian Institute of Family Studies.

Glezer, H. (1984b). Changes in marriage and sex-role attitudes among young married women: 1971–81. In *Proceedings of the Australian Family Research Conference* (Vol. 1, pp. 201–255). Melbourne: Australian Institute of Family Studies.

Glezer, H. (1988). *Maternity leave in Australia*. Melbourne: Australian Institute of Family Studies.

Glezer, H. (1993, February). *To tie or not tie the knot: Pathways to family formation*. Paper presented to the fourth annual Australian Family Research Conference, Sydney, Australia.

Glezer, H., Edgar, D., & Prolisko, A. (1992, May). *The importance of family background and early life experiences on premarital cohabitation and marital dissolution*. Paper presented at the Conference on Family Formation and Dissolution: East and West Perspectives, Taipei.

Glick, P. (1988). Fifty years of family demography. *Journal of Marriage and the Family, 50*, 861–874.

Glick, P., & Lin, S. (1986). Recent changes in divorce and remarriage. *Journal of Marriage and the Family, 48*, 737–748.

Goering, K. (1992, July 27). Singles shying away from saying "I do." *Chicago Tribune*, pp. 8–9.

Goode, W. (1956). *Women in divorce*. Westport, CT: Greenwood Press.

Goode, W. (1963). *World revolution and family patterns*. New York: Collier Macmillan.

Goode, W. (1964). *The family*. Englewood Cliffs, NJ: Prentice-Hall.

Goode, W. (1984). Individual investments in the family collectivity. *The Tocqueville Review, 6*, 1.

Goody, J. (1983). *The development of the family and marriage in Europe*. Cambridge: Cambridge University Press.

Green, R. (1978). Sexual identity of 37 children raised by homosexual or transsexual parents. *American Journal of Psychiatry, 135*, 672–691.

Guttentag, M., & Secord, P. (1983). *Too many women?* Beverly Hills: Sage.

Hacker, A. (1988, October 13). Getting rough on the poor. *New York Review of Books*, pp. 12–17.

Hajnal, J. (1985). European marriage patterns in perspective. In D. V. Glass & D. E. Eversely (Eds.), *Population in history* (pp. 101–143). London: Edward Arnold.

Hanlan, J. (1984). *Mozambique: The revolution under fire*. London: Zed Books.

Hanson, S. L., Myers, D. E., & Ginsburg, A. L. (1987). The role of responsibility and knowledge in reducing teenage out-of-wedlock childbearing. *Journal of Marriage and the Family, 49*, 241–1256.

Harris, M. (1980). *America now*. New York: Touchstone.

Hart, N. (1976). *When marriage ends*. London: Tavistock.

Hartley, S. F. (1975). *Illegitimacy*. Berkeley: University of California Press.

Hartley, S. F. (1980). Illegitimacy in Jamaica. In P. Laslett, K. Oosterveen, & R. M. Smith (Eds.), *Bastardy and its comparative history* (pp. 379–396). London: Edward Arnold.

Hartmann, H. (1981). The unhappy marriage of Marxism and feminism: Towards a more progressive union. In L. Sargent (Ed.), *Women and revolution* (pp. 1–42). London: South End Press.

Headlam, F. (1984). Marital breakdown: Reactions to separation and post-separation experiences of adults. *Proceedings of the Australian family Research Conference* (pp. 226–255). Melbourne, Australia: Institute of Family Studies.

Hendry, J. (1981). *Marriage in changing Japan*. London: Croom Helm.

Herbert, A. P. (1934). *Holy deadlock*. London: Methuen.

Herlihy, D. (1961). Church property on the European continent 701-1200, *Speculum, 36*, 81–105.

Herlihy, D. (1987). The family and religious ideologies in medieval Europe. *Journal of Family History, 12*, 3–18.

Her Majesty's Stationery Office. (1992). *Mortality statistics 1990, perinatal and infant: social and biological factors* (Series DH3 No 24). London: Author.

Hetherington, E. M., & Arasteh, J. (1988). *Impact of divorce, single parenting and stepparenting on children*. Hillsdale, NJ: Lawrence Erlbaum Associates.

Hewlett, S. (1987). *Lesser life*. New York: Warner.

Hinde, R. A. (1984). Why do the sexes behave differently in close relationships? *Journal of Social and Personal Relationships, 1*(4), 471–502.

Hoem, B., & Hoem, J. (1987). *The Swedish family: Aspects of contemporary developments* (Stockholm Research reports in Demography No. 43). Stockholm: Stockholm University.

Hoem, B., & Hoem, J. (1988). *Dissolution in Sweden: The breakup of conjugal unions to Swedish women born in 1936-60* (Stockholm Research Reports in Demography No. 45). Stockholm: Stockholm University.

Hofferth, S., & Hayes, C. (Eds.). (1987). *Risking the future: Adolescent sexuality, pregnancy and child-bearing* (Vol. 2). Washington, DC: National Academy Press.

Hopflinger, F. (1985). Changing marriage behaviour: Some European comparisons. *Genus, 16*, 41-64.

Hrdy, S. B. (1981). *The woman that never evolved.* Cambridge, MA: Harvard University Press.

Hrdy, S. B. (1986). Empathy, polyandry and the myth of the coy female. In R. Bleier (Ed.), *Feminist approaches to science* (pp. 119-146). New York: Pergamon.

Huggins, J., & Blake, T. (1992). Protection or persecution? In K. Saunders & R. Evans (Eds.), *Gender relations in Australia: Domination and negotiation* (pp. 42-58). Sydney: Harcourt Brace Jovanovitch.

Humphries, J. (1977). Class struggle and the resistence of the working class family. *Cambridge Journal of Economics, 1*, 241-258.

Illich, I. (1983). *Gender.* New York: Pantheon Books.

Indra, M. A. (1955). *The status of women in ancient India* (2nd ed.). Benares: Motil Banarasidass.

James, P. (Ed.). (1990). *T. R. Malthus' essay on the principle of population.* Cambridge: Cambridge University Press. (Original work published 1798)

Johansson, S. R. (1984). Deferred infanticide: Excess female mortality during childhood. In G. Hausfater & S. B. Hrdy (Eds.), *Infanticide: Comparative and evolutionary perspectives* (pp. 463-486). New York: Aldine.

Jones, E. F., Forrest, J. D., Goldman, N., Hensaw, S. K., Lincoln, R., Rosoff, J. I., Westoff, C. F., & Wulf, D. (1985). Teenage pregnancy in developed countries: Determinants and policy implications. *Family Planning Perspectives, 17*, 53-663.

Jordan, A. (1989). *Lone parent- and wage earner? Employment prospects of sole-parent pensioners* (Social Security Review Background/Discussion Paper No. 31). Canberra: Department of Social Security.

Jordan, P. (1985). *The effects of separation on men: "Men hurt"* (Family Court of Australia Research Report No. 6). Brisbane: Brisbane Registry FCA.

Kamerman, S. (1984). Women, children and poverty: Public policies and female-headed families in industralised countries. *Signs, 10*, 249-271.

Kamerman, S. (1992, November). *Family income and social policy.* Paper presented to the 54th annual conference on the National Council on Family Relations, Orlando, FL.

Kanowitz, W. (1969). *Women and the law: The unfinished revolution.* Albuquerque: University of New Mexico Press.

Kaplan, G. (1992). *Contemporary western European feminism.* Sydney: Allen & Unwin.

Katz, C. (1989). *The undeserving poor: From the war on poverty to the war on welfare.* New York: Pantheon Books.

Kendig, H., & McCallum, J. (1990). *Grey policy.* Sydney: Allen & Unwin.

Kharchev, A. G., & Matskovskii, M. (1981). Changing family roles and marital instability. In G. Lapidus (Ed.), *Women, work and family: New Soviet perspectives* (pp. 191-217. New York: M. E. Sharpe.

Khera, S. (1981). Illegitimacy and mode of land inheritance among Austrian peasants. *Ethnology, 20*, 307-323.

Khoo, S-E. (1987). Living together as married: A profile of de facto couples in Australia. *Journal of Marriage and the Family, 49*, 185-191.

Kiernan, K., & Wicks, M. (1990). *Family change and future policy.* London: Family Policy Studies Centre.

Kilbride, P., & Kilbride, J. (1990). *Changing family life in East Africa: Women and children at risk.* University Park and London: Pennsylvania State University Press.

Kitson, G., & Raschke, H. (1981). Divorce research: What we know; what we need to know. *Journal of Divorce, 4*, 9–37.

Kitzinger, S. (1978). *Women as mothers.* London: Fontana Books.

Kollontai, A. (1977). *Selected writings of Alexandra Kollontai* (A. Holt, Trans.). New York: Norton.

Kumagai, F. (1983). Changing divorce in Japan. *Journal of Family History, 8*, 85–107.

Lancaster, J. B. (1984). Evolutionary perspectives on sex differences in the higher primates. In A. Rossi (Ed.), *Gender and the life course* (pp. 3–27). New York: Aldine.

Lancaster, J. B., & Lancaster, C. B. (1987). The watershed: Change in parental-investment and family-formation strategies in the course of human evolution. In J. B. Lancaster, J. Altmann, A. S. Rossi, & L. R. Sherrod (Eds.), *Parenting across the life span: Biosocial dimensions* (pp. 187–206). New York: Aldine De Gruyter.

Lapidus, G. (Ed.). (1981). *Women, work and family: New Soviet perspectives.* New York: M. E. Sharpe.

Laslett, P., Oosterveen, K., & Smith, R. M. (Eds.). (1980). *Bastardy and its comparative history.* London: Edward Arnold.

Law Commission. (1966). *Reform of the grounds of divorce: The field of choice* (Command Paper 3123). London: Her Majesty's Stationery Office.

Lenin, V. I. (1951). *The woman question: Selections from the writings of Karl Marx, Friedrich Engels, V. I. Lenin and Josef Stalin.* New York: International Publishers.

Lerner, G. (1986). *The creation of patriarchy.* New York: Oxford University Press.

Levine, R. (1978). Comparative notes on the life course. In T. Hareven (Ed.), *Transitions: The family and the life course in historical perspective* (pp. 287–296). New York: Academic Press.

Levinger, G. (1965). Marital cohesiveness and dissolution: An integrative review. *Journal of Marriage and the Family, 227*(1), 19–28.

Lewis, R., & Spanier, G. (1979). Theorizing about the quality and stability of marriage. In W. Burr, R. Hill, F. Nye, & I. Reiss (Eds.), *Contemporary theories about the family* (Vol. 1, pp. 268–294). New York: The Free Press.

Loengard, J. S. (1985). "Of the gift of her husband": English power and its consequences in the year 1200. In J. Kirshner & S. F. Weniplex (Eds.), *Women of the medieval world* (pp. 215–255). Oxford: Basil Blackwell.

Lopata, H. Z. (1973). *Widowhood in an American city.* Cambridge, MA: Schenkman.

MacDonald, M., & Sawhill, I. (1978). Welfare policy and the family. *Public Policy, 26*, 89–119.

Macfarlane, A. (1986). *Marriage and love in England 1300–1840.* Oxford: Basil Blackwell.

Mair, L. (1969). *African marriage and social change.* London: Frank Cass.

Majors, R., & Gordon, J. (1991). *The American black male: His recent status and his future.* New York: Nelson-Hall.

Malinowski, B. (1930). Parenthood, the basis of social structure. In V. Calverton & S. Schmalhausen (Eds.), *The new generation* (pp. 113–168). New York: Macauley.

Malthus, T. R. (1970). *A summary view of the principle of population* (A. Flew, Ed.). Harmondsworth, Middlesex, U.K. (Original work published 1830)

Mason, P. (1970). *Patterns of dominance.* Oxford: Oxford University Press.

Mazumdar, V. (1978). "Comment on Suttee." *Signs, 4*, 269–273.

McDonald, P. (Ed.). (1986). *Settling up: Property and income distribution in divorce in Australia.* Sydney: Prentice-Hall.

McDonald, P. (1987). *The rise in ex-nuptial births.* Paper presented at the second Australian Family Research Conference, Melbourne.

McGoldrick, M., Anderson, C., & Walsh, F. (1991). *Women in families.* New York: Norton.

McGregor, O. (1970). *Separated spouses: A study of the matrimonial jurisdiction of magistrates' courts.* Duckworth: London.

McGuire, M., & Alexander, N. J. (1985). Antifamilial insemination of single women. *Fertility and Sterility, 43*, 182–184.

McIvor, G. (1993, March 11). Sweeping welfare cuts for Sweden urged in report. *Sydney Morning Herald*, p. 6.

McLanahan, S. (1985). Family structure and the reproduction of poverty. *American Journal of Sociology, 90*, 873–901.

McLanahan, S., & Booth, K. (1991). Mothers-only families. In A. Booth (Ed.), *Contemporary families: Looking forward, looking back* (pp. 405–428). Minneapolis: National Council on Family Relations.

McLanahan, S., & Bumpass, L. (1988). Intergenerational consequences of family disruption. *American Journal of Sociology, 94*, 130–152.

McLanahan, S., Sorensen, A., & Watson, D. (1989). Sex differences in poverty, 1950-80. *Signs, 15*, 102–122.

McRobbie, A., & Nava, M. (Eds.). (1984). *Gender and generation*. London: Macmillan.

Meyer, D. (1962). Foreword. In H. Ibsen, *Ghosts*. London: Rupert Hart-Davis. (Original work published 1881)

Meyer, J. (1980). Illegitimates and foundlings in pre-industrial France. In P. Laslett, K. Oosterveen, & R. M. Smith (Eds.), *Bastardy and its comparative history* (pp. 249–263). London: Edward Arnold.

Mitterauer, M., & Sieder, R. (1983). *The European family*. Chicago: University of Chicago Press.

Montague, M., & Stephens, J. (1985). *Paying the price for sugar and spice*. Canberra: Australian Government Publishing Service.

Morgan, S., Lye, D., & Condran, G. (1988). Sons, daughters and the risk of marital disruption. *American Journal of Sociology, 94*, 110–129.

Moskoff, W. (1983). Divorce in the U.S.S.R. *Journal of Marriage and the Family, 45*, 419–425.

National Council on Family Relations. (1990, December 10). NCFR Report. Minneapolis: Author.

Newcomb, M. (1986). Cohabitation, marriage and divorce among adolescents and young adults. *Journal of Social and Personal Relationships, 3*, 473–494.

New legal protection for women in Nicaragua. (1987). *Update, 6*, 10.

Noller, P., & Fitzpatrick, M. (1990). Marital communication in the eighties. *Journal of Marriage and the Family, 52*, 832–843.

Norton, A., & Glick, P. (1986). One parent families: A social and economic profile. *Family Relations, 35*, 9–18.

O'Neill, B. J. (1983). Dying and inheriting in rural Tras-os-Montes. *Journal of the Communities Society of Oxford, 14*, 44–74.

O'Neill, W. (1967). *Divorce in the progressive era*. New Haven, CT: Yale University Press.

Organization for Economic Cooperation and Development. (1987). *Proceedings of the Conference of National Experts on Lone Parents: The Economic Challenge of Changing Family Structures*. Brussels: OECD.

A pagan sacrifice. (1987, October 15). *India Today*, pp. 58–61.

Pampel, F., & Tanaka, K. (1986). Economic development and female labor force participation: A reconsideration. *Social Forces, 64*, 599–619.

Pateman, C. (1986). The marriage contract. In N. Grieve & A. Burns (Eds.), *Australian women: New feminist perspectives* (pp. 172–181). Melbourne: Oxford University Press.

Peers, J. (1985). Workers by hand and womb—Soviet women and the demographic crisis. In B. Holland (Ed.), *Soviet sisterhood* (pp. 116–144). Bloomington: Indiana University Press.

Peristiany, J. G. (Ed.). (1976). *Mediterranean family structures* (pp. 116–144). Cambridge: Cambridge University Press.

Pleck, J. (1977). The work–family role system. *Social Problems, 24*, 417–427.

Popenoe, D. (1987). Beyond the nuclear family: A statistical portrait of the changing family in Sweden. *Journal of Marriage and the Family, 49*, 173–183.

Popenoe, D. (1988). *Disturbing the nest*. New York: Aldine de Gruyter.

Potash, B. (Ed.). (1986). *Widows in African society: Choices and constraints*. Stanford: Stanford University Press.

Pringle, R. (1993). Women in the professions. In N. Grieve & A. Burns (Eds.), *Australian women: Feminist issues in the '90s*. Melbourne: Oxford University Press.

Qvist, J., & Rennermalm, B. (1985). *Family formation* (Urval No., 17). Stockholm: Statistika Centralbyrån.

Rabb, T., & Rotberg, R. (1971). *The family in history.* New York: Harper Torchbooks.

Raymond, J. (1987). *Bringing up children alone: Policies for sole parents* (Social Security Review Issues Paper No. 3). Canberra: Australian Government Publishing Service.

Reddaway, P. (1993, January 28). Russia on the brink? *New York Review of Books,* pp. 30–35.

Rheinstein, M. (1972). *Marriage stability, divorce and the law.* Chicago: University of Chicago Press.

Rich, G. W. (1978). The domestic cycle in modern Iceland. *Journal of Marriage and the Family, 40,* 173–183.

Richardson, H. H. (1925). *The fortunes of Richard Mahony.* London: Heinemann.

Roberts, G. W., & Sinclair, S. (1978). *Women in Jamaica: Patterns of reproduction and family.* London: Research Institute for the Study of Man.

Roll, J. (1989). *Lone parent families in the European community.* London: Family Policy Studies Centre.

Rossi, A. (1985). Gender and parenthood. In A. Rossi (Ed.), *Gender and the life course* (pp. 161–192). New York: Aldine de Gruyter.

Rossi, A. (1987). Parenthood in transition: From lineage to child and self-orientation. In J. B. Lancaster, J. Altmann, A. S. Rossi, & L. R. Sherrod (Eds.), *Parenting across the life span: Biosocial dimensions* (pp. 31–84). New York: Aldine De Gruyter.

Rugh, A. B. (1984). *The family in contemporary Egypt.* New York: Syracuse University Press.

Salman, M. (1978). *Arab women.* New York: New York Wire Service.

Sarantakos, S. (1984). *Living together in Australia.* Melbourne: Longman Cheshire.

Scanzoni, J., & Szinovacz, M. (1980). *Family decision-making: A developmental sex-role model.* Beverly Hills: Sage.

Sen, A. (1990a). Gender and cooperative conflicts. In I. Tinker (Ed.), *Persistent inequalities: Women and world development* (pp. 123–149). Oxford: Oxford University Press.

Sen, A. (1990b, December 20). More than 100 million women are missing. *New York Review of Books,* pp. 61–66.

Shammas, C. (1980). *Women and inheritance in the age of family capitalism.* Paper presented to the American Historical Association meeting, Washington, DC.

Short, R. V. (1978). The evolution of human reproduction. *Proceedings of the Royal Society,* B195, 3–24.

Shorter, E. (1975). *The making of the modern family.* London: Collins.

Slater, M. (1986). Sons and levirs. In B. Potash (Ed.), *Widows in African societies.* Stanford, CA: Stanford University Press.

Sluzki, C. (1982). The Latin lover revisited. In M. McGoldrick, J. K. Pearce, & J. Giordano (Eds.), *Ethnicity and family therapy* (pp. 492–498). New York: Guilford.

Smith, R. (1956). *The negro family in British Guiana.* London: Routledge Kegan Paul.

Smout, C. (1980). Aspects of sexual behaviour in nineteenth century Scotland. In P. Laslett, K. Oosterveen, & R. M. Smith (Eds.), *Bastardy and its comparative history* (pp. 192–216). London: Edward Arnold.

Social Trends 21. (1991). London: Central Statistical Office.

Sonin, M. (1981). Socioeconomic problems of female employment. In G. Lapidus (Ed.), *Women, work and family: New Soviet perspectives* (pp. 23–32). New York: M. E. Sharpe.

South, S. (1988). Sex ratios, economic power, and women's roles: A theoretical extension and empirical test. *Journal of Marriage and the Family, 50,* 19–31.

South, S., & Trent, K. (1987). *Sex ratios and women's roles: A cross-national analysis.* Paper presented at the annual meeting of the Population Association of America, Chicago, IL.

Stack, C. B. (1973). Sex roles and survival strategies in an urban black community. In M. Z. Rosaldo & L. Lamphere (Eds.), *Woman, culture and society* (pp. 113–128). Stanford, CA: Stanford University Press.

Stack, C. B. (1974). *All our kin: Strategies for survival in a black community.* New York: Harper & Row.

Stack, S. (1992). The effect of divorce on suicide in Japan. *Journal of Marriage and the Family, 54,* 327–334.

Staples, R. (1982). *Black masculinity: The black male's role in American society*. San Francisco: The Black Scholar Press.

Staples, R. (1985). Changes in black family structure: the conflict between family ideology and structural considerations. *Journal of Marriage and the Family, 47*, 1005-1014.

Stark, E. (1986, October). Young, innocent and pregnant. *Psychology Today*, pp. 28-35.

Statistics Sweden. (1991). Personal communication. Stockholm: Statistics Sweden Population Research Office.

Stein, D. K. (1978). Women to burn. *Signs, 4*, 253-268.

Strawn, J. (1992). The states and the poor: child poverty rises as the safety net shrinks. *Social Policy Report, 6*, 1-19.

Taylor, R. J., Chatters, L., Tucker, M., & Lewis, E. (1991). Developments in research on black families. In A. Booth (Ed.), *Contemporary families: Looking forward, looking back* (pp. 275-296). Minneapolis: National Council on Family Relations.

Thomson, E., & Colella, U. (1992). Cohabitation ad marital stability: Quality or commitment? *Journal of Marriage and the Family, 54*, 259-268.

Thorne, B., & Yalom, M. (1982). *Rethinking the family*. New York: Longman.

Thornes, B., & Collard, J. (1979). *Who divorces?* London: Routledge Kegan Paul.

Trivers, R. L. (1972). Parental investment and sexual selection. In B. Campbell (Ed.), *Sexual selection and the descent of man* (pp. 136-179). Chicago: Aldine.

Trost, J. (1977). Sweden. In R. Chester (Ed.), *Divorce in Europe* (pp. 35-52). Leiden: Martinus Nijhoff.

Trost, J. (1985). Remarriage. In L. Cseh-Szombathy, I. Koch-Nielsen, J. Trost, & I. Weda (Eds.), *The aftermath of divorce: Coping with family change: An investigation in eight countries* (pp. 51-74). Budapest: Akademiai Kiado.

Trussell, J., Hankinson, R., & Tilton, J. (Eds.). (1992). *Demographic applications of event history analysis*. Oxford: Clarendon Press.

United Kingdom. (1985). *Labor force survey*. London: Her Majesty's Stationery Office.

United States of America. Bureau of the Census. (1985). *Statistical Abstracts of the U.S., 1986* (106th ed.). Washington, DC: U.S. Government Printing Office.

United States of America. Bureau of the Census. (1992). *Poverty in the U.S., 1991*. Washington, DC: U.S. Department of Commerce.

United Nations. (1968, 1978, 1988). *United Nations demographic yearbook*. New York: United Nations.

van de Kaa, D. (1987). Europe's second demographic transition. *Population Bulletin, 42*, 1-59.

Viazzo, P. P. (1986). Illegitimacy and the European marriage pattern: Comparative evidence from the alpine area. In I. Bonfield, R. M. Smith, & K. Wrightson (Eds.). *The world we have gained: Histories of population and social structure* (pp. 100-121). Oxford: Basil Blackwell.

Voegeli, W. (1983, February). *Single women and their families: The case of Germany*. Paper presented to the fourth annual Australian Family Research Conference, Sydney.

Wagatsuma, H., & De Vos, G. (1984). *Heritage of endurance*. Berkeley: University of California Press.

Walker, S. (1985, March). Why I became a single mother. *Ladies Home Journal*, pp. 22-24.

Walker, T. W. (1986). *Nicaragua, the land of sand*. Boulder: Westview Press.

Waring, M. (1988). *Counting for nothing*. Sydney: Allen & Unwin.

Weideger, P. (1985). *History's mistress*. Harmondsworth, Middlesex: Penguin.

Weitzman, L. (1985). *The divorce revolution: The unexpected social and economic consequences for women and children in America*. New York: The Free Press.

White, L. (1990). Determinants of divorce. *Journal of Marriage and the Family, 52*, 904-911.

Willenbacher, B., & Voegeli, W. (1985). *Multiple disadvantages of one-parent families in the Federal Republic of Germany*. Paper presented to the fifth International Conference of the International Society on Family Law, Brussels.

Wilson, W. J. (1987). *The truly disadvantaged: The inner city, the underclass and public policy*. Chicago: University of Chicago Press.

Wolcott, I. (1984). From courtship to divorce: Unrealised or unrealistic expectations. *Proceedings of the Australian Family Research Conference* (Vol. 3). Melbourne:Australian Institute of Family Studies.

Wolfe, A. (1989). *Whose keeper? Social science and moral obligation*. Berkeley: University of California.

Women's association addresses machismo in Nicaragua. (1985). *Update, 4*, 33.

Women's International Resource Exchange. (1985). *Nicaraguan women: Unlearning the alphabet of submission*. New York: Author.

Worsoe, V. (1988). *Sati*. Unpublished masters thesis, Department of Anthropology, University of Sydney.

Yamaguchi, K., & Kandel, D. (1987). Drug use and other determinants of premarital pregnancy and its outcome: A dynamic analysis of competing life events. *Journal of Marriage and the Family, 49*, 257–270.

Yang, J. E. (1992, May 20). Clinton finds new voice of emotion; Quayle decries "poverty of values." *Washington Post*, p. 1.

Zelizer, V. A. (1985). *Pricing the priceless child: The changing social value of children*. New York: Basic Books.

Author Index

Subject Index